P9-APW-493

Technology, Education—Connections
The TEC Series

Series Editor: Marcia C. Linn
Advisory Board: Robert Bjork, Chris Dede, BatSheva Eylon,
Carol Lee, Jim Minstrell, Mitch Resnick

Creating and Sustaining Online Professional Learning Communities
Joni K. Falk and Brian Drayton, Editors

Designing Coherent Science Education:
Implications for Curriculum, Instruction, and Policy
Yael Kali, Marcia C. Linn, and Jo Ellen Roseman, Editors

Data-Driven School Improvement:
Linking Data and Learning
Ellen B. Mandinach and Margaret Honey, Editors

Electric Worlds in the Classroom:
Teaching and Learning with Role-Based Computer Games
Brian M. Slator and Associates

Meaningful Learning Using Technology:
What Educators Need to Know and Do
Elizabeth A. Ashburn and Robert E. Floden, Editors

Using Technology Wisely:
The Keys to Success in Schools
Harold Wenglinsky

CREATING AND SUSTAINING
ONLINE PROFESSIONAL
LEARNING COMMUNITIES

EDITED BY

Joni K. Falk and Brian Drayton

FOREWORD BY

MARCIA C. LINN

JUN 1 0 2010

TEACHERS
COLLEGE
PRESS

Teachers College
Columbia University
New York and London

MONTGOMERY COUNTY PUBLIC SCHOOLS
PROFESSIONAL LIBRARY
850 HUNGERFORD DRIVE
ROCKVILLE, MARYLAND 20850

WITHDRAWN

Published by Teachers College Press, 1234 Amsterdam Avenue, New York, NY 10027

Copyright © 2009 by Teachers College, Columbia University

All rights reserved. No part of this publication may be reproduced or transmitted in any form or by any means, electronic or mechanical, including photocopy, or any information storage and retrieval system, without permission from the publisher.

The work reported in this volume was supported by: the National Science Foundation Grant Nos. 9812831, 0088027, 0335334. Any opinions, findings, conclusions or recommendations expressed herein are those of the Author and do not necessarily reflect the views or policies of the funding agency.

Library of Congress Cataloging-in-Publication Data

Creating and sustaining online professional learning communities / edited by Joni K. Falk and Brian Drayton ; foreword by Marcia C. Linn.
        p. cm. — (Technology, education-connections—the TEC series)
    Includes bibliographical references and index.
    ISBN 978-0-8077-4940-1 (pbk. : alk. paper) 1. Teachers—In-service training—United States. 2. Teachers—Computer networks—United States. 3. Teachers—Professional relationships—United States. I. Falk, Joni K. II. Drayton, Brian.
    LB1731.C692 2009
    371.12—dc22

                                                                2008055078

ISBN: 978-0-8077-4940-1 (paperback)

Printed on acid-free paper
Manufactured in the United States of America

16 15 14 13 12 11 10 09   8 7 6 5 4 3 2 1

For my parents Miriam and Marcus Kaplan,
who do wonderfully well without ever using a computer,
For my daughters Leora, Avital, and Shira,
who can't go a day without one,
and for my husband, Rodney, who has accompanied me in
my journey, and supported me throughout.
—Joni Falk

For Darcy, *mo chride*,
and for Micah and Abraham, *maicc mo chridi*.
And remembering John and Barbara Drayton,
who would've liked to hold a copy.
—Brian Drayton

Contents

Foreword

Online communities evoke excitement, anger, boredom, dissent, and commitment—often all at the same time! They have undergone rapid and unpredictable changes over the past 40 years. *Creating and Sustaining Online Professional Learning Communities* explores the varied, conflicting, productive, and unexpected ways that online communities can contribute to teacher professional development and offers concrete solutions. This book continues a promising trajectory to find effective ways to use online tools. It builds on the intriguing innovations and unanticipated consequences of advances in online communication. From the earliest opportunities, users of electronic networks have sought to connect to each other both one-on-one and in groups.

In 1971, for example, when email using the @ sign became available to users of the ARPANET, it rapidly became what many called the "killer application." Today we debate who—or what—is being killed by this application. Many see email as a battleground between persuasive folks who use nefarious techniques to reach a largely unwilling audience and colleagues who become frustrated when their legitimate messages get filtered into the junk mailbox.

Initially electronic bulletin boards allowed users of networks to get information posted by developers. By 1979 the Usenet emerged as a network-wide discussion board where participants could describe unintended consequences of system updates and seek answers to vexing problems. Thirty years later the Usenet has developed into a quirky, threaded discussion tool supporting numerous public and moderated communities on everything from esoteric computer glitches to efficient toilet repair techniques.

With the advent of public access to the Internet came new online tools and emergent communities. In 1985 the Whole Earth 'Lectronic Link (WELL) was created as an interactive bulletin board system designed to stimulate formation of virtual communities. The WELL spawned communities dedicated to improving teaching, as well as communities for everything from model train aficionados to fans of the Grateful Dead.

PLATO, the online computer-assisted instructional system started at the University of Illinois, quickly added various online communities starting in the 1970s. One addition to PLATO was a form of chat called Talkomatic, a name I have assigned to various family members over the years. Although intended to provide technical assistance to users, Talkomatic became an instant hit as a place to flirt with other users. Recent innovations such as YouTube, Facebook, LinkedIn, Second Life, and Match.com take this tradition in unimagined directions.

Many designers have experimented with online communities for professional development, often building on past practice, inspired by theorists such as Dewey or Vygotsky, and implementing concepts such as communities of practice. Up until recently, few of these efforts have either succeeded or persisted. Fortunately, designers are learning from these experiments and constantly conducting more investigations. *Creating and Sustaining Online Professional Learning Communities* brings us up-to-date on these efforts.

For example, many studies show that teachers benefit from observing other teachers deal with complex dilemmas and discussing their observations. Designers have tried to achieve the same effect with videotaped lessons. Observing experts serve an ace in tennis, use a potter's wheel, or lead a group of students as they experiment with objects that float and sink can be a learning experience when embedded in comprehensive instruction. But, if just watching a talented teacher were sufficient for learning to teach, professional development would be much more successful.

To capitalize on the benefits of face-to-face social networking, designers have set up numerous online forums, discussion groups, and other collaborations. Access to the ideas of more experienced users has been a mainstay of online communities but can go the way of the Talkomatic. Experts differ in their ability to articulate their ideas. In addition, users often complain that they already know what the expert recommends but cannot change their own behavior. And, why should talk alone lead to change—as many teachers point out, talk is far from sufficient to change algebra problem-solving behavior.

Besides converting successful techniques to online options, designers are also experimenting with new technologies, such as digital libraries, datamining, and recommender software. For example, from comprehensive services like Amazon to specialized sites for music, restaurants, or dating, recommender systems use information from participants to match users with promising choices. Imagine the opportunities for reviewing curriculum materials.

The authors of *Creating and Sustaining Online Professional Learning Communities* triumph over the challenge of finding effective combinations of advances in technology, advances in understanding the nature of leaning, and research on professional development. They identified many unintended consequences and successful transformations that result when designs are implemented in varied settings. This book brings all these threads together, draws on an impressive range of diverse approaches to the challenge, and offers readers helpful, pragmatic, and principled insights. The book underscores the need to work *behind the scenes*, tinkering with the design of online communities, responding to emergent user activities, and incorporating lessons learned by others to sustain communities. Everyone who is interested in understanding, improving, or designing online communities will find this book rewarding.

Marcia C. Linn

Acknowledgments

We wish to express our thanks to the chapter authors, both for their contributions to this volume and for the rich dialogue and interchange that we have had over the years about the development and understanding of electronic communities. Collectively, the authors bring a great insight about ways to harness the vast potential of the Internet with the power of community engagement in order to create professional learning environments online.

We also wish to thank our institution, TERC, Inc., and the Center for School Reform, for ongoing support for our work. TERC, Inc., founded in 1965, is a nonprofit research and development institute located in Cambridge, Massachusetts, dedicated to the improvement of math and science education for all learners.

Each of the communities represented in this volume has evolved as the Internet has grown, as new interactive tools have been released, and as the public's comfort with interacting online has increased. Given the constant growth and change inherent in this work, it is never clear when to stop and assess what one has learned and when to share that knowledge with others who are creating, facilitating, and assessing such environments. We would like to thank Michael Haney from the National Science Foundation for encouraging us to take stock of the lessons learned by multiple long-running projects that have cut new ground. Throughout Mike's tenure as a program officer at NSF, he has played a large role in encouraging a wide range of innovative work in technology and education, and he has played an essential role in the development of our own work. From him we have always received challenging questions, high standards, unceasing curiosity, optimistic collegiality, and an unwavering focus on the life and growth of teachers and students. We would also like to thank Elizabeth VanderPutten of the National Science Foundation, who has been our program officer for both MSPnet and MSPnet Phase II. We have been very fortunate to have had her support and sage advice as we grappled with the technical, political, and conceptual challenges inherent in creating an electronic community for the varied and diverse constituencies involved in NSF's Math, Science Partnership initiatives.

We are grateful to Marcia Linn, the series editor, for her vision, encouragement, and support of this project. We are also grateful to Aureliano Vazquez, Meg Lemke, and the editorial team at Teachers College Press.

Each educational environment described in this book was actualized through a collaborative team effort. While lead staff may hold an initial vision, it is transformed by staff who bring expertise in the following areas: programming, Web architecture and design, community outreach, content management, facilitation of dialogue, research, and evaluation. They are the people behind the URL, the human faces behind the technology. They may be invisible to users, but they subtly influence the culture and the dynamics of the learning that takes place. While we cannot mention all the staff on each of the teams in this volume, the editors would like to specifically thank Jon Obuchowski, Quang Le, and Shaileen Pokress; Kathryn Hobbs, Kimberly Patton, Tara Robillard, and Maria Ong; and Lance Lockwood, Jay Feldman, and Elizabeth Applebee for their pivotal contributions to MSPnet and to the virtual conference described in Chapter 7. Finally, we would be remiss not to mention the pivotal role played by community participants who not only browse and search but who also actively contribute to the dialogue, content, and learning that takes place.

Many of the projects described in this book were supported by grants from the National Science Foundation, including NSF/MSP 0335334, NSF/DUE 0634149, NSF/DRL 9980081, NSF/ESI 9911770, NSF/DRL 0088027, and NSF/DRL 9812831. Any opinions, conclusions, or recommendations, expressed in this book are those of the authors and do not necessarily reflect those of the foundation.

Joni Falk
Brian Drayton

CREATING AND SUSTAINING ONLINE PROFESSIONAL LEARNING COMMUNITIES

Introduction

Brian Drayton and Joni K. Falk

For the past 2 decades a growing number of professional developers, educators, Web designers, and programmers have collaboratively developed electronic communities to facilitate professional learning in the areas of mathematics and science. This book presents the work of a group of trailblazers who have been engaged in the creation of such communities over a long time. In sharing their insights and decisions, they cast light on the building and scaffolding of many aspects of online communities: content selection, creation and management, site architecture, administrative structures, tools and interactive features to be deployed, facilitation of discourse, and the development of online leadership. These developers have been learning from their experience, assessing the success of their projects, and at the same time engineering future projects to take advantage of a greater suite of interactive functionalities, faster data transmission rates, nearly ubiquitous access, and a growing pool of users with ever-greater Web sophistication and expectations.

The initial impetus for this book came from Dr. Michael Haney of the National Science Foundation, who was determined to learn from the collective experience of projects aimed at creating electronic communities for math and science professional development. He hoped that such a book could help make explicit the implicit decisions that were being made by creators of math and science professional development. To this end, the editors invited colleagues who had a long history of experimentation with such learning communities to a retreat at the Essex Conference Center in Essex, Massachusetts, in October 2005. During 2 days of congenial and vigorous colloquy we explored how our ideas about professional development and learning affected our decisions as we designed, facilitated, and evaluated the success of our different online learning environments over the course of their evolution so far. This book grew out of these conversations.

The authors of these chapters—the developers and researchers of these communities—are educators first and foremost. While each of the authors is knowledgeable about site design, and about new technologies and collaborative Web tools, their work is deeply influenced and informed by scholarship that has unfolded over the past 3 decades about how professional learning takes place, particularly for math and science educators.

The projects in this book have provided varying forms of professional development to university provosts; science, math, and education professors; and K–12 administrators and mathematics and science teachers, among others. The subject of the professional development ranges from exploring content knowledge, to pedagogical practices, to the nature of educational change. However, we believe that the lessons learned will be of interest to anyone designing, sustaining, or studying electronic learning environments, regardless of the specific subject matter.

This book bridges the worlds of Web development and research on professional learning communities for educators. The bridge between these two worlds manifests itself in the human infrastructure that scaffolds the users' interactions and the online activities in which they participate. This human infrastructure administers the site, constrains or seeks to expand the site's membership, envisions the nature of site content, determines how content will be presented and managed, facilitates collaboration, and determines the modes of these interactions. The focus of this book is on the human infrastructure that is often less than visible to the user; hence the title "Behind the Scenes."

The communities presented in this book were created during a period of burgeoning research and debate about professional learning, which was proceeding in parallel with the marked technical and social advances related to telecommunications and the Internet. The projects discussed in this book were all influenced, to varying degrees, by three streams of research: research about (1) the learning and knowing that educators need, (2) the necessity of situating that learning in a distributed knowledge framework, and (3) the power of professional communities to drive or support professional learning. Since these ideas may be less visible to the surfer of these sites than are the technology and content, we begin by briefly addressing each of these ideas in turn and draw out their implications for electronic communities.

CONCEPTUAL FRAMEWORKS

The Nature of Teachers' Work and Implications for Professional Learning

Starting in the 1970s, seminal work by researchers as diverse as Mary Budd Rowe, Hugh Meehan, Seymour Sarason, and Susan Philips began to provide a deeper analysis of the nature of teaching, taking into account its cognitive, cultural, and emotional complexities—in parallel, and in dialogue, with kindred studies of student learning. This line of research brought out the kinds of decision making and strategic deployment of content and pedagogical knowledge that are required of teachers moment-to-moment. A teacher's work came to be seen as a systematic practice, a kind of expert knowledge (Ball, 1997; Carter, 1990; Munby, Russell, & Martin, 2001; Shulman, 1987).

As with other kinds of expertise, teachers' expertise involves the development of a large fund of deployable skills, disciplinary content, and pedagogical knowledge, based both on formal learning (e.g., during college or preservice teacher education) and on learning from practice. Teachers deploy their content knowledge and pedagogical strategies in the context of their understanding of the background, needs, and diversity of their particular students. Simultaneously, they employ classroom management strategies to keep the students engaged and to shape the social climate of the class. They teach, facilitate discourse, and listen, in order to assess their students' prior knowledge and understanding: the contextualized backdrop upon which new information will be placed. Their practice includes the ability to gauge their students' engagement level and to determine, moment-to-moment, how and when to introduce new material, to provide greater depth, or to retreat and review. Shulman (2004) suggests that the complexity of teachers' work can be compared with that of a hospital emergency room.

This reality has important implications for those who wish to provide professional development for teachers. Since much expertise is tacit, and not readily verbalized, it was recognized early on that teachers' professional development must include strategies for reflection about practice—making the tacit explicit, so that it could be worked with and made subject to conscious choice and change. Since teachers' work involves a mixture of classroom culture building, disciplinary and pedagogical content, and insight about children's learning, their professional learning should not treat each of these components as separate and unrelated modules that could be addressed by brief workshops or institutes. Rather, focused work on one or another aspect of teaching needs to be contextualized and to become part of teachers' practice to some extent.

In this approach to professional development, teachers become essential resources for one another's professional development. In the end, this is a fundamentally democratic view of the educator, learning with and from colleagues about the substance of their work. This in turn has implications for the kinds of learning that should take place when professional development is situated in electronic communities, including the exchange of subject-matter knowledge and the "wisdom of practice." For example, sites can be targeted to identify particular elements or classroom techniques (e.g., "inquiry" in science or the integration of Web-based resources in teaching). They also can provide a way to explore aspects of professional knowledge and practice (e.g., "pedagogical content knowledge" or "teachers' ways of knowing" mathematics or science).

Theoretically informed electronic communities can support professional learning as well by enabling the identification and exploration of areas of professional knowledge, making them accessible to reflection and change.

Learning Situated in Practice

Another field of theory and investigation was taking shape and attracting more and more attention during this time, that is, the study of situated cognition in general, and the study of the knowledge characteristic of practice in particular (craft or professional practice, and then, more broadly, any well-defined kind of activity). The sociocultural approach founded in the work of Vygotsky and others conceives a professional knowledge, thinking, and practice as socially situated and distributed. That is, one's knowledge is inextricably bound up with one's tools, resources, and collaborators: what she does, the tools she uses, the people she collaborates with, the ends she seeks, and so on. Thus, a professional or expert carries out her work in the midst of an adapted system of mediational means.

The interacting web of habits, relationships, and tools is used and improved piecemeal, and often not revised or evaluated from a systemic perspective.

The activity theorist Leont'ev and researchers such as Scribner, Cole, Latour, and Woolgar have fruitfully examined the way that a person's purpose or intent shapes her collaborations, acquisition and use of tools, and evaluation of success and effectiveness. The cohering element is the user herself, the center of her cognitive and social network.

Thus, professional learning situated in practice should take account of this network of tools and intentions, so that it can be evaluated and possibly changed, either by improving the coordination of the resources across which the practice is distributed, by augmenting the elements, or by changing them, bearing in mind the professional's goals and purposes, and the typical challenges encountered in the workplace.

Moreover, users tend to build up their practice by the addition of one and then another element as needed—a new database tool, a new piece of equipment, a new journal or reference work, a new professional ally (Huberman, 1993). For this reason, community Web sites need to balance the designers' vision with users' flexible and creative use of resources. "Going about technology design from this set of perspectives is far from standard in human–computer interaction research. Often design proceeds from a gadget-centric viewpoint divorced from a context of use" (Nardi, 2002, p. 529).

Communities of Practice

In the sociocultural view of learning, one's work and learning are mediated by tools and resources—and a critical part of this "surround" is collaborators and colleagues: the professional community. This realization has opened a wide field of interest in communities of practice and related notions, such as communities of interest and of action. Investigators in this area tend to approach the vexed question of the meaning of "community" in a way that frames it in terms of *participation*—specific professional practices, characteristic activities and tools, characteristic values, and typical performances.

A person may belong to several such communities—a scientist in education may, for example, belong to a community of scientists, and another of educational researchers, and also to communities not related to her work. As Wenger (1998) points out, this multiple, simultaneous belonging can be an important source of enrichment for a community, when people play the role of "broker" in importing ideas, points of view, questions, and practices from outside the specific community of practice.

Furthermore, this approach suggests some characteristic pathways for continued professional learning. Lave and Wenger (1991) posit a typical trajectory of entry, from legitimate peripheral participation toward participation in the center, core, or heart of the community. This trajectory, with its corollary view of learning as change in participation, thus provides a structural view of how professional learning can be fostered by participation in a community of people who share the same practice.

Electronic communities have come to explore two important roles in the context of communities of practice (or of interest). In the first place, they may further the life of an existing community; in this case, online communication may enhance (and be enhanced by) existing patterns already established offline. In the second place, a Web site may make possible the creation of a community that does not yet exist, by connecting people and enabling them to explore the possibility of a shared practice.

When a community's membership or focus is carefully restricted, trust and mutual knowledge develop relatively quickly. If, on the other hand, a community is more heterogeneous in membership or focus (or both), this diversity can increase the likelihood of the brokering of expertise, ideas, and tools among the participants; difference then can drive learning. In this case, there is a greater need for the facilitators to foster a culture of respect among diverse constituencies.

Electronic communities also can be designed so that different levels of participation are possible, leadership of different kinds can emerge, and participants can build shared knowledge and standards for their practice. Since evaluation, debate, and exchange are essential to a professional community, the increasing number of interactive tools have added to the potential power of Web-based communities as resources and settings for learning.

THE CONTENTS OF THIS BOOK

The book is divided into two parts. Part I comprises chapters on long-running electronic communities that have a broad, growing membership base. The members have a large role in shaping the professional learning that takes place. The chapters in Part II describe professional development experiences that are more targeted and constrained. They engage smaller populations for a more well-defined period (e.g., a semester, a 10-day conference) in activities such as sharing classroom practices, engaging in an online course, or participating in a virtual conference.

Part I: Community Forums

Chapter 1, by Joni Falk and Brian Drayton, describes a Web site, MSPnet, that serves as the "electronic infrastructure" for school reform projects funded by the National Science Foundation's Math and Science Partnership program. The partnerships represent collaborations between institutions of differing kinds—higher education research scientists and mathematicians, school districts, nonprofit educational organizations, schools of education. Furthermore, while its membership is limited to MSP members, MSPnet must support dissemination to the public at large, while preserving a sense of community and trust for the site members.

MSPnet's design reflects the complex, nested nature of these partnerships, but also provides mechanisms by which new communities can emerge according to the needs or purposes of participants. Allowing for this hybrid of predefined and emergent communities has required innovations in the design of the Web architecture (e.g., the role of permissions or access control structures), the kinds of tools that are built to serve both predefined and emergent community structures, and the development of distributed methods for facilitation and leadership. Success has included both participation (frequency and depth of use of tools and resources) and co-construction (building the libraries and resource areas, creating emergent groups for learning or collaboration).

Chapter 2, by Bertram C. Bruce, argues for the importance of an alternative vision of a learning community. The Inquiry Group, starting with a lunchtime discussion about inquiry and science education, has unfolded over time and come to include derivative communities using a flexible Web-based toolkit to explore diverse subject domains well beyond the original focus on inquiry-based science. Bruce's chapter describes ways in which the Inquiry Group communities have been co-constructions by the participants as part of authentic inquiry—using "inquiry" in Dewey's comprehensive sense. Bruce suggests that the basic metric of success for such a community is that people who are involved with it continue to participate, to use the community and its tools to facilitate their continued inquiries. Evidence of this kind of success emerges from the story of successive or parallel lines of inquiry, on topics ranging far from the original focus on inquiry in science and math education.

Chapter 3, by Wes Shumar, describes the Math Forum, a diverse site for math educators, math learners, and anyone interested in mathematics. It is founded on the idea that what all math people share is an interest in doing math—problem solving and mathematical reasoning. The focus of this chapter is on the ways that the community, and its growing resource base, takes shape and is renewed: "the production of participation." Participation, as measured in various ways, is a foundational metric of an online community's success. In the Math Forum, engagement with mathematics is the reason for participation, but participation reliably must take several forms if the community's contents and resources are to continue to be maintained and refreshed.

Chapter 4, by Flora McMartin, examines yet a different model for the center of an online community, a digital library. In this case, MERLOT, the community aspect is essential to the populating and value of the library, as it consists of annotated or reviewed resources for college and university faculty to support and encourage the use of online resources. The online community was designed to incorporate basic elements of academic practice such as peer review. The structured community designed to implement this avatar of academic behaviors in the end includes elements both of a library and of a professional journal or society. The culture of the site is recognizably a reflex of academic culture, but the implementing community is not yet self-renewing in the way that academic societies are. How powerful a "glue" is the shared interest in the use of online resources for college teaching?

Part II: Communities Interacting in Targeted Professional Learning Environments

Chapter 5, by Rebecca K. Scheckler and Sasha A. Barab, examines the development of a culture of inquiry in the Inquiry Learning Forum (ILF). The ILF's online component (e-ILF) is an electronic community constituted to support participating science teachers in Indiana as they explore their understanding and implementation of inquiry-based science in K–12 classrooms. In addition to commonly used tools such as discussion forums, the e-ILF also makes possible "virtual classroom visits" in the form of videos of the teachers' classrooms. In this way, teachers' isolation is diminished, and they benefit from the opportunity to see other teachers in action. This, then, can enrich the discussions of practice and related issues. The authors explore how John Dewey's theories of inquiry, of habit, and of sociability can provide an analysis of dynamics within their learning community. This analysis in turn can inform the way the community is facilitated and evaluated.

Chapter 6, by Andee Rubin and Sue Doubler, presents us with an exploration of how community—or some community processes—can be constituted in a short time in the context of an e-course for teachers. Contrary to many online courses, "community" is inherent to the design of Investigating Physics. Rubin and Doubler's treatment emphasizes the role of scientific values and modes of discourse (including graphical representations) in shaping the culture of the online community. The course structure, credit requirements, and other design features unique to Investigating Physics provide incentives to participation not present in the other communities in this book, for which participation is itself a basic criterion for success. Community structure to a significant degree is dictated by the learner–teacher relationship of the course, yet as the chapter shows, when natural phenomena and collaboration are central to the activity of the community, multiple sources of authority emerge (as in an inquiry-based classroom).

Chapter 7, by Joni K. Falk, Soo-Young Lee, and Brian Drayton, draws on lessons learned from creating virtual communities for scientists, educators, researchers, evaluators, and district and school administrators engaged in large-scale mathematics and science reform projects. There is a paucity of data on effective means to foster deep, reflective discourse within interactive, online conferences, despite the increased affordances provided by the Internet for collaborative work across distances. This chapter begins to fill in that gap.

The chapter explores the interaction of content and structure in fostering interactive dialogue, the role of novel structures such as an interactive poster hall in fostering collaboration, the role of moderators and discussants in enabling reflective discourse, and benefits and drawbacks of virtual conferences when compared with traditional ones.

ORGANIZING THEMES

When the authors included in this volume met, we found that we shared certain ideas that influenced our work, and explored how these ideas contributed to the development of very different online professional development environments. Our discussion, and the chapters that emerged in this book, related to four groups of questions.

   1. *How do the content and the context (online course, virtual conference, community forum) affect the type of professional experience that one encounters?* One way in which these communities vary, is in the nature of their *content*. The narratives make clear that the content present on a site is shaped by several different characteristics, including the site's community, purpose, and processes. Indeed, the contrasts among these sites are to an interesting degree a matter of relative emphasis, despite obvious specific differences.

   These sites differ in the degree to which the content is constrained. For example, Rubin and Doubler, in their Investigating Physics course, cover a well-defined corpus of knowledge related to the basic physics of motion. The Math Forum, while focused on mathematics teaching and learning, covers a broad variety of topics for a broad array of constituencies. Some are parents; others, students who enjoy doing math; still others, educators seeking better ways to represent a lesson. Perhaps furthest along this spectrum, Bruce in Chapter 2 offers a toolkit and a philosophical framework through which very different constituencies can explore unrelated interests.

   Another dimension that affects the content is the degree of emphasis on the sharing of resources as opposed to the sharing of craft knowledge. The latter seeks to encourage practitioners to share information, techniques, and subject matter of specific importance to the work in which they are immersed. The role of this in a particular community may not be evident at first glance. In MERLOT (McMartin), for example, what strikes a visitor first is the collection of resources being exchanged, but the value of these resources is significantly enhanced by the annotations and comments from community members about how they have used the resources, including such qualities as potential effectiveness as a teaching tool and ease of use for students or teachers. In a related vein, a visitor to MSPnet might be struck by the wealth of resources on math and science reform within the library and resource centers. However, members on MSPnet would use private forums to exchange draft work in progress, challenges, and strategies with their colleagues.

   In addition to variations in content, the professional online experiences represented in this book provide multiple *contexts* within which discourse is facilitated. Each of these sites makes use of "implementation metaphors," which enable the user/participant to quickly grasp what participation can mean, what kinds of interactions will be available, and what sort of topics may be offered. For example, people who attend a "virtual conference," as described by Falk, Lee, and Drayton, bring from their experience of face-to-face conferences an expectation that there will be ways to interact with peers around their work, as in a poster presentation; there will be presentations from leaders in the field, as in keynote addresses; there will be thematic, focused exploration of common problems in the field, as in the form of panel discussions; and there will be conversations. Judicious use of such expectations enables the user to feel at home with the electronic environment quickly and efficiently. In the case of an online course (Rubin and Doubler), schedules, grades, feedback from teachers, and so on, provide incentives to full participation, as well as guidance about some specific ways to interact. The Inquiry Learning Forum (Scheckler and Barab) builds on spatial imagery to enable teachers to "tour" one another's classrooms as one more channel of exchange. These metaphors in combination enhance the quality and quantity of information and meaning that are available to participants.

2. How is professional development influenced by different site architectural structures, choices of collaborative tools, models for facilitation of interaction, and administrative structures? The designer's vision of the purpose of the professional development, as well as the nature of the content and context, as explored above, influence the suite of collaborative tools that are employed. For some—e.g., the Math Forum (Shumar) and MERLOT (McMartin)—text exchanged through discussions and the posting and sharing of resources was the primary mode of exchange. For others, video (the Inquiry Learning Forum, Scheckler and Barab) or graphical representation (Investigating Physics, Rubin and Doubler) assumed a central role in promoting discourse.

In some cases, the use of tools is carefully scaffolded behind the scenes; the administrators design when a graphical representation will be introduced or when a video will be uploaded and shared. For others, the community is given a suite of tools to deploy as the need arises. For example, in the Inquiry Group (Bruce) constituents can choose from a toolbox of functionalities. Similarly, within working groups on MSPnet (Falk and Drayton), users can choose to utilize an interactive calendar, a threaded discussion, a file-sharing tool, or a survey tool. New functionalities such as Web-video conferencing, whiteboards, and wikis soon will be incorporated into this suite of tools. This approach allows users to choose the tools with which they are comfortable and that best serve their purpose for communicating with different groups of people at different times.

Finally, the authors' understanding of the ways professional learning is actualized (strictly peer-to-peer, expert-to-novice, a mixture of expertise from different fields, or a combination of these), or the need to constrain the content or focus of exchanges, influenced the design for facilitation, moderation, and administrative functionalities. Thus, some communities (e.g., MERLOT, McMartin) encouraged wide participation, but made use of the customs of academic peer review, coordinated by a project core, to ensure quality control and to warrant the value of contributed content. MSPnet combined some centralized facilitation by project staff, but also fostered distributed leadership and facilitation among its many constituent groups, including small emergent communities that could be formed online by individuals, working parties, or others sharing work or topical interest.

3. How are community interactions influenced by size, coherence of membership, structure, and the presence of offline interactions? What are effective mechanisms to support a community, to sustain it, and to deepen members' interactions online? The nature of an electronic community is a blend of vision and experience, of design and emergence. The way people can join it, inhabit it, and learn through it reflects important design decisions and has implications for the facilitation and "metabolism" of the organism: its internal and external processes of change and growth. For example, if an electronic community is an outgrowth of an offline community, this can ensure pre-existing patterns of collaboration, personal acquaintance, and at least some aspects of shared culture. For example, the virtual conference on sustainability (Falk, Lee, and Drayton) convened people who had shared in an online community (LSC-Net) for several years, but a significant number of the participants had also met one another face-to-face during preceding traditional conferences.

The criteria for participation also shape how the community will take form and evolve. Groups with restricted membership (the Investigating Physics course, Rubin and Doubler, or MSPnet, Falk and Drayton) have an easier time creating a sense of trust since their members know the relative size and composition of the group of people with whom they will be interacting. This "semiprotected" sense of community can foster frank exchange of resources, insights, and questions that are safest "backstage" (to use Goffman's term)— explorations of issues and dilemmas, strategies and methods (Goffman, 1959). This is more difficult to achieve in communities that are open.

Another way in which these projects vary, is in how homogeneous or heterogeneous the membership is with respect to professional backgrounds and purposes, scope of action, and typical collaborative patterns; the chapters in this book vary along this dimension as well. For example, if the site has multiple constituencies, the way its design reflects the relationships among the constituencies can play a significant role in nurturing the community, providing resources, and supporting its goals. If the membership is homogeneous as to professional focus (e.g., science teachers, as in the Inquiry Learning Forum, Scheckler and Barab) or interest (mathematics, as in the Math Forum, Shumar), the community structures can differentiate to support a range of interactions within an established practice or topic group. If, on the other hand, the membership is heterogeneous (as in MSPnet, Falk and Drayton, or the Inquiry Group, Bruce), then supporting communications within and between the nested communities is a key task for facilitators and will have structural implications as well.

Finally, structures and facilitation will shape and be shaped by the administrative structures and the leadership that emerges from within the community, and this dependency is explored in each of the chapters that follow. Some of these communities provide a range of pathways for members to participate and contribute. MSPnet (Falk and Drayton) and the Inquiry Group (Bruce) enable leadership to emerge within several levels or areas of their communities, and leadership can range from contributing content to creating and facilitating small communities of interest or practice. MERLOT (McMartin) has a concentric structure from "patron" (resource user) to "core," which allows members to move from peripheral to central roles in the identification and peer reviewing of materials on the site.

4. *How does one assess the success of such an effort over time?* A consideration of measures of success for these communities leads directly back to the goals and vision underlying each one. It is interesting to note that none of these projects makes a case for its value on the basis of "numbers served," but all take for granted that active participation is necessary evidence of value or at least usefulness. The narratives present a variety of measures beyond this, which reflect the role of exploratory, research-driven projects, even if a service or product is an ultimate goal. Concretely, by its very nature, a Web-based project preserves some of the story of its community and the resources it has accumulated, making them available for the next generation of investigators and users.

The kinds of participation that emerge during the project's development are another outcome, harder to measure, but with a definite impact on the capacity of the participants to carry forward their work. The growth of expertise, the density of interconnecting ties, the greater experience with new collaborators—all these are presented as returns on investment, different forms of enrichment of the professional development community. Continued use of the tools developed, the connections made, and the ideas tested and propagated, is additional evidence that in fact professional learning has occurred and has been integrated into the practice of the participants. Change in participant quality is as important to measure as number of participants; neither is reducible to the other's terms.

Given the breadth of types of communities and forms of professional development represented, the readers of this book might naturally find themselves asking which method is best: constrained or open content; online course or community forum; an intimate or broad and open community? We can save you the suspense—there is no one right answer. Yet, each of the authors provides some reflection on this question, and it is our hope that the way they thought about and measured the success of their venture, will inform others who are in the process of creating and joining a professional learning community.

It is interesting that the chapters in this book are not technically oriented. That is, while they discuss tools and techniques, their focus is much more on structures of thought and practice—centered in fact on the abiding values of professional practice and growth. Because the implementers of these communities have been able to focus on the learning structures, the cultural dynamics, the nature of participation, and the values and benefits exchanged, they have, over time, begun to exploit some of the affordances of telecommunications and related technologies to alter some basic assumptions about professional learning. Consequently, they seem to be moving beyond the implementation of an electronic representation of "offline" professional learning and exploring new territory. For example, many Web-based professional development programs essentially reproduce in online form the accustomed roles of professor and student. Yet telecommunications implicitly allows free movement between all nodes of a network, in a fashion analogous to the way hypertext allows the reader to create many paths through a corpus of information or narrative. The natural language for a learning network of this kind is the language of community. For the potential to be realized, however, three crucial changes are needed. First, there must be a change in consciousness, as participants actually take advantage of the possibility for multivocal conversation and exchange. Second, a cultural change is required, as participants (the community of designers and learners) develop processes for sociability (trust building, presentation of self, protection or control of exposure, development of habits or customs to facilitate constructive exchange). Finally, the community needs to use explicitly the power of distributed knowledge and cognition, accumulating resources and tools appropriate to the professional practice(s) of its members.

The reader is encouraged to reflect on the ways in which the idea of community has contributed to the various cases discussed here. More particularly, how has the technology and the work behind the scenes made possible the growth of community engagement? How in turn have these diverse communities changed the nature of professional learning? While each of them has evaluated its success in different ways, their persistence and generativity are strong evidence of the success of the past 20 years of explorations in technology-enabled professional learning.

REFERENCES

Ball, D. L. (1997). Developing mathematics reform: What *don't* we know about teacher learning—but would make good working hypotheses? In S. Friel & G. Bright (Eds.), *Reflecting on our work: NSF teacher enhancement in K–6 mathematics* (pp. 77–111). Lanham, MD: University Press of America.

Carter, K. (1990). Teachers' knowledge and learning to teach. In W. R. Houston (Ed.), *Handbook of research on teacher education* (pp. 291–310). New York: Macmillan.

Goffman, E. (1959). *The presentation of self in everyday life*. New York: Anchor Books.

Huberman, M. (1993). The model of the independent artisan in teachers' professional relations. In J. W. Little & M. W. McLaughlin (Eds.), *Teachers' work: Individuals, colleagues, contexts* (pp. 11–50). New York: Teachers College Press.

Lave, J., & Wenger, E. (1991). *Situated learning: Legitimate peripheral participation*. Cambridge: Cambridge University Press.

Munby, H., Russell, T., & Martin, A. K. (2001). Teachers' knowledge and how it develops. In V. Richardson (Ed.), *Handbook of research on teaching* (4th ed., pp. 877–904). Washington, DC: American Educational Research Association.

Nardi, B. (2002). Activity theory and design. In T. Koschman, R. Hall, & N. Miyake (Eds.), *CSCL 2: Carrying forward the conversation* (pp. 529–532). Mahwah, NJ: Lawrence Erlbaum Associates.

Shulman, L. (1987). Knowledge and teaching: Foundations of the new reform. *Harvard Educational Review*, 57(1), 1–22.

Shulman, L. (2004). The wisdom of practice: Managing complexity in medicine and teaching. In L. Shulman (Ed.), *The wisdom of practice: Essays on teaching, learning, and learning to teach* (pp. 249–272). San Francisco: Jossey-Bass.

Wenger, E. (1998). *Communities of practice: Learning, meaning, and identity*. Cambridge: Cambridge University Press.

PART I

Community Forums

The Web sites analyzed in Part I are broad-based sites offering a range of tools and activities to their users, whose learning is motivated by their own emergent professional or intellectual needs. The professional development that the sites enable, therefore, is "informal" in the sense that the content and timing, among other features, are based in each learner's questions: There is no specified common core of knowledge, no curriculum or assessments involved in participation. The sites therefore share important characteristics in common, which also can be seen as the source of characteristic shared problems or challenges.

Each of the communities served is heterogeneous along several dimensions. For example, the Web sites serve a variety of constituencies, whose needs may change over time, whose ease with the technology varies, and whose interactions with other constituencies are more or less under negotiation. All these kinds of variety are the source of innovation. As members gain experience with the tools and with the kinds of interactions built into the design, new possibilities or limitations of the environment become evident and can be articulated in relationship to, or in terms of, the existing tools and functionalities and the users' purposes. Thus the initial design, resources, and facilitation make reflection, revision, and experiment necessary.

Each of these sites has a structure that reflects important characteristics of the community being served and the kinds of activities the participants need/hope/want to engage in: for MSPnet, the partnerships and projects in which members participate; for the Inquiry Group, the inquiry circle; for the Math Forum, the problem, a fundamental kind of activity that is shared by all; for MERLOT, the scholarly processes of peer review. These structures provide orientation for new members and reflect basic commitments of each community. Yet from these foundations, each project, in its development over time, has incorporated new technologies and new metaphors for participation.

While it stands to reason that these sites will be very different, given the variety of their origins, some of the differences turn out to be interesting

15

for anyone seeking to understand or create such sites. Some common challenges to which each project has made different responses include:

- How to enable diverse kinds of participation.
- How best to integrate online and offline dimensions of the community.
- Where leadership happens, and how it arises.
- How the roles of the designers/maintainers of the site should evolve and complement emerging leadership among the members.
- Balancing designed versus emergent activities, groupings, and tools.
- Addressing the questions of quality and of sustainability over time, in the context of continued technological innovation and technical skill among participants.

To differing degrees, each of these is addressed explicitly or embodied tacitly in the narratives here presented, and the areas of both contrast and similarity are instructive.

CHAPTER 1

MSPnet: Design Dimensions for Nested Learning Communities

Joni K. Falk and Brian Drayton

INTRODUCTION

MSPnet (http://mspnet.org) was created to serve multiple, nested communities composed of university faculty, K–12 educators, administrators, and professional developers who were engaged in efforts to improve math and science education. The site was launched in January 2004 as part of a large-scale, educational change initiative, the Math and Science Partnership (MSP) program, funded by the National Science Foundation (NSF). To date, the site has served over 5,000 members; nearly 3 million pages have been viewed by more than a million visitors to the site. This chapter looks behind the scenes at design decisions that have shaped the users' experience in this learning community.

Some of the questions that we faced as we began this effort were: Are professional communities best served by large umbrella organizations that have a breadth of membership and access to large bodies of research and resources, or by fostering smaller communities that are more targeted to address specific concerns and interests? Can communities of practice be pre-defined, or must they emerge spontaneously and change over time? What are the interactions between content, tools, and leadership structures online? When does a centralized facilitation model serve professional community sites best, and when are they best served through a distributed leadership model?

It is our hope that this chapter will serve to stimulate others who intend to create or participate in communities that provide avenues for professional growth. In doing so, we would like to move beyond the architecture of MSPnet to share the debates, values, decision points, and dichotomies that ultimately affect the users' experience.

STRATEGIES FOR PROFESSIONAL DEVELOPMENT ONLINE

It is difficult to speak in general terms about community sites for professional development, or even about that subset of sites that serve educators. That is because each site has a vision that lies behind its creation, and the vision influences both the design of the site and how the site's success will be measured. This vision often is not fully articulated but rather is embodied in the site's architectural design, the content that appears on it, the facilitation structures, the membership structures, and the suite of tools that is offered.

To be less abstract, therefore, let's start by considering the Tapped In project (http://tappedin.org) at one end of a spectrum and ERIC, the Educational Resource Information Center, at the other (http://www.eric.ed.gov). Tapped In, launched in the mid-1990s, offers teachers and organizations virtual buildings and meeting rooms where groups can make use of an advanced technology environment and a suite of interactive tools to communicate and collaborate. The vision of the creators of Tapped In was to invite educational professionals "to be tenants in the TI environment and use it to help accomplish their own TPD [teacher professional development] agendas" (Schlager, Fusco, & Schank, 2002, p. 133). Their hope was that it would be used by many different organizations and constituencies for their own purposes; consequently, the site itself is content free. The activity on the site is not intended to produce an accumulated corpus of knowledge or research evidence for the field at large.

At the other end of the spectrum, consider ERIC (Education Resource Information Center, http://www.eric.ed.gov) an online digital library of education research and information sponsored by the Institute of Education Sciences (IES) of the U.S. Department of Education. ERIC provides access to bibliographic records of journal and non-journal literature indexed from 1966 to the present." ERIC's vision is to provide the public with easy retrieval of and broad access to research; its vision does not include the provision of collaborative opportunities. The Computer Science Corporation provides centralized leadership in building and managing the collection.

In comparing these two, we see that Tapped In uses the online medium as a tool to promote collaboration, but the specific content of that collaboration is undetermined. Facilitation of groups is decentralized; the professional development that takes place is for and by the participants who are directly engaged in the collaboration. By contrast, ERIC provides professional development by creating a corpus of knowledge that can inform the field at large. Although all of the documents have been collected from the field at large, the Computer Science Corporation tightly manages the content of the site, as well as its the organization, updating, and quality control, with advice from content experts and a steering committee. Most important from the users' perspective, Tapped In is a place to meet and communicate, while ERIC is a place to retrieve information.

Since the creation of Tapped In and ERIC, the Web has continued to evolve, technological advances are constantly changing the landscape of Web site design, and user expectations have changed as well. People have become accustomed not only to browsing, but also to editing, chatting, conferencing, and buying products online. Sophisticated permissions (access control) systems now enable sites to provide varied levels of access to different users, so that one user's view of a site can be quite different from another's. Some users may see a "read only" view of a site, whereas other users may have permission to post, edit, and manage information. Sites also have begun to track user preferences and are able to customize what the user sees in response to previous behavior patterns.

The explosion of new interactive capacities with more complex and flexible content management systems has opened the door to many hybrid designs that combine features of both retrieval/storage and communication/collaboration systems. While there are still sites that specialize in providing access to digital libraries, and others that offer only collaborative environments, hybrids are increasingly common. Sites that typically were identified with the retrieval of information (online journals, newspapers) have begun to include places for user comments and discussions. Conversely, sites associated with collaboration increasingly have embraced content as well. One extraordinary site, launched in 2001, is Wikipedia, an encyclopedia written collaboratively by people around the world. Wikipedia is a perfect example of a marriage between interactivity and content delivery. With the rise of these more advanced functionalities, and consequent hybrid designs, no longer is one forced to choose between content and collaboration: Mechanisms have evolved to integrate both.

In addition to the blending of content and interactivity, systems have developed to allow users to have control over the groups with whom they choose to communicate. A prime example of this is facebook.com (http://www.facebook.com/) launched in 2004, a site that provides students with multiple social networks, some that are predefined (e.g., their university affiliation) and others that are emergent (e.g., a group of students whose favorite book is *The Lord of the Rings*).

The increased capabilities to combine features that optimize content retrieval, content creation, and collaboration, and to customize users' experience according to their preferences, history, and community affiliations, have created new possibilities that must be taken into account when creating learning communities for professional development. We suggest that there are four dimensions that strongly influence decisions on the nature of the architectural design, content, the suite of tools, expectations for dissemination, and leadership structures in any community for professional development. All of these decisions in turn will shape the nature of the participants' experience.

These dimensions are:

1. The nature of the community: Will the users experience the community as a large professional association (such as AERA and NSTA), or will they see themselves as a part of a small community where they know and can identify the other members of the group? Will the community be predefined (for example, all members that belong to a particular university or department), or will it emerge out of shared interest (a group of teachers from different schools interested in exploring 5th-grade student work together)?
2. The nature of the professional development experience: Will the users anticipate that the professional experience will be more similar to visiting a specialized library, or to attending a meeting with colleagues? What role will a specific corpus of content play in participants' professional experience? Will the site result in a growing knowledge base, resource center, or library that users can read, share, and contribute to? Or is the site intended to provide rich virtual meeting spaces where ideas are exchanged and collaborative work is done, but where no specific product is necessarily anticipated?
3. The nature of the audience and of the "products": Do the users anticipate that the site will serve to disseminate content to a broader audience (as tends to be the case for professional associations), or do they anticipate that the content that emerges will be protected and shared only with members who are a part of a well-defined community? Members' understanding of the private versus public nature of the community will affect the types of documents that will be produced and shared.
4. The focus of leadership and facilitation: Does control over membership, moderation, and knowledge management reside centrally, or is it distributed within each subcommunity or emergent group?

As the rest of this chapter will show, MSPnet was developed intentionally to be a hybrid on all four of the above dimensions; that is, while the dimensions seem to offer divergent options, the diverse needs of our community required that we combine elements that might seem to be in tension. Thus, MSPnet's design is intended to provide the user with the sense of belonging to a large community, while still offering smaller predefined and emergent community spaces. The participants' professional experience blends the retrieval of resources, research, and information, with modes of interaction that promote rich exchanges with colleagues around craft knowledge, contextual knowledge, and emerging experiences. While some of the knowledge shared on the site is for participants' eyes only, there is also the expectation on the part of the funder and participants that the site will result in a corpus of knowledge to be shared with the field at large.

Finally, the site combines both a centralized and a distributed leadership model. Hybrid models are rich and challenging. They provide the users with more choices in how they will interact, with whom, and for what purpose. They also run the risk of confusing the users about the site's primary purpose. These trade-offs will be discussed later in the chapter.

SETTING THE SCENE: THE MATH AND SCIENCE PARTNERSHIPS

There is no one perfect design for online professional development Web sites. The design, the content, the suite of interactive tools, and the community infrastructure must be deeply informed by the community that is being served. In designing MSPnet, our first task was to understand the Math and Science Partnership program, and then to understand the needs of multiple constituents who were a part of this community. Hence, before proceeding to describe the site design, it is important to provide a brief overview of the Math and Science Partnership program.

The NSF was created by Congress in 1950 to further America's growth and development in science and engineering. NSF's educational directorate has funded many innovative, large-scale educational change programs to improve STEM (science, technology, engineering, and mathematics) education. These programs have included Urban Systemic Initiatives, State Systemic Initiatives, Local Systemic Initiatives, and most recently the MSP program. What sets the MSP program apart from its predecessors is its emphasis on engaging science and mathematics faculty in higher education institutions to create partnerships with K–12 school districts. In addition to universities and school districts, partnerships often include corporate and business partners, community organizations, state educational agencies, and informal science organizations. Each of these partnerships is a complex entity stretching across institutional boundaries, work cultures, and sometimes even state boundaries.

NSF has funded over 80 such partnership projects (72 of which are currently active) that have brought together approximately 450 K–12 school districts and 150 institutions of higher education across the United States. While some of these projects are modest in scope, others are extremely ambitious; they range in their funding from $150,000 to $35,000,000 each.

These projects cumulatively make up the community that MSPnet serves. The projects are divided into four types.

- Comprehensive partnerships are typically largest in scope and aim to implement change across the entire K–12 continuum.
- Targeted partnerships focus on improving student achievement in either mathematics or science and focus on a narrower grade range.
- Institute partnerships focus on developing science and mathematics intellectual leaders and master teachers, school- and district-wide.
- RETA (Research, Evaluation, and Technical Assistance) projects assist partnership awardees in the evaluation and/or implementation of their work.

While the projects vary significantly in scope and size, all projects share some common goals—articulated by NSF as the program's five key features. They are: (1) to improve the capacity of schools to provide challenging curriculum; (2) to increase the quality, quantity, and diversity of mathematics and science teachers; (3) to support partnerships between scientists and mathematicians at higher education institutions and K–12 school districts; (4) to provide evidence-based design and outcomes to increase our understanding of how to improve student achievement; and, last, (5) to sustain institutional change in participating K–12 school districts and higher education institutions. These five key features of the program provide overarching goals for projects to discuss at conferences and online.

The MSP program is a major research and development effort. It is recognized that there is still a paucity of research on the factors and conditions necessary for effective partnerships between higher ed and K–12 to emerge and become self-sustaining. There was an assumption from the beginning that all constituents would learn from one another as they worked together in new combinations (Ramaley, 2003). Hence, it was anticipated that successful projects would serve as models, document their process, and publish research so that successes within this program could be widely replicated to improve mathematics and science nationwide.

MSPNET'S "MISSION" WITHIN THE NSF MSP PROGRAM

MSPnet was funded to be the electronic infrastructure for this large national initiative. There were many expectations for what such a community would achieve, which we clarified through a needs assessment with a wide range of stakeholders. For NSF's MSP program, our funder, it was critical that MSPnet eventually could provide an archive of the lessons learned from the cumulative experience of all of the projects involved. Principal investigators were interested in communicating with leaders of other projects to see how they were handling commonly faced challenges. Project directors wanted a space to communicate with their collaborators and partners within their project. Although some of the projects had Web sites of their own, they often lacked the capabilities to build in collaborative functionalities. Hence, our initial needs assessment with multiple constituencies revealed that MSPnet needed to serve a variety of functions, which included:

1. *Serving as a dissemination vehicle*: Given that this program was a research and development effort that would inform others in the field, it was critical to develop a dissemination vehicle, where lessons learned from these projects could be gathered, archived, and disseminated to the public at large. In addition, as this program is a part of the No Child Left Behind Act, it has a political dimension to it, and there is broad public interest in the program's progress.

2. *Providing a mechanism for project leaders to learn from one another*: Leaders of each of the MSP projects had a need to access and learn from the resources, research, tools, strategies, and challenges of other projects. Given that all of the projects were engaged in a similar enterprise, they faced common challenges and sought to know other projects' solutions. This form of learning from one another is indeed a form of professional development, and it is best done within a protected space. While it was decided that many research articles and resources would be shared with the public, it also was determined that discussions between leaders of the MSPs would take place in a protected environment for members only.

3. *Providing each project with its own interactive space*: Each MSP project is in itself a complex community made up of faculty from higher education and from multiple K–12 school districts. Some of the MSPs have hundreds of affiliated staff members and reach thousands of teachers. Each MSP had a need for its own interactive Web presence that would be used to engage constituents in dialogue, provide teachers with ongoing professional development, and provide staff at different institutions with a way of sharing files and collaborating. Inter-project collaboration was even more sensitive than cross-project collaborations. These spaces needed yet further insurance that dialogue and files shared would be seen only by members of the project, until the project chose to share them within a larger community.

4. *Allowing for emergent communities to arise*: Finally, within each project smaller communities began to emerge that had needs for a collaborative space where they could share documents, discussions,

events, and announcements. These groups could not be predicted by the designers of MSPnet at the outset. Sometimes a group might consist of a project's leadership team; sometimes it might be a group of teachers who had made a commitment to share student work; sometimes it might be a cross-section of teachers, a scientist, and an administrator who chose to extend their face-to-face workshops to online follow-up discussions. Many of these groups wanted an even more secure environment. They needed a space to collaborate that could be private and not visible even to other members within their project.

To address these challenges we had to come up with creative approaches to our design of a community infrastructure, to the interactive tools that, in part, would shape our users' professional development experience, and to the level of support required to facilitate distributed leadership.

These multiple needs had a great impact on our thinking about a Web-based infrastructure that could serve all of them. They forced us to recast our understanding of the four dimensions proposed above, in light of the specifics of the MSP program.

1. *What is our vision of community?* Could the site serve to connect all of the MSPs in a large community of practice while also providing each MSP project with its own site and independent identity, and privacy?
2. *How do we envision the professional development that will take place?* Could we engage users in collaboratively creating a growing digital library of research and resources while at the same time engaging them to use the site as a vehicle for collaboration?
3. *Could we serve multiple audiences and bear in mind the needs and constraints relevant to each?* Could we become an effective dissemination vehicle for the public without marring a collaborative culture where projects could share unfinished products, drafts, unmet needs, and challenges?
4. *Who would assume administrative responsibility?* Could we provide the centralized scaffolding necessary to engage all projects and to connect them with one another's work while also creating a distributed leadership model where each project would be responsible for the administration, membership, management, and facilitation of its own space?

Below, we address each of these in turn and relate its impact on our architecture, our tools, our content, and our users' experience.

Our Vision of Community

Some communities seem to have clearly defined boundaries and articulated procedures for joining. Such communities may be defined by neighborhood boundaries, affiliation in an organization, or membership within a religious group. From an organizational perspective, the community is clear. It contains all those who fit a certain set of criteria. If a person lives on a certain street, he is *ipso facto* part of a neighborhood community; someone living outside the boundaries is not. We will refer to such communities as "predefined." An individual is not likely to initiate such a community but rather to join one. A single individual may belong to several of these predefined communities, and these multiple affiliations combined will make up the individual's community network.

Yet there is a competing construct that is taking shape on the Web. This construct places each individual at the center of his or her own community network. Rather than seeking predefined networks to join, a person creates his or her own network, which is composed of friends, colleagues, buddies, associates, and so on. In this notion, the individual is the center of his or her own universe, and community is defined through varied networks and experiences. These communities are emergent, and a person can belong to many that intersect or overlap; boundaries may still be important, but take on meanings that vary with each association (Cohen, 1985). They form spontaneously, out of shared interests, personal relationships, and tasks.

On the Internet, both forms of community exist. The NARST or AERA Web site is a professional community that has clear rules for membership. The community is pre-existing. A visitor comes to join the community rather than to create it. However, visitors to http://facebook.com see the construct where the individual is at the center of creating his or her own communities. Students can identify those who love the same book as they do, and discuss it, or those who share an interest in bicycling during the weekends. Students form networked communities that are composed of their friends and their friends' friends.

The Math and Science Partnership community, and, by extension, the MSPnet community, has important characteristics of a predefined community. Membership within the community is acquired by an affiliation with one of the NSF-funded MSP initiatives. When a new project is awarded, senior staff instantly are invited to become members of MSPnet. Conversely, colleagues who may share many similar interests but who are not associated directly with an MSP project cannot obtain membership. Hence, membership within MSPnet is contingent on being directly affiliated with one of the MSPs.

This, perhaps, is not very different from being a part of a university community. A chemistry and a mathematics professor at a given university are part of the same university community, even though they may feel a stronger kinship with others in their own disciplines who may be at other institutions. Externally defined community structures have the virtue of bringing together people who may not know of one another or of one another's work. This benefits individuals by enlarging their social and intellectual network of colleagues. The downside of communities so constituted is that they may not feel "authentic" to their members. It may feel like belonging to a community by default rather than as a result of a considered choice.

Membership on MSPnet has grown steadily from an initial 350 members in January 2004 to over 5,000 members. This large group includes those working on large comprehensive projects and on more targeted efforts, those providing institutes, as well as members of projects providing research, evaluation, and technical assistance. The community's membership includes the leadership teams of each project as well as staff and participants representing a diversity of project roles. Thus, it includes physics professors at a university and elementary school teachers. It includes college provosts and K–12 administrators. What unites them is their engagement in a Math and Science Partnership project, and through this effort an interest in improving students' STEM education from elementary school through college.

Within the membership there are smaller, predefined subcommunities in which people are more likely to be working with one another for a common goal. Project membership varies greatly in size from one project to another, with one project having as many as 755 members and one research-oriented project having as few as two. The community of members within a project is certainly more coherent along certain dimensions. These members will likely share goals, activities, meetings, products, research agendas, and the motivation to see their project succeed.

While staff within a project may include college faculty and elementary school educators, they are engaged in an active partnership through their involvement in the project, and thus there is greater motivation to communicate and collaborate, despite institutional and cultural differences. Forming relationships between higher education and K–12 is an essential part of engagement in the MSP effort. While the project community is smaller and more intimate than the MSPnet community at large, it also is predefined by a participant's affiliation and employment.

Yet, within the predefined structure of the MSP program, the designers of MSPnet saw the need to build in flexibility that would allow emergent communities of practice to arise and fit within the constraints of the access control system. These communities could not be predefined; their membership could not be foreseen. Some examples of such emergent communities might be a group of teachers who spent the summer at a workshop and now want to continue their discourse, a leadership team that is charged with collaboratively writing an annual report, or evaluators on different projects that want to discuss the tools that they use. These small groups usually have a specific purpose or task in mind, and membership consists of people who have a vested interest in the particular activity taking place.

Members are likely to know one another personally and are most likely to form a true community of practice or action, as they share a greater understanding of one another's context and practice. If drafts, unfinished work, ideas in progress, and unmet needs are to be shared, they will likely be shared in such smaller, more intimate (and more protected) communities.

As you reflect on this structure, you may find yourself thinking about the communities to which you belong, or about those that you serve, and may realize that in some aspects those communities are quite similar to the community described in this chapter. Your communities, like this one, may be very large yet contain many smaller subcommunities. Consider, for example, a very large corporation where employees share, at some level, a sense of belonging, a common purpose, and a shared vision. Within this large group of managers and employees, there may be departments, centers, or projects that define a more closely knit group of people. Moreover, within each of these units there are likely to be groups who work more intensely together and who share a stronger bond. Perhaps these are people who work within the same building or who share the same job responsibilities, or perhaps they are brought together through personal friendships that have emerged in the workplace over time.

This structure of communities within communities within communities is very common. A sense of belonging to a very large group, corporation, university, or organization certainly brings many benefits to the individual. Such an affiliation provides a sense of identity and belonging to a large enterprise, of which the collective impact can feel even greater than the sum of individual or small-group efforts. Belonging to a large professional community brings members into contact with engaging people and ideas that they may not have had access to otherwise. These large communities have the benefit of providing rich networks and a wealth of resources. In this way, large communities can provide excellent forums for professional development, especially if professional development is defined to include increased exposure to related research and resources generated by others.

Smaller communities, defined by membership in a department or a project, provide different potential benefits. The smaller scale will not provide the breadth of exposure that a larger community might, but there is likely to be greater depth in exchanges. Smaller communities are more likely to share or at least to be aware of participants' needs, concerns, and challenges.

The view of community described above was the basis for the MSPnet architecture. At the center is the MSPnet Hub, which connects all projects, as shown in Figure 1.1. The Hub contains a library with a rich array of papers pertaining to STEM education, and a resource center with evaluation instruments and useful Web sites pertaining to the work of the MSPs. When building a resource that will serve the community, scale is indeed beneficial. As all projects can contribute to the holdings in this area, the Hub library and the resource center are far richer than they would be if they were built by any single project. Project leaders can contribute research that they have written about their project, and it will be shared with all other projects and, if they so choose, with the public at large. Likewise, each project learns from reading the contributions of others.

The Hub project showcase highlights the work of each MSP project, so that individual members can see how their project's effort fits into a larger national initiative. The public can (and does) access the project showcase and because of its national scope it attracts many more visitors than any one project could. Annual face-to-face conferences are archived in the Hub, so those who could not attend in person can watch the videos of the keynote speakers. The Hub also serves a communication purpose for the project leaders, who have a special interest in learning about how their counterparts in other projects are handling administrative, logistical, communication, recruitment, and other challenges. Here the leadership teams can use the "Search and Mail" functionality to find their counterparts in other projects and communicate by sending individual or group e-mails. An online event center

FIGURE 1.1. Schematic representation of MSPnet's nested communities

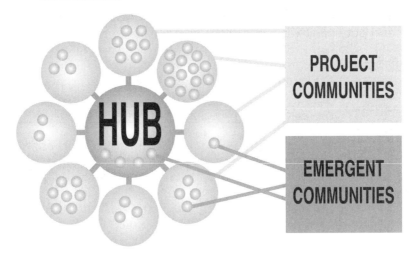

provides the opportunity for speakers to present in video or text format and to hold an online discussion with members of different projects. An interactive calendar informs all members about upcoming events and conferences.

In addition to the Hub, MSPnet provides a Web site for each project, which mirrors most of the functionality available in the Hub. Each project has its own library and resource center. It has its own project showcase, which highlights press releases, project reports, and multimedia presentations. Projects have their own "Search and Mail" functionality (to search for people within the project and to send group or individual e-mails to names reurned by the search). Whereas the Search and Mail functionality within the Hub searches through a database of people associated with all of the MSP projects, the Search and Mail within each project is confined to a database of members of that project. Also, like the Hub, each project space has its own interactive calendar.

While each project has its own URL, the project spaces are intricately interwoven with the Hub. A member logging in sees a page that shows both the Hub and the individual project space.

Clicking on the MSPnet Hub tab as shown in Figure 1.2, allows a member to navigate within the Hub, a space shared by all projects. Clicking on the tab labeled with a project's name (in this case, PRISM, see Figure 1.3) changes the left menu, and brings the user to their project's space. Not only is the content different, but he or she is now interacting with a smaller community composed of members from their own project.

With one click, project members can copy items from the Hub library or the Hub resource section to their project's library or project's resource

FIGURE 1.2. Hub home page, showing key navigation paths within and between Hub and project community pages

FIGURE 1.3. An example of a project home page within MSPnet

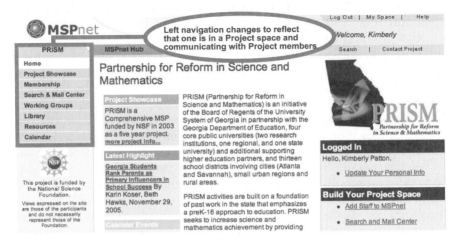

sections as shown in Figure 1.4. In addition, when members of a project add new items to their library or resource center, they are asked whether they want these items to be shared in the Hub as well. All items posted in each project's showcase are harvested and displayed in the Hub.

When MSPnet was first launched, members of the Hub or members of any project space could participate in discussion forums. While these forums provided discussion functionality to members of predefined groups, they did not allow emergent groups to form and to collaborate. In order to provide the user with greater control to decide who they wanted to communicate

FIGURE 1.4. Hub library metadata page with a button to copy item to a project library

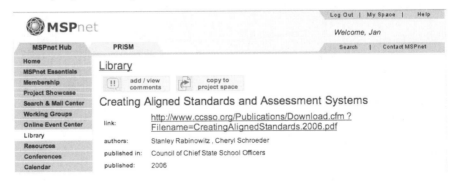

with—and to provide a greater suite or tools with which to communicate—we converted discussion forums to a more robust functionality called working groups.

Each working group can control its own membership, its own agenda, and its own level of privacy. Working groups can choose the tools that they need for their purpose. They can elect to utilize a threaded discussion, an interactive calendar, a file manager, a survey tool, or a Web-conferencing tool. They can choose whether the group should be private (which will result in its being invisible to MSPnet members who do not belong to the working group), project-wide (other members of the project can apply to join), or site-wide (members of any MSP project can apply to join).

By interlinking Hub space, project spaces, and working group spaces, the architecture now provides users with seamless navigation as they move from a larger community space to a more restrictively defined one and then, often, to a still smaller community that they have created for a particular purpose.

When in the Hub, the user experiences the advantages of belonging to a large professional association. The scale of the Hub provides exposure to new ideas, new people, new contacts, and new resources that one may never have sought out intentionally in a small community. The project space provides the user with a feeling of belonging to a smaller community where members share common activities, goals, and deadlines. Last, Working Groups provide individuals with the ability to create emergent communities as the need arises and to specify the people who are invited and the visibility of the items that are posted.

Even though users of MSPnet interact in multiple communities, MSPnet also works to ensure that their experience is not fragmented. Users receive one customized digest every night that tells them of new relevant activity that has taken place within the Hub, within their project spaces, and within their working groups.

The Nature of the Professional Development Experience

The term *online professional development* often calls to mind "distance learning" through online courses. Such courses release participants from the need to be physically in attendance, while still providing a corpus of material, a professor, and other students with whom one may be able to interact. The best of such courses have found ways to foster lively interaction among students and teachers (see Chapter 6). Yet, too often, this mode of professional development tries to replicate traditional classroom environments rather than enabling new modes of professional development made possible by the technology.

Online learning communities represent a different model of professional development, which can be substantive and deep, although it may lack a specific corpus of information that will be transmitted and assessed. Participants most often do not receive credit for their engagement—their motivation is based on professional need or personal interest. In online learning communities, people and their purposes, the tools and resources that they deploy, and the patterns of facilitation that affect their interactions are all part of a dynamic system or ecology. Content, action, knowledge creation, and the building and maintenance of community processes are mutually interdependent and shaped by social and historical context. This approach, often called "sociocultural" or "situative" (Greeno, 2006), bears in mind the realities of professional life and learning, in which knowledge is distributed among people and their tools and resources (Salomon, 1993); practice is collaborative and is mediated by artifacts like documents, models, or Web sites; and learning and practice are inseparable (Lave & Wenger, 1991; Scribner, 1997; Wenger, 1998).

The Internet provides a rich learning environment where such a mix of professional development activities can occur. It combines a medium for storage and archiving of information, new ways to broaden an individual's professional network and communication with colleagues, tools for substantive collaboration, and vehicles for dissemination. Such an environment can provide increased access to resources and research; access to a community of colleagues to discuss, comment on, and critique the value and applicability of the research; access to role models and project models, collegial support when facing challenges, a safe environment in which to share work in progress and to collaborate with others; and a pathway to disseminate one's work to a larger audience. (For a discussion of such benefits in an online learning community for students, see Bruckman, 2004 and 2006.) In addition, the archival nature of the Web can make the results of shared discourse available to others who did not participate in specific events; thus, even the record of substantive discussions becomes a resource for later inquirers.

Yet these benefits are certainly not ensured by the existence of the Web (or by any particular Web site). They need to be considered carefully when building a site's architecture and functionality, and when considering the behind-the-scenes activities that will take place to facilitate, moderate, and nurture such professional development. We turn to MSPnet now, to provide a concrete example of how such professional development occurs.

The Value of Resources for Professional Development

The online environment often is associated with a communication space, but it also provides a rich collaborative storage medium, where a community of colleagues with a shared interest can collectively build a library and resource center for one another. With the growth of the Internet there is no shortage of resources, and many will complain of information overload. Hence, access to increased resources may seem unnecessary. But a collectively built library and resource center does not provide *more* resources, but rather *shared* resources that are of interest to a community of people engaged in the same or similar endeavors.

The collective can always provide richer breadth than an individual (or even an individual project) can, so when using the Internet in this way, a larger community is better than a smaller one. Hence the Hub library and resource center, to which all projects can contribute, are far richer than the library and resource center of any individual project.

A second, important advantage of a collectively built archive is that it provides a forum in which colleagues can discuss and critique resources. Here the value of a smaller, more intimate community becomes more essential. While a larger audience is great for the harvesting of resources, an individual may want to know the people with whom he engages in dialogue about these artifacts. The participative dialogue that continues beyond the reading of the resource, enables one to understand not only what the research says, but also how and when it is being applied, and whether and how the results are being replicated. Hence, while a particular resource on MSPnet can be copied from the Hub to a project space (or uploaded from a project space to the Hub), the comments that are attached to an article are visible only to a single community. If a resource is posted within a project and shared within the Hub, comments posted within the project will *not* be copied and shared with the larger community. In this way, the architecture of MSPnet maximizes the potential for building a collective resource while providing smaller communities in which the dialogue takes place.

The Value of a Social Network and Communication Tool for Professional Development

The value of a large social network is that it enables individuals to converse with others who are not in their immediate social circle. So, for example, a child born on 9/11 can find other children born on this date to support one another in figuring out how to celebrate on a day associated with a national tragedy (D. Gruen, personal communication, 2004), and students across the country can discuss their love of *The Lord of the Rings* on Facebook, even though they may never meet.

Likewise, educators have the need to converse with those encountering similar issues whom they do not know and may never meet. Again, larger communities are better for this purpose than smaller ones, and they provide a greater breadth of interest and experience. Being a member of such a community allows each participant permission to find others within the network who can offer advice, resources, and support.

Here is an example of how this may occur on MSPnet. An evaluator, engaged with assessing an elementary science professional development program, wants to query others who are doing similar work to see whether they can recommend an evaluation instrument. To do so, the evaluator might go to the Search and Mail feature within the Hub, where, by querying the large database, she can gain access to many other evaluators whom she has never met. She would search for "evaluators," "elementary," and "science," and the results of that search would reveal 71 individuals. She then could send an e-mail to all or any subset of this group through the site, or save the group as an e-mail group for later use. This functionality instantly allows the individual to find others engaged in common work across a large community.

The Search and Mail center also facilitates finding project models and strategies. For example, a person may be interested in how different projects within the MSP community are implementing lesson study within their professional development program. By searching on "Lesson Study" within the project database field, he quickly can identify nine projects that are doing so. He then can learn more by reading the project abstracts, reports, and multimedia presentations within the MSPnet's project showcase or by sending an e-mail to the leaders of these projects.

Each project also has its own Search and Mail for networking within the project community. For example, a member of the PRISM project (which has the largest single project membership on MSPnet) will find that she can communicate with 86 K–12 administrators, 10 principal investigators (PIs) and project directors, or 21 advisory board members through the Search and Mail functionality. Conveniently, when one replies to a message sent through the site, the reply goes directly to the sender's personal e-mail (precluding the need to keep checking back on the site).

Another kind of communication and participation is not necessarily initiated by the participant, but can resemble the learning that takes place as a result of being in a room where an important conversation between colleagues is taking place. For example, recently there was an active discussion within the Hub on "Teacher Content Knowledge," a discussion that was visible only to members of MSPnet who are on their projects' leadership teams. Forty members visibly participated by posting 88 messages in the discussion. Yet 304 distinct members accessed the discussion, which received 4,030 hits. So there were far more people "in the room" and listening in on the conversation than the people who left a visible trail. One MSPnet member said, "Did you read the post by Deborah Meier? I loved it. The whole conversation was worth it for that one post alone." Our archives show that this member did not post to the discussion, but that did not prevent him from benefiting from the dialogue and this post in particular. This ability to hear the voice of others, without being seen and heard, is indeed professional development afforded through a learning community. It is worth noting that Deborah Meier, a professor of education at New York University, a founder of the Mission Hill School in Roxbury, Massachusetts, and a widely respected progressive educator, is a role model for many. Her voice carries weight. Those who posted to the conversation, as well as those who listened in, did not know that she and several other very notable leaders in the field would take part. But once these leaders joined, MSPnet members were given greater access to role models with whom they might not have felt comfortable conversing on their own.

The Value of a Collaborative Tool for Professional Development

Collaboration in a professional community with an electronic component often begins in face-to-face conversations and then continues online. Usually people collaborate with people whom they know of, or have met in person, and hence it is most natural that collaboration online will occur within smaller communities. This can take the form of a group of teachers who spent a week together during the summer engaged in professional development, continuing their dialogue online throughout the year. It also can take the form of someone sharing a draft document and asking for feedback, or anticipating that another member of the group will collaborate by writing a second section of the document. The sharing of work in progress requires trust and an expectation that the work will be judged as a draft and not a final product. On MSPnet this most commonly happens within working groups, which we have referred to as emergent communities. These working groups can be site-wide, enabling all MSPnet members to see the contents of the files shared and the discussions posted; project-wide, enabling all members of a project to see the activity; or private, enabling only the invited members to see the dialogue exchanged and files shared.

On MSPnet 284 of these working groups have been created to date. They contain over 4,542 files. It is interesting to note that the creators of these groups tend toward restricting access and visibility, with only 10 of these groups being site-wide, while 135 are project-wide and 139 are completely private. When privacy increases and the people within the group are known to one another, it creates a milieu that fosters experimentation, risk taking, and the sharing of drafts and ideas still in formation.

The Value of a Dissemination Tool for Professional Development

We often think of professional development in one category and dissemination in quite another, but in fact for the educators and academicians in our network, the dissemination of work is part of their concept of professional development. This perhaps surprising idea makes more sense when one bears in mind that "dissemination" involves more than the act of broadcasting a document. For those creating the materials, it is a multistage process, in which a document is developed, critiqued, and refined, often within successive groups with differing vantage points on the material—including some consideration of the needs and questions of the intended audience. In this way, dissemination (as with a plant's setting seeds) involves a long process of growth, development, and ripening.

MSPnet provides a pathway for dissemination of materials in this broader sense. When a document is in its draft stage or an instrument is being tested, it can be shared with trusted colleagues in a private working group. When a member is ready, it can be shared with project colleagues or with colleagues throughout the MSPnet network, but not with the public at large. At this stage, the member may receive feedback from others in the community before allowing anyone on the Internet to Google the document. Then, when ready, the creator of the document can change the visibility setting to permit the public at large to access the document, and it will be announced in an electronic newsletter.

Recently, this process worked nicely when approximately 40 researchers prepared papers that were to be presented at a face-to-face MSP evaluation summit. The papers were made available on the site for MSPnet members only. At the conference, the papers were discussed, and moderators of each session offered feedback. The authors then revised their papers and, after doing so, extended the visibility of their papers, making them available to the public at large.

The Relationship Between the Documents
Shared and the Intended Audience

Do you remember the last time you presented your work at a conference? You were likely to arrive before your presentation was due to start, to get a feel for the culture of the conference and for the people in the room. Perhaps without being totally conscious of it, you took in how engaged the audience looked, how formal they appeared, the types of questions that they tended to ask. In your own session, before you began, you probably took note of how many people were in the room, and whether some of the attendees were colleagues and friends or all were new faces. You might have noted whether the attendees looked tired or wide-awake, whether they would appreciate a bit of humor to lighten the introduction, or whether they seemed ready to dive right into the substance. All of these cues are far more difficult to ascertain on the Internet, yet knowing our audience, how our words will be used, by whom, and for what purpose remain essential questions that affect how we present our ideas.

Now let us think about your collegial conversations. When discussing a challenge, you might speak very casually and openly to a close colleague, might present the problem in a more formal light when speaking to a larger group, and might offer additional context and formal structures when committing your ideas to print. The audience size, intimacy, history or relationships, and purpose affect how we talk.

Many newspaper articles have noted that youth seem less inhibited than one might expect when expressing themselves on online public forums. Almost anyone can blog, and many, quizzically, share intimate facts about their lives on sites such as myspace.com. Not infrequently, this has resulted in employers finding out unflattering details revealed online by potential employees. It has left people wondering whether somehow the technology has erased the boundaries of public and private; perhaps for some it has.

This is not the case for the members of MSPnet. These members are very aware that they represent an MSP project that is part of a program at NSF created as part of the No Child Left Behind Act. They are aware that the articles they publish on MSPnet's Hub, the resources and tools that they share, will be scrutinized by many, including program officers at the Foundation, and that the quality of their work possibly may have an impact on their project and on their own ability to attract future funding. The Hub provides the opportunity to disseminate their work, to become more well known, and to contribute to the field at large. At the same time, however, the high-stakes environment puts a damper on open discussions that would allow members to seek advice, appeal for help, and speak of inhibitors to success and of unexpected roadblocks. These members, perhaps unlike the youth who spill their personal life on social networks, realize that they are leaving a public record.

Therefore, it is imperative that MSPnet have a continuum of public to private forums in which work of different kinds is shared. When a member posts an article to his project library, he can designate its level of visibility, and by doing so choose to share it with project members only, with all site members, or with the public at large. As a result, a member of a particular project will have greater access to documents than will those who are members of a different MSP project. Likewise, members of any MSP project will have access to more documents than will the public at large.

Although it is not as easy to visualize the audience on MSPnet as it would be in a conference room, a person knows that if an article he writes appears in the Hub, it will be accessible to all projects, and if designated as such, it also will be accessible to the public at large. Within a project space, a person knows that she can make an article visible to project members only, to all site members, or to the public. If she wants a more private forum, she can create a private working group that is visible to invited members only.

It has been our experience that the nature of the audience has an impact on defining the types of documents that are shared. The MSPnet's Hub documents tend to be more formal and more finished. Documents exchanged within project spaces, and even more so within private working group spaces, are more casual in style, and as a result are more ripe for collaborative input, critique, sharing, and further development.

MSPnet's sophisticated system combines a *permissions control* system (which assigns access privileges to individuals based on their project affiliation and their role within the project) with a *visibility control* system (by which individual resources and articles in the library can be denoted as public, site-wide, or project-wide). This dual system has enabled MSPnet members both to find ways to disseminate work widely but judiciously and to have safe haven for private sharing.

Yet while this sophisticated system solves some problems, it creates others. When I log in, the underlying database recognizes my project affiliation and that I am an administrator of my project. It also recognizes the working groups (those that are site-wide, project-wide, and invitation-only) to which I belong.

Once I log in, I have access to all of *my* working groups. When my colleagues log in, they will see the site differently. We have found that, despite repeated reminders and cues on the site, people forget that the way they see the site is *not* how others see it. A member may sense a moment of panic, "If I see this, then it is on the Internet and everyone can see it. Oh no!" When an individual is moving between a multitude of tasks and Web sites, it is hard to remember that this site is customized, and what he sees is not necessarily available to others within the project, within the MSP community, or to the public at large. This is still a challenge with which we are grappling.

The Administration and Facilitation of This Structure of Nested Communities

We have seen that many factors influence the types of documents that are discussed and shared within a professional development community. Some of these are more apparent than others to the user. For example, users know instantly that the library is more amenable to reading and browsing, and the Search and Mail center is more amenable to communicating. Other factors are less evident but still exert an influence over users' interactions. For example, the level of privacy within collaborative spaces influences the nature of what is shared. Private groups will tend toward casual interactions, whereas public areas will prompt more formal contributions.

Other features that influence interaction are not built into the site at all, but in fact are embedded in the human infrastructure behind the scenes. One such factor is the structure of online leadership. Our design of MSPnet, with a Hub that connected multiple nested communities, created the necessity both for a centralized support team for the Hub as well as for the development of online administrators from each of the project spaces.

Within the Hub

MSPnet staff play a large role in facilitating and scaffolding interactions on the site. This role is ongoing and hence has implications for sustainability of such community sites. Our role includes being the convener, the collector, the moderator, the organizer, and the disseminator of information.

> *The convener:* Through communication with projects, and being the recipients of "contact" messages, we were often in a position to recognize areas of interest across multiple projects. Knowledge of staff across multiple projects allowed us to cajole leaders from several projects to facilitate a discussion while sharing their different perspectives.
>
> *The collector:* Many projects have stories to tell, but often the project members are not aware that their stories are indeed of interest to others outside their project. From a centralized position, we could call for research articles, work in progress, and case studies.
>
> *The moderator:* While discussions in the Hub most often were co-moderated by content experts in the field, there was often a need for oversight of the discussion. Were people's voices and multiple points of view being acknowledged, were the moderators consistent in signing on, were conversation threads mutating without closure to any particular idea, was there a time to close the discussion and to provide a synthesis?
>
> *The organizer:* Knowledge management, and organization, is essential to building a site where materials can be found easily by its users. As MSPnet has over 12,000 pages, the content needs to be well structured so that the user can navigate without feeling overwhelmed. Some of the organizational structures, put in place for users, are automated. For example, as new material is added, the site automatically highlights the additions on the header pages of the library, the resource center, and the project showcase. See http://hub.mspnet.org/index.cfm/library. In addition to ensuring

an intuitive navigation, and highlighting new material, there is a need for ongoing human attention to the content and its organization on the site. Staff need to ensure that material posted by the community has landed in the appropriate location and that it has the necessary metadata tags, keywords, and copyright permissions. In addition, there is a need to review that the material posted within the Hub is relevant to the work and interests of a broad constituency of members from across projects.

The disseminator: Automated e-mail digests help to keep members informed about new posts to their working groups. Beyond these, however, there is a need to keep the community as a whole informed of new events, library articles, resources, and additions to the project showcase. Through weekly e-newsletters, the community is not only told of new articles but provided with an abstract of each document, which helps members to judge whether it is worth their while returning to the site. We have found a consistent spike in usage during the 24-hour period that follows our weekly e-newsletter.

Within the Project Spaces

Our role here is quite different. Here we saw the need for each project to have ownership, control, and responsibility over its own project space. To do this, each project was asked to assign one to two people to the job of project administrator. Each project administrator had the ability to approve or decline requests for membership, assign levels of access (according to members' roles within the project), change the project's home page, manage working groups, and edit or hide posts to discussions, resources, the library, and the project's calendar.

Optimally, the administrators of each project would take on the role of convener, collector, moderator, organizer, and disseminator, yet our experience has shown that often this is not the case. Project leaders often have expressed a desire to have interactive functionality available to them for discussion groups, for sharing files, for building a library of articles and resources, and for sharing calendar events and news. Yet often they underestimated the human factor and the necessity to designate an individual who would attend to the site, to the building of content, and to the facilitating of interaction.

Projects do not necessarily have the human resources, technical skill, or expertise to provide the behind-the-scenes scaffolding, to prompt active participation from users, to call for contributions to their site, to spend the time to provide organizational oversight, to send newsletters to announce new highlights, and so on. Acknowledging this fact, we sought to provide the projects and their administrators with additional centralized support that would enable them to refresh the look and information on their sites with a minimum of effort. For example, each project can add material to its project's space either by posting through an online form or by simply copying material from the Hub space to the project space. The home page of each project is automatically refreshed to highlight any new post within the site's library, project showcase, or resource center.

This centralized support, coupled with decentralized administration, has met with some measure of success. Of the 79 projects, 74 have posted information to one of the four key areas—the library, resources, project highlights, or working groups. Sixty projects have posts within their project highlights section, 66 projects have posted articles within their project's library, 46 projects have posted events on their project's calendar, and 33 projects have made use of functionality within their working groups. Only five projects have not posted within their project space at all.

Projects vary greatly in their use of their space and in their investment in getting staff to participate. At the high end, one project has over 700 members, whereas at the low end, one project has only two. The success of project spaces is significantly affected by the attention, expertise, and experience of the projects' administrators. It is the administrators who will recruit and attract new members, call for papers, create events such as follow-up activities after workshops, and solicit moderators for discussions. Members or projects that do not have active project spaces, with active administrators, still participate in MSPnet, but are more likely to rely primarily on the resources, discussions, articles, and so on, provided through the Hub.

Providing interactive tools for users, intuitive navigation, and administrative "back-end" functionality is a necessary but insufficient catalyst for community interaction. Professional communities often need the nurturing, the facilitation, the moderation, and the content management that supplement excellent technology with a personal, coaching, guiding hand. As a result, we have begun to provide administrator workshops that focus on technical and techno-pedagogical skills needed for facilitating online communities. In addition, we are conducting case study research on the relationship between project leadership and the forms of leadership that emerge online.

SUMMARY

Learning communities embody an understanding of professional development that is very different from an approach built around courses or workshops (online or offline). Participants in online learning communities are both the recipients and the providers of professional development. Participants return week after week, month after month to exchange resources, share research, network with colleagues, disseminate their findings, and dialogue with peers who are engaged in similar endeavors. They do so without the clarity that a definite curriculum provides and without the motivation of a grade or promise of credit. Their ongoing participation can never be taken for granted. It is nurtured by the relationships that participants build within a community or within multiple nested communities. The nature of participants' interactions will be further shaped by a vision of professional development, coupled by tools and functionality that support that vision. Further, interactions continuously are influenced by participants' judgment of who is listening and responding; hence, it is imperative to be able to control not only what is posted, but also the audience with whom a post will be shared. Finally, the behind-the-scenes administration, content management, facilitation, and moderation subtly but profoundly affect site content, activities, tone, and dialogue. Administrators need both the skills for online leadership, as well as the local connection to the work and the people being served.

In this chapter we discussed four dimensions to consider when designing learning communities. The first is the design of the community infrastructure. Will the participant feel a part of a small community, which has the advantage of being more cohesive, intimate, and personal, or will she feel a part of a large professional organization, which affords greater access to shared research and resources? Our model in MSPnet provides an example of a site architecture that provides for both of these experiences and allows the user to easily navigate between smaller communities of practice and larger learning networks. In addition to the user being able to move between these communities, the site architecture allows artifacts to be copied easily from one community to another, while dialogue about each artifact remains community-specific.

Beyond the question of the size and nature of the community, we also addressed how communities arise and discussed the value of predefined versus emergent communities. Are participants best served by the availability of ready-made professional development structures that an individual can join, or should communities arise based on particular needs, network, and tasks that emerge?

MSPnet has a particularly large and complex predefined structure as it provides "predefined" community spaces for each of the 80 MSP projects. This architectural infrastructure approximates the community's structure offline. It provides a way for each member to find a useful "place" in the online structure, including ways to present herself, find and "meet" others, and get involved in useful activities. The predefined structure therefore can serve as a "bootstrapping" operation, enabling new users to quickly get oriented and find some value in participation. Especially at an early stage of the community's development, and also for new members joining over time, the "sociability" and intelligibility of the site are critical (Preece, 2000). Predefined structures can help in this orientation function. Yet as members feel more at home, and seek to turn the site to their own particular uses, the predefined structure will feel like a limiting model, unless it also includes some capacity for "improvisation," or emergent activities.

Our second dimension addresses the nature of professional development within learning networks. One strand of this professional learning environment is the community's identification, sharing, and evaluation of resources, papers, and research, and discussions about these artifacts. Another is the access to a greater network of human resources: the opportunity to communicate with colleagues with a shared history, to meet new colleagues, and to be in the company of role models. Some communications will be in the form of direct exchanges, while others will be more akin to "listening in" to the dialogue of others. A third strand is engagement in collaborative efforts where a participant may share work in progress, ask for or offer advice, share challenges, define values, or wrestle with ideas. While some collaboration may result in serious research efforts, other tasks may be as mundane as a team leader writing a memo to share a proposed workshop agenda. Yet even the latter may provide the opportunity for recalibration, negotiation, and articulation of values and ideas. Last, the online environment provides a form of publishing where work can be disseminated and shared, an activity that we argue is part of professional development.

Our third design dimension relates to the importance of giving a participant the ability to specify and control his audience. Doing so allows a participant to know if he is addressing a small group of colleagues behind closed doors or sending out a broadcast that will be accessible to thousands. Within MSPnet the diversity of the community is even greater than first appears, because as a participant moves from one space (e.g., a project's working group) to another (e.g., Hub working group), he may be moving from a smaller community with whom he is closely affiliated to a much larger community with whom he is far less familiar. As he moves from protected or well-defined community spaces to more public ones, his communication is apt to become more carefully phrased, and he is likely to take fewer risks. He will take greater care to provide context to audiences who are less informed about his work and to avoid jargon understood only by his colleagues. As the audience grows, he will be less likely to share drafts and products that are still under development, and he will be more hesitant to express ideas that could be mischaracterized or deemed politically insensitive. Thus, as the audience changes from private to public, the participant adjusts his expectations about how the audience will understand and interact with his work, and this in turn changes the actual content of what the participant chooses to impart. Hence there is a feedback loop between presenter and audience in which content and context are intimately intertwined.

Enabling participants to limit and define their audience is crucial to establishing a safe environment for collegial exchange. For this reason, MSPnet's structure keeps track of contexts (in terms of permissions and visibility), with the result that a member can determine and view who is included in a new working group, or which groups will have access to papers that are posted within a project's library.

This makes an important contribution to the user's experience, because context (or intended audience) helps the user shape the activity and its products: Will this collaboration take shape as a no-holds-barred, brainstorming session in private with a small team, or will the collaboration result in an annual report for NSF, parts of which will be posted on the project Web site for public view?

Such choices are a matter of practice; in making them, the participants also are deepening their understanding about their purposes, guiding values, and role within their projects. Therefore, it is important that the design of a learning network take into account the important element of *agency*: recognizing that people's participation is an expression of their own interests, needs, or duties. In these decisions, as in the development of the products themselves, values and principles, goals and methods, are negotiated and then made concrete and visible on the Web site for the intended audience. Further, the products of each such activity are themselves contextualized in the MSPnet system, and the change of context requires, if only to a small degree, some reflection about a participant's purposes and the purposes of the resource being moved or copied.

Our last design dimension examines the relationship of centralized control and distributed administrative leadership. Because MSPnet serves the whole NSF MSP program, centralized technical development and overall facilitation are necessary to maintain a certain level of coherence and consistency in technical performance across the whole MSPnet "universe." Therefore, there is a significant effort, behind the scenes, in content management, content dissemination, facilitation, moderation, and community support and engagement. The centralized staff has an indispensable role that is akin to metacognition: understanding the emergent dynamics across the whole community of communities, and "reflecting" that understanding in its own facilitation and administrative work.

At the same time, we are committed to having a distributed administrator and leadership structure, so that each project space and emergent community has local control and is able to shape its content, professional development experiences, and membership structures to meet its own community's needs and culture. Distributed leadership can promote investment and active participation. We have found that as leadership and facilitation increasingly are distributed within the MSPnet community, ideas for technical innovation are more likely to arise from the experience and interests of the active online leaders invested in developing their own communities. One challenge in creating nested communities with distributed administration is that the expertise of administrators varies markedly between projects. A project's commitment to online leadership, facilitation, administration, and moderation has a great impact on the communities' engagement and viability. Our understanding that online leadership needs to be cultivated and supported has created an imperative for MSPnet staff to launch a continuing effort to support the growth of skilled distributed administrators.

As the community matures, the MSPnet staff continues its original mission, but increasingly in collaboration with the active and innovating membership. Thus, as we have found, for ourselves as much as for the members, the work itself is inherently a learning process—we are ourselves a community in professional development.

REFERENCES

Bruckman, A. (2004). Coevolution of technological design and pedagogy in an online community. In S. A. Barab, R. Kling, & J. H. Gray (Eds.), *Designing for virtual communities in the service of learning* (pp. 239–255). Cambridge: Cambridge University Press.

Bruckman, A. (2006). Learning in online communities. In R. K. Sawyer (Ed.), *The Cambridge handbook of the learning sciences* (pp. 461–474). Cambridge: Cambridge University Press.

Cohen, A. (1985). *The symbolic construction of community*. London: Tavistock.

Goffman, E. (1959). *The presentation of self in every day life*. New York: Anchor.

Greeno, J. G. (2006). Learning in activity. In R. K. Sawyer (Ed.), *The Cambridge handbook of the learning sciences* (pp. 79–96). Cambridge: Cambridge University Press.

Lave, J., & Wenger, E. (1991). *Situated learning: Legitimate peripheral participation*. Cambridge: Cambridge University Press.

Preece, J. (2000). *Online communities: Designing usability, supporting sociability*. Chichester, UK: Wiley.

Ramaley, J. (2003). *Visions for MSP Learning Network*. Address delivered at MSP awardees meeting, Washington, DC.

Salomon, G. (Ed.). (1993). *Distributed cognitions: Psychological and educational considerations*. Cambridge: Cambridge University Press.

Schlager, M. S., Fusco, J., & Schank, P. (2002). Evolution of an online education community of practice. In K. A. Reninger & W. Shumar (Eds.), *Building virtual communities: Learning and change in cyberspace* (pp. 129–158). Cambridge: Cambridge University Press.

Scribner, S. (1997). Thinking in action: Some characteristics of practical thought. In E. Tobach, R. G. Falmagne, M. B. Parlee, L. M. W. Martin, & A. S. Kapelman (Eds.), *Mind and social practice: Selected writings of Sylvia Scribner* (pp. 319–337). Cambridge: Cambridge University Press.

Wenger, E. (1998). *Communities of practice: Learning, meaning, and identity.* Cambridge: Cambridge University Press.

CHAPTER 2

"Building an Airplane in the Air": The Life of the Inquiry Group

Bertram C. Bruce

The question, "How can professional development be supported through an online community?" has assumed increasing importance because of growing needs and promising possibilities to address professional development needs. On one side, the demands on lifelong learning have increased in response to changing technologies, demographics, and workplace demands. On the other side, the tools to support online communities have become both more robust and more accessible, making possible continuing support even among dispersed communities.

Recognition of this situation has led to the organizing themes for this book: How can professional development be supported through an online community? What is the nature of the professional development? What is the nature of the community? What values shaped the online tools? What was the behind-the-scenes facilitation? What was the nature of the online and offline interactions? These questions are all legitimate and significant. However, they apply best to a top-down model for development, in which tools are developed, community participation is solicited, and developers facilitate community actions, all aimed at fostering inquiry for a target community. As important as it may be, this model is only one way in which online communities develop.

This chapter considers another approach, one that turns some of those quite reasonable questions inside out. It tells the story of what I'm calling the Inquiry Group, which has supported professional development through both online and offline means, thriving for more than 25 years. Many other projects have been designed to foster online professional development communities, but the story of the Inquiry Group looks quite different. For a start, it is questionable whether *group* is the best term, when perhaps *community* or *assemblage* might be used instead. In any case, we'll explore here its nature, the reasons for the differences between this story and that of other more intentional development efforts, and the implications for studying online community building.

MODELS FOR DEVELOPMENT OF ONLINE COMMUNITIES

> The reason that simultaneous top-down/bottom-up strategies are essential is that dynamically complex societies are always full of surprises. Only the negotiated capacity and strengths of the center and the locals, in combination, are capable of pushing for improvement while retaining the capacity to learn from new patterns, whether anticipated or not. (Fullan, 1994, p. 24)

There are many ways that online communities are designed, built, and supported. This book is premised on the need to understand more about the diverse ways that happens. As I seek to describe one community with which I have been involved, I find that the questions described above are helpful up to a point, but then become perplexing. The problem derives from a set of issues revolving around agency, intentionality, and process. This can be explained best by contrasting two models for development. I should note at the outset that I know of no project that fully accords with either of these; most are a mix of models, with changes over time. Moreover, as Fullan (1994) has shown, hybrid models are often the most effective and long-lasting. Nevertheless, it will be helpful to sketch the two extremes in order to communicate the reasons for my perplexity.

Let us consider first the *top-down model*. This model arises in various ways. In one scenario, researchers, system developers, policy makers, and funders recognize a professional development challenge, for example, to help teachers learn about new approaches to science education, particularly in situations in which they are geographically dispersed. Following various conferences, workshops, e-mail discussions, planning meetings, and the like, a request for proposals is issued by a foundation or government agency. People in universities and research institutes, who may have had some inkling already about the possible funding, now write proposals to secure funding for specific projects. The proposal defines the professional development goals and the nature of the community to be served or supported. The proposers make initial contacts with potential user communities.

Once a project is awarded, the proposers, who are now *developers* or *facilitators*, proceed to build or adapt online tools, to encourage participation from the target community, and to enter into the cycle of formative evaluation, observing interactions and seeking to improve the tools or community processes. In the course of the project, the values that shaped the online tools, which were articulated in the proposal, are further refined or even reshaped in the light of experience. Because of complex and changing circumstances, the developers find that they are doing many things they hadn't expected to do. This typically results in behind-the-scenes facilitation and a growing understanding of the complexities of both online and offline interactions.

This model is not restricted to funded projects; the defining feature is that the primary actions are those of the facilitators.[1] Moreover, they establish a beginning point independent of the lived experience of the members of the target community. The project does not come into being until the funding or authorization is secured. It runs a course from there until its completion, when it is evaluated and, typically, terminated. In the model, the project is foreground and the community is background.

When a top-down approach enlists participation in the community, it can become what Zacklad calls a *community of action*. This description applies to

> dealing with small groups which actively and thus to some extent rationally pursue explicit goals while relying on a tightly woven fabric of relationships to promote mutual sympathy and the mimetic learning that is assumed to characterize primary groups and communities of practice. (Zacklad, 2003, p. 193)

Communities of action work toward two kinds of goals simultaneously. The first are *service goals*, which involve transforming an external situation, for example, designing a new use of technology for learning. The second are *integration goals*, which involve constructing an internal social milieu allowing its members to develop mutual knowledge and identities. These two categories of goals reflect the fact that community is a necessary means for transformation of the situation, but as a part of that situation, it too is transformed.

As an alternative, consider more *bottom-up models*.[2] Here, the community is foreground and various projects may or may not contribute to the background. The community exists, grows, faces difficulties, and otherwise lives, independent of a particular funding cycle. Actions such as "specify need" or "identify population," may still be carried out, but they have at most a descriptive, a posteriori function, not a performative, a priori one. When we then talk about behind-the-scenes facilitation, we see that it is done as much by community members themselves as by funded developers. Rather than considering one project with a well-defined beginning, end, purpose, and audience, we need to consider the story of the community and the way it appropriates various tools, environments, projects, and professional facilitators, along with its other activities. Thus, in the bottom-up approaches, both agency and intentionality shift from the "expert" to the "client."

A bottom-up approach reflects a *community of practice* (Lave & Wenger, 1991) with less explicit goals for either service or integration. Rather than principled design, the process appears more akin to "building an airplane in the air." As a result, questions about when it begins or ends, and whether it reaches its goals, make less sense. A revised set of questions then arises.

1. What is the nature of the professional development that various community members seek?
2. How does the community evolve?
3. How do the values of community members shape their creation or adaptation of online tools and environments?
4. How do community members facilitate content sharing, reflective discourse, and other kinds of exchanges?
5. How do they engage in both online and offline interactions?
6. How do they evaluate their activities?

I say that the questions are turned inside out, because they flip who is doing what with or to whom. That flipping is integral to the definition of inquiry within the community and to the significance of online communities for professional development. In order to answer these questions, we need to understand more about the story of the Inquiry Group. In the next section I describe some of the activities of the group. The action of members shows how the community has evolved, how members create and adapt online tools, how they share and interact both online and offline, and how they evaluate their activities. In most cases, this is most evident through actions they take to further the work of the group.

THE STORY OF THE INQUIRY GROUP

The *Inquiry Group* is a term I use for an assemblage of people, organizations, projects, and technologies, united by common participation, values, and experiences. It is unlikely that people would say that they joined or left the group on a particular date, or even that they knew for sure the extent to which they belonged. Nevertheless, there are threads that have tied this community together for over 25 years. One thread is a significant overlap of people as various projects developed. As with a small, place-based community, people come and go on particular activities, but over time most of the faces become familiar.

There are various Inquiry Group activities, and only some of them are highlighted in the account below. The activities described are simply representative of the kinds of things that people in this loose consortium do. What results is a montage of how the group continues to *reinterpret*, *adapt*, and *reinvent* online environments to serve its needs (Eglash, Croissant, Di Chiro, & Fouché, 2004).

The Nature of the Professional Development That Various Community Members Seek

If pressed to identify a beginning point for the Inquiry Group, we might look to Dialogues in Methods of Education (DIME) (Bruce & Easley, 2000). This group formed in 1981 for discussion about problems in education, especially in math and science. The members included mostly classroom teachers, but also administrators, scientists, educational researchers, and parents.

In the mid-1980s DIME members began to use Free Educational Mail (FrEdMail), an Apple II e-mail application. Al Rogers, a teacher, had created it for other teachers. In 1985, Rogers also set up the first FrEdMail network. The program did not require any special technical skills to operate, which was appropriate since the primary users were classroom teachers. People in DIME used it for their own communication, but also implemented Science Network News within it. This was a means for elementary school students to ask questions of university scientists. Unlike some similar-sounding systems of today, it saw the children as full participants in the process of investigating scientific questions and sought to show the commonality between ordinary and expert thinking.

Research in schools by DIME members has found that the top-down model, in which experts identify goals, articulate methods, and then work to inculcate those goals and methods, simply doesn't work, unless one has quite limited aspirations for inquiry.

> Early in this research they [DIME members] learned that when experts demonstrated their best methods in the teachers' own classes, they relied on backgrounds of mathematical ideas and a confidence with mathematical dialogue that the teachers did not share. Thus, teachers were often unable to emulate these innovative teaching methods. Moreover, the teachers were not learning how to learn as teachers. Demonstration and imitation was not an effective way to foster learning to teach. (Bruce & Easley, 2000, p. 249)

DIME members met frequently in the first year, but later less often. They now meet twice a year, drawing participants from several states and abroad. Online tools now include a wiki (http://www.uiuc.edu/goto/dime), a newsletter, and a listserv. Although the structure has never been formalized beyond a brief description on the wiki, the persistence of the group represents a community construction of meeting structures and an appropriation of technologies that address professional development needs perceived by members and that members evaluate as useful for their work. Members continue to participate for a variety of reasons, including friendship and emotional support, professional validation, and finding ways to think outside of professional boxes.

The Evolution of the Community

While DIME continued to meet, some of its members began a weekly discussion group, called the Inquiry in Teaching and Learning Lunch. Linda Duke was concerned with thinking and communicating through art. She asked, and prompted others to ask, questions such as, "What does art have to do with everyday life?" "With how we learn and grow?" "How does thinking about meaning in art relate to other kinds of thinking—in science, literature, or relationships with others?" Linda was then education director at an art museum. She was involved with a program to promote visual thinking strategies, a creation of cognitive psychologist Abigail Housen and museum educator Philip Yenawine (1993). Linda wanted to share her work as well as to learn from others. In particular, she knew of work by Margery Osborne and others in science education on the relations between art and science. Others in the local community had a similar need to find places for dialogue about fundamental questions of thinking and learning, which often did not fit well within conventional coursework or organizational practices.

Responding to these needs, the group decided to start a brownbag lunch series. About 30 people attended an initial meeting and set up the following schedule for the first few meetings of the Inquiry Lunch: City planning as a theme for science learning, learning about the human body/bioengineering, the Visual Learning Initiative, gender and mathematics, a summer science program (Grow in Science), and distance learning. As this list indicates, topics varied; often there was no topic set ahead of time at all. People came from diverse departments on campus, as well as from schools and museums. The glue was a shared interest in inquiry and a belief that the definition of inquiry would best grow out of shared activity and dialogue.

It must be emphasized that the Inquiry Lunch was no idyll of inquiry, with delightful discussions spiraling ever onward and upward. Instead, there were inevitable conflicts, debates about content and format, confusions, missed meetings, people who came for a while then dropped out—all the usual problems one might find. Over the years, there may even have been more such problems due to the lack of a tradition, a rigid hierarchy, any extrinsic incentives, explicit objectives, or a designated coordinator. But participants nevertheless found value in the dialogues, creating and growing through the interactions. In contrast to what occurs in many projects that appear similar, the definition of inquiry, the goals, and the measures of success were created by the participants. About the only framing was in an initial invitation message, which said:

> Although the specific topics will evolve on the basis of the interests of the participants, we expect that there will be a focus on promoting inquiry-centered learning, as well as on studying the processes of teaching and learning in classrooms, museums, summer programs, and other settings. Some of the terms that may emerge are "discourse", "practices", "child-centered", "constructivism", "integrated curriculum," "whole language", "project-based learning", and "minds-on". . . . We're trying to provide a space for dialogue about more divergent and student-centered kinds of teaching and learning. (e-mail, February 14, 1995)

This meant that the Inquiry Lunch was an aberration in terms of the top-down model for professional development. There were no clear goals, so it is difficult to measure and evaluate success in achieving them. Moreover, there were no key personnel, timelines, materials, and activities. One might argue that the groups would have benefited from a more explicit structure, but articulating that would entail costs as well as benefits. In this context, one fundamental cost is a reduced conception of the very inquiry-based learning that the project seeks to support. In other words, the more the project specifies its objectives, methods, and evaluation, the more it limits possibilities of inquiry for the participants.

The Inquiry Lunch continued, although its name and composition changed several times. Now called the Community Inquiry Research Group, it continues to meet weekly, with people calling in to participate from diverse places, including in Europe. Discussions are recorded, presentation materials are shared in an iLab online space, and discussion continues in an associated listserv. Eventually, it more or less merged with DIME, with one set of activities being more local and one set more regional or national.

How the Values of Community Members Shape Online Tools and Environments

Although the Inquiry Lunch may have thrived on its lack of structure, there were always pressures to institutionalize it. In 1996, a new graduate-level course was designed to continue the dialogue in a for-credit mode. In the course, students developed curriculum elements (from small resources or activities to course modules). Initially, the units were text-based and free-form.

As part of their work in the first class, Trudy Morritz and George Reese designed a Web site to share the course projects. Students then could read and comment on one another's work as well as experience any interactive elements of the projects. Success of the Web site over successive iterations of the class led to a growing database of what we called Inquiry Units. These units supported investigations into phenomena of all kinds, including teaching and learning. Discussions soon led to articulating an inquiry cycle: Ask—Investigate—Create—Discuss—Reflect. The cycle draws loosely from Dewey's (1933) five-step analysis of effective inquiry, and his view of the natural impulses of a child—inquiry, communication, construction, and expression (Dewey, 1900).

Inquiry Units are now based on the cycle. They can be created and edited using a Web form, and may have hyperlinks, images, and uploaded files, including videos and spreadsheets. There is a comment feature to encourage dialogue about the units. There is also a spin-off feature that allows a user to customize a unit for another purpose, with the original unit remaining unchanged. There is a link-back path to go from a unit to its parent and to that unit's parent, thus ensuring credit to the original creators and a history of changes.

The cycle represented in the Inquiry Units became a boundary object to facilitate communication across disciplinary and work divides (Star & Griesemer, 1989). It expressed values that group members held about inquiry as a creative process and also as one requiring a supportive community with common values.

How Community Members Facilitate Content Sharing, Reflective Discourse, and Other Kinds of Exchanges

The increasing use of Inquiry Units in project and community settings serves to position inquiry as an activity that pervades life activity, not simply formal learning. This was a refrain among Inquiry Group members. Over the past 10 years the Inquiry Units have evolved from a simple means for teachers to share curriculum units with other teachers into a general mechanism for people in community centers, libraries, schools, universities, workplaces, and other settings to engage in collaborative inquiry. Features for co-authorship, comments, document sharing, and group and community support emerged through an open, participatory process of reflective inquiry, not through a centralized design process.

Along with more basic tools, such as listservs, static Web sites, and wikis, the Inquiry Page shown on Figure 2.1 becomes a means to facilitate content sharing within and across organizational boundaries. It also supports reflective discourse. Interestingly, this has occurred not so much because of the explicit "reflect" component in the inquiry cycle, but rather more through

FIGURE 2.1. The Inquiry Page

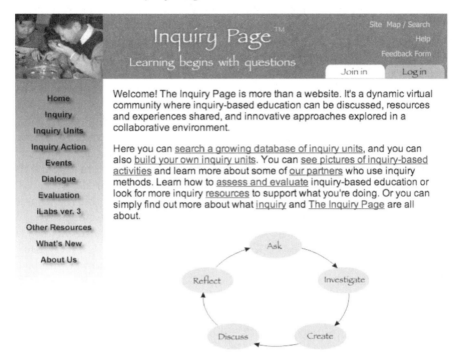

Based on John Dewey's philosophy that education begins with the curiosity of the learner, we use a spiral path of inquiry: asking questions, investigating solutions, creating new knowledge as we gather information, discussing our discoveries and experiences, and reflecting on our new-found knowledge.

the simple mechanism of having work presented and shared in an online, searchable space.

The Web site is used by teachers, librarians, students, parents, and people involved in a wide variety of community action. University courses and full programs, Web sites, various research projects, dissertations, and international connections have grown out of the original project. It has spun off other activities, including Community Inquiry Laboratories (or iLabs), *StoneSoup* (Robins, 1999, 2002, 2003; Snow, 2005), and inquiry workshops. Other university staff and students, as well as participants in many parts of the world, have played a major role in its ongoing development and are considered owners and creators as well. In addition, local participants meet weekly to engage in a participatory design process.

How Participants Engage in Both Online and Offline Interactions

As discussed above, the story of the Inquiry Group is one of shifting and overlapping interactions through a variety of media and meeting structures, only some of which have been described here. In addition to the more core interactions, the personal relationships and orientations have carried over to other contexts. These provide additional opportunities for both online and offline interactions.

For example, the East St. Louis Action Research Project sets up community technology centers with recycled computers and Internet access for community organizations and churches (Choksi, 1997). Volunteers have used the Inquiry Units to share challenges and solutions to setting up the technology centers, as well as ideas for libraries for teenagers, help for the aged, and economic development.

In another setting, African-American women in north Champaign have been working together to take charge of their own families' health care needs through the Afya project (Bishop, Bazzell, Mehra, & Smith, 2001). Participants have created personal health plans, which were facilitated by their use of Inquiry Units. As they entered units online, they had ideas about how to improve the interface and about how to make the structures more useful for their purposes. The individual and collective effort to address everyday problems did, in fact, lead to online community building and also to improved software design. Possibly, the principal value of the software was in how it provided a common focus for the community. In this way, neither means nor ends predominated, but existed in dynamic interrelationship with one another, connected through an inquiry process (Dewey, 1938). Templates created by women in the project became available for other users of the Inquiry Page, as did their model workshops.

In the Chickscope project, involving elementary, middle, and high school teachers, students incubate eggs and raise chickens in the classroom, create magnetic resonance images of the developing embryos (using Web-based remote instrumentation), and in the process learn about incubation and poultry raising, scientific methods, mathematics, embryology, genetics, evolution, biomedical imaging, poultry breeds and economics, research ethics, and diverse other topics. The common focus on chicken incubation facilitated the development of a community of inquiry. But the diversity of topics meant that no one in that community came close to knowing all there was to know. Inquiry Units became a handy way to conceive inquiries into specific topics as well as into the development of learning communities. Continuing meetings in the spirit of the Inquiry Lunch became opportunities to learn about inquiry in the broad sense as well as to acquire a deeper understanding of the development of living organisms.

These ideas are evident in another project, the Ethnography of the University Initiative (EUI) (Abelmann, Kelleher, & Mortensen, 2005), in which undergraduate students engage in research about their own lived experiences. The students address issues such as the experience of Korean students in American universities, the transition from high school to university, or violence in American society. As they do this, they create Inquiry Units to represent the results of their ethnographies. This use significantly extends what was originally a curriculum development tool.

The ethnography use, in turn, has led through a participatory design process to major additions and improvements in the software. Users *appropriate* the technology to meet their own needs. They use it not only for diverse purposes, but as participatory designers, they become active creators, rather than passive recipients of someone else's idea of what the technology should be (Bruce & Rubin, 1993; Eglash, Croissant, Di Chiro, & Fouché, 2004).

EUI has created hundreds of Inquiry Units in more than 50 courses. The project has invested its own resources to add features to the Inquiry Page to better address its needs. These changes in turn have become available to all other users. The continuing engagement and use are one measure of success. EUI now holds annual student conferences and functions as a learning group for students, staff, and faculty interested in what it means to conduct research on universities as institutions.

Experiences of EUI, especially the need for group support, led to extending the Inquiry Page to include Community Inquiry Labs. These are online environments for communities to use to support communication, collaboration, and content management. The iLabs software includes Inquiry Units as well as other tools, such as calendars, contact lists, and document centers (Bishop et al., 2004).

How Community Members Evaluate Their Activities

Participants in the Inquiry Group often were involved in well-structured projects, as discussed above, or in formal teaching. In those settings they tended to follow the structural norms. But it was crucial to have other settings in which they were freer to ask questions that challenged the dominant model for any given project.

As an example, consider the strawberry milkshake machine (Brown, Beck, Frazier, & Rath, 1996). In a summer science camp, there was an activity involving water and tubes, ostensibly to help children investigate siphons and, more fundamentally, water pressure. In response to the teacher's open-ended invitation to make the "water work for you," two 5th-grade girls decided to construct a (fantasy) strawberry milkshake machine. Below is an excerpt from their dialogue and interaction.

Mary: All we do is pour a little bit more strawberry in it [Sue gets a small plastic cup from the back table and asks Mary to "put it in here"], and a little bit of ice cream, and then [Sue puts the cup she had gotten down right next to the large plastic cup, apparently to give Mary another chance to put the shake in there], done. Shake it up [tries covering the large plastic cup with the small plastic cup Sue had gotten and seems to think it's too small, so she empties out another large plastic cup holding pencils and rulers and uses it inverted as a top for shaking], and give it to the window [hands the shake toward the imaginary window to the left of the screen].

A typical evaluation of a science program might identify the strawberry milkshake machine episode as being off-task, probably suggesting remedies such as stronger scaffolding for learning. Somewhat more expansively, David Brown (2000), the lead investigator, described this as a "fantasy context of engagement which provided an overall stability within which other modes of engagement (particularly engineering and performance) made frequent appearances" (p. 37). But even that account implies that the value of the activity lies outside itself, that it's okay to make strawberry milkshake machines because that establishes good ways of working together or necessary "messing about" time (Hawkins, 1965).

These ideas were discussed in the Inquiry Lunch, but participants also felt free to say, "it's great to see children having fun," without the nagging feeling that the fun must be justified in terms of project objectives. At a recent DIME meeting, this theme recurred, with Robert Louisell performing his own composition, "The Old Playground," and leading a discussion about the value of unstructured play. The freedom of those discussions is itself a kind of messing about and often led to deeper examinations of the nature of inquiry. Some might say that it manifests Feyerabend's (1975) description of the scientific method as "anything goes." Yet oddly, the very freedom led to a deeper focus: an opening up of the process of inquiry, encompassing phenomena that never should have been marked out of bounds.

LESSONS LEARNED

Inquiry is the controlled or directed transformation of an indeterminate situation into one that is so determinate in its constituent distinctions and relations as to convert the elements of the original situation into a unified whole. (Dewey, 1938, p. 108)

The various experiences of the Inquiry Group offer a number of lessons about how online or hybrid communities develop and can be supported. This sec-

tion considers some of these lessons, drawing also from John Dewey's definition of inquiry as the process of transforming situations. Dewey's theory
provides a useful framework for considering the wide range of goals and
activities we see here.

Deweyan Inquiry

There are many ideas packed into Dewey's definition of inquiry. It articulates a process common to the inquiry of a scientist, a teacher, a small child,
or a community group. Moreover, this inquiry can be both physical and
mental. Thus, putting on a coat to get warm would constitute inquiry. Furthermore, it pertains to a full range of moral, aesthetic, emotional, physical,
as well as cognitive dimensions. This is in contrast to Peirce's notion, which
separates fact from value and does not construe ordinary actions as inquiry
(Talisse, 2002).

An essential aspect of the definition is that it sees inquiry as involving
transformation of situations, not simply learning new concepts or acquiring
decontextualized skills. Thus, it involves embodied action in the world as much
as it does thinking; it means changing the world, including creating the means
to enhance further inquiry. There is an underlying assumption of an ever-
changing world. The goal is then not to remove all doubt, but rather to continually shape an individual's own situation in order to achieve greater unity.
Dewey's idea is thus akin to biological homeostasis, in which organisms survive
by regulating both their internal systems and their settings in order to adapt to
a complex, sometimes hostile, and ever-changing environment.

Another aspect of Dewey's definition is that action brings into existence
future values. In the top-down model presented earlier, developers typically
have in mind a particular kind of professional development they wish to
enhance. They articulate values they wish to promote and mechanisms to
further those values. Thus, values tend to precede action. For Dewey, inquiry
is both a physical and a mental act. Our actions in the world lead us to reconstruct prior understandings. In that way, values emerge from doing. For
the Inquiry Group, professional development goals were not prior to the
group activities, but often developed as a result of actions with vague or, at
best, tentative and shifting purposes.

Individual and Collective Inquiry: Boundary Objects

How can inquiry involve the possibility of learning with and from others,
while at the same time addressing individual situations? Participants in the
Inquiry Group learned several times about the dual nature of standardiza-
tion. On the one hand, it tends to regularize and thus limit inquiry. On the
other, it facilitates communication and thus enables the very collaboration

that fosters inquiry. Accordingly, there has been an effort to devise structures that are flexible enough to encourage divergent thinking, yet substantive enough to facilitate dialogue. Such is the definition of *boundary objects* (Star & Griesemer, 1989). It was not a problem that these objects might be interpreted or used differently in diverse settings. "Boundary objects are objects which are both plastic enough to adapt to local needs and the constraints of the several parties employing them, yet robust enough to maintain a common identity across sites" (p. 393).

For example, the inquiry cycle arose initially to facilitate creating Inquiry Units. Over time, the cycle itself became a focal point for discussions. It became, for better or worse, a representation of inquiry and has been reproduced widely in books, articles, and course Web sites. To this day, there are people who see it as overly constraining, and others who ask for more structure. Moreover, there is a wide variation in the way it is used.

The cycle plays an important role in structuring specific inquiries as well. It helps to turn vague difficulties into specific representations of the problem and possible solution paths. In that sense, it supports what Dewey (1938) calls "the controlled or directed transformation of an indeterminate situation . . . into a unified whole" (p. 108).[3] Specific Inquiry Units then might be considered as boundary objects for problem solving or inquiry in particular domains.

Control of the Process: Design as Inquiry

In the previous section, I identified some participants by name, both to credit their work and to show that leadership does play a role even in bottom-up processes. However, the latter is most accurately characterized as a process in which many people have served as leaders, and the line between developers or facilitators on one side and participants or clients on the other has existed in only tenuous ways.

Who controls or directs inquiry transformations? The process we have experienced through the Inquiry Page development is akin to *participatory design*, which "places a premium on the active involvement of workplace practitioners (usually potential or current users of the system) in design and decision-making processes" (Computer Professionals for Social Responsibility, 2005, par. 1). But participatory design often is reduced to a process of obtaining information from users so that the "actual" designers can make more informed and usable decisions. Users and developers then are seen as two distinct categories, each with special, almost disjoint sets of expertise. Mechanisms are developed (focus groups, surveys, user testing, workplace task analysis, iterative design, etc.) to help users to communicate their knowledge to developers. Much of what has occurred with the Inquiry Group is what we call instead, *inquiry-based design*.

Under the conception of inquiry-based design, there is no a priori assumption that *any* computer system would be used, designed, or redesigned. Moreover, users and developers are participants in a community of inquiry. Some of the teacher users had much greater technical know-how, such as about Web site design, than did the university participants. The university people in turn were often as much teachers and users as those who might be designated as such. We did not see communication among participants as a means to better design. Instead, we saw design, when and if it emerged, as the outcome of collaborative problem solving; a new technology was a fortuitous by-product.

This argues that users should be empowered to participate actively in design, development, implementation, distribution, use, and evaluation of resources, not simply as informants. As Dewey argues, they need to enter into the *process of authority*. Accordingly, the online tools and environments here could be conceived not as fixed elements to achieve predefined ends, but rather as tools for inquiry, which themselves are transformed through the inquiry process. Through contributions to content, participatory design, and appropriation into new situations, participants are not merely passive recipients, but active creators of the very system that promotes their own inquiry.

Continual Development: Pragmatic Technology

How does inquiry relate to ever-changing situations, including shaping those situations? The process of the Inquiry Page development may be described as *pragmatic technology* (Hickman, 1990). Typically, we conceive a technology as a tool to solve a problem, for example, a toaster to toast bread. We then ask about whether the technology is appropriate or effective for a given task. In the realm of learning technologies, we often see a process in which users are taught, cajoled, even paid, to make use of a new technology to solve problems they never realized they had. Alternatively, the problems they do have remain unaddressed and unsolved.

The pragmatic technology perspective steps back from the idea of pushing a particular technology and instead places inquiry at the center. In that way, it conceives technologies as representing the outcome of problem solving, not the a priori means. In that sense, the idea of holding a piece of bread over a fire is a technology for toasting, the same as laying it on a rack in an oven. Viewed this way, technologies become stages in an inquiry process. Each surmounting of a problem becomes a new technology, whether in the form of a procedure or technique, a term, a set of guidelines, or a physical device. That technology in turn provides the means for enlarged or enhanced problem solving in the future. Technologies thus may be seen as the creation or reflection aspect of the inquiry cycle, taking us to a new, expanded, or deeper asking.

From the perspective adopted here, the best test is the growth and development of the community, and participants' continued efforts to change it. As Feyerabend (1975) argues concerning progress in science, it is not the lack of falsification that determines scientific truth, but the continued willingness of participants to modify and extend the theory. The analogue here is that the evolving system itself becomes a measure of the development of the community.

Because participants are encouraged to define their own goals and ways of using the Inquiry Page, we need diverse metrics for impact. One general measure is continued engagement, which we believe reflects participants' judgment that the tools and the project as a whole address their needs. For example, the Afya project used the Inquiry Units initially for creating personal "spiritual health plans," meaning a holistic approach to managing health for themselves and their families. This was coupled with workshops in which Sisternet members discussed these plans and provided mutual support. Later, they created "intellectual health plans," "fitness plans," and "financial plans." More than 200 Inquiry Units thus have been created by individuals or by groups within that community. We record data such as page visits and workshop attendance, but continue to work with community partners to define appropriate measures for their community needs.

Unified Whole: Defining Inquiry

The National Science Education Standards (NSES) (National Research Council, 2000) defines *scientific inquiry* as

> the diverse ways in which scientists study the natural world and propose explanations based on the evidence derived from their work. Scientific inquiry also refers to the activities through which students develop knowledge and understanding of scientific ideas, as well as an understanding of how scientists study the natural world. (p. 23)

That definition is typical in that it emphasizes the *ways* or *activities* that either scientists or students of science use to learn.

It is beyond the scope of this chapter to critique that definition, but it should be noted that this definition is not the only one. It is noteworthy that despite direct or indirect citations to the work of John Dewey, definitions of inquiry most compatible with the NSES may trivialize Dewey's key insights about inquiry as an embodied, participatory, social, moral, and critical process. The very idea of standards developed in isolation from the lived experience of students and teachers, and without their active participation, would have been problematic for Dewey.

Within the Inquiry Group, a major activity over the years has been to continually refine and extend the understanding of inquiry itself. This is evident in three themes, none of which is unique to the project, or proposed as universal, but instead developed in forms appropriate to the situations encountered here. They serve to describe the learning of all the participants, regardless of their formal roles as users, developers, students, or teachers.

One theme is that inquiry is inherently *a cross-disciplinary, collaborative, and participatory process*. In this perspective, ownership of the process of development is both a means and an end. Rather than setting out specific objectives for professional development or change, the approach has been to work together to create an environment that is supportive of the diverse kinds of inquiry in which participants engage. Thus, it is not a case of bringing people into an interactive environment, but rather of collaborating with them to build it. Knowledge construction depends on community processes— sharing and building on one another's work.

A second core theme is *respect for diversity*, meaning that each individual should be recognized for his or her own abilities, interests, ideas, needs, and cultural identity. Dialogue across differences is not a necessary evil, but the generative force behind change and growth. Every situation is unique; as Dewey argues, there is *no absolute value* in education. Nevertheless, we can all learn from the experiences of others. Our ordinary experiences are fundamental, but it is through reflection on experience and dialogue that individuals are able to grow and prepare for enlarged experiences in the future.

A third theme is that underlying specific community or pedagogical aims is the goal of helping all participants to develop a *critical, socially engaged intelligence*. Dewey argues that creation, not acquisition, ought to be the measure of a civilization, and this perspective applies to the individual as well. In other words, acquiring skills or knowledge is of little import if it doesn't enable the individual to contribute to the community and to the development of those around him or her.

A COMMUNITY OF PRACTICE

Many projects have worthwhile goals and work humanely and creatively to realize them. These goals might include fostering collaborations among teachers, preservice teachers, and scientists; facilitating scientific investigations using the Internet; enabling the use of new technologies in science classrooms; promoting standards-based curriculum materials; or preparing teachers for incorporating inquiry-based learning and teaching in science and mathematics classrooms. Our schools would be significantly better if those goals were even partially attained.

But there is a fundamental inconsistency inherent in this top-down approach. As Ella Flagg Young argued in her early work in the Chicago schools, one cannot force teachers to teach democracy (Smith, 1979; Tanner, 1997). Nor is it enough to let them teach it. She would ask instead: How can teachers teach democracy if they work in a system in which they have so little say in what they teach and how they teach? How can they then communicate to children what it means to work across differences, to take responsibility for one's actions, and to participate creatively and actively in the society around them? Thus, for Young, and her mentor, John Dewey, teaching democracy was inseparable from living democracy.

There is a risk in the top-down model that a role such as participating in the community will become separated from those of building the community or evaluating the project. Building the tools for community can be removed from living in the community; finding tools for inquiry can be apart from inquiring, and that in turn can be apart from learning about inquiry. As actions are parceled out to participants—developers, evaluators, teachers, students, and so on—the forms of understanding are as well. Thus, one group is to learn about inquiry in the science classroom, while another is to learn about design of online communities. This quite natural division of labor has its value of course, but it also sets limits on everyone's inquiry and on their feelings of ownership and participation.

In an inclusive community of practice, roles exist as well, but they are fluid and open to continual renegotiation. The activities of the Inquiry Group show that there is much more room in the process of authority than we often acknowledge. Correspondingly, one major impact has been on the individuals involved (Williamson, 2003), rather than on formal organizational structures. Along with this recognition is the notion that inquiry flowers most when understanding and action come into dynamic and reciprocal relationship with each other. The Inquiry Group has developed without a mission statement, major funding, explicit rules, membership dues or criteria, or institutional standing. Despite, or maybe because of, this openness, various activities have been energizing, often spawning others, and it has continued in various forms for over 25 years, thus demonstrating both sustainability and scalability.

CONCLUSION

Members of the Inquiry Group have sought to understand inquiry-based learning through both formal research and informal dialogue. They use mechanisms such as workshops and social Web sites to facilitate inquiry. In response to the reasonable question: "What did *we* do behind the scenes to make it work for *them?*" the Inquiry Group changes the pronouns. Instead of *we* as the actors and *them* as the recipients, it sees *we* and *them* as co-equal, if not identical, and their differences as sources of strength, not deficits to over-come. This extends across realms of learning, technology design, teaching methods, and evaluation. An appropriate question, then, is, How do the In-quiry Page (and iLabs) align with the central values of the inquiry process (a cross-disciplinary, collaborative, and participatory process; respect for diver-sity; development of a critical, socially engaged intelligence), and how does the continual process of supporting and improving the online resources in turn contribute to participants' growth with respect to these values?

Both the successes and the failures of the Inquiry Group derive from an underlying question throughout. That question, which we can answer only in part today, is a response to the one above, and is an appropriate conclusion to an ongoing process: What happens when users are not merely recipients of a design for inquiry, or even informants for the design, but instead *become a part of the process of authority throughout*? In other words, what if we imag-ine development *as* inquiry for all involved, not development *for* inquiry?

NOTES

1. This is not to deny that users may play some role through participatory design and other mechanisms.

2. It is difficult to come up with a neutral term to highlight a kind of distrib-uted, situation-specific development with less organized planning. I considered linear/branching, waterfall/sashimi (terms from software design), standard/nonstandard, and standard/organic. Chapter 1 by Joni Falk and Brian Drayton analyzes these ideas further.

3. I am grateful to Brian Drayton for pointing out how the inquiry cycle serves this "problematizing" or "intellectualizing" role.

REFERENCES

Abelmann, N., Kelleher, W., Jr., & Mortensen, P. (2005, January 21). *Ethnogra-phy of the university cross-campus initiative.* Progress report, University of Illinois at Urbana–Champaign. Retrieved April 21, 2007, from http://www.eotu.uiuc.edu/EOTUMODEL/Documents/cci-report-for-web.pdf

Bishop, A. P., Bazzell, I., Mehra, B., & Smith, C. (2001, April). Afya: Social and digital technologies that reach across the digital divide. *First Monday,* 6(4). Retrieved October 27, 2008, from http://www.uic.edu/htbin/cgiwrap/bin/ojs/index.php/fm/

Bishop, A. P., Bruce, B. C., Lunsford, K. J., Jones, M. C., Nazarova, M., Linderman, D., Won, M., Heidorn, P. B., Ramprakash, R., & Brock, A. (2004). Supporting community inquiry with digital resources. *Journal of Digital Information*, 5(3), Article No. 308, 2004-08-24. Retrieved October 27, 2008, from http://jodi.tamu.edu/

Brown, D. E. (2000, April). *Merging dynamics: An integrating perspective on learning, conceptual change, and teaching, and its implications for educational research*. Paper presented at the annual meeting of the American Educational Research Association, New Orleans.

Brown, D. E., Beck, D., Frazier, R., & Rath, A. (1996). *Siphons and strawberry milkshake machines: Is fantasy in science inquiry a valuable context or an unwanted distraction?* Paper presented at the annual meeting of the American Educational Research Association, New York.

Bruce, B. C., & Easley, J. A. (2000). Emerging communities of practice: Collaboration and communication in action research. *Educational Action Research*, 8(2), 243–259.

Bruce, B. C., & Rubin, A. (1993). *Electronic quills: A situated evaluation of using computers for writing in classrooms*. Mahwah, NJ: Lawrence Erlbaum Associates.

Choksi, B. (1997). *Evaluating the use of information technology in the East St. Louis Action Research Project (ESLARP)*. Retrieved April 20, 2007, from http://lrs.ed.uiuc.edu/Students/b-choksi/ESLARP/

Computer Professionals for Social Responsibility. (2005, June 1). Participatory design. Retrieved November 14, 2006, from http://www.cpsr.org/issues/pd/

Dewey, J. (1900). *The school and society*. Chicago: University of Chicago Press.

Dewey, J. (1933). *How we think: A restatement of the relation of reflective thinking to the educative process* (Rev. ed.). Boston: Heath.

Dewey, J. (1938). *Logic: The theory of inquiry*. New York: Holt Rinehart & Winston.

Eglash, R., Croissant, J., Di Chiro, G., & Fouché, R. (2004). *Appropriating technology: Vernacular science and social power*. Minneapolis: University of Minnesota Press.

Feyerabend, P. (1975). *Against method*. London: Verso.

Fullan, M. G. (1994, September). Coordinating top-down and bottom-up strategies for educational reform. In R. J. Anson (Ed.), *Systemic reform: Perspectives on personalizing education* (pp. 7–24). Washington, DC: Office of Educational Research and Improvement (ERIC Document Reproduction Service No. ED 376557).

Hawkins, D. (1965). Messing about in science. *Science and Children*, 2(5), 5–9.

Hickman, L. A. (1990). *John Dewey's pragmatic technology*. Bloomington: Indiana University Press.

Lave, J., & Wenger, E. (1991). *Situated learning: Legitimate peripheral participation*. Cambridge: Cambridge University Press.

National Research Council. (2000). *Inquiry and the national science education standards: A guide for teaching and learning*. Washington, DC: National Academy Press.

Robins, J. (1999). StoneSoup: A distributed collaboratory using software agents. (Unpublished manuscript)

Robins, J. (2002). StoneSoup: A contextualized portfolio system. *Proceedings of Computer Support for Collaborative Learning: Foundations for a CSCL community* (pp. 538–539). Hillsdale, NJ: Erlbaum.

Robins, J. (2003). *The role of a mediating information structure in a contextualized system.* Unpublished doctoral dissertation, University of Illinois at Urbana–Champaign.

Smith, J. (1979). *Ella Flagg Young: The portrait of a leader.* Ames, IN: Educational Studies.

Snow, J. (2005). *StoneSoup: Technology innovation, introduction, and use to support learner-centered education.* Unpublished doctoral dissertation, University of Illinois at Urbana–Champaign.

Star, S. L., & Griesemer, J. R. (1989). Institutional ecology, "translations," and boundary objects: Amateurs and professionals in Berkeley's Museum of Vertebrate Zoology, 1907–1939. *Social Studies of Science, 19,* 387–420.

Talisse, R. (2002, Spring/Summer). Two concepts of inquiry. *Philosophical Writings, 19/20,* 69–82.

Tanner, L. N. (1997). *Dewey's laboratory school: Lessons for today.* New York: Teachers College Press.

Williamson, J. (2003). *Teachers as change mediators in educational reform.* Unpublished doctoral dissertation, University of Illinois at Urbana–Champaign.

Yenawine, P. (1993). *What do you see?* [Videotape on teaching in art galleries]. Chicago: Art Institute, Department of Education.

Zacklad, M. (2003). Communities of action: A cognitive and social approach to the design of CSCW systems. In M. Pendergast, K. Schmidt, C. M. Simone, & M. Tremaine (Eds.), *Proceedings of the 2003 international ACM SIGGROUP conference on supporting group work* (pp. 190–197). New York: ACM.

CHAPTER 3

Communities, Texts, and Consciousness: The Practice of Participation at the Math Forum

Wesley Shumar

This chapter is an exploration of one of the earliest interactive educational Web sites, the Math Forum (http://mathforum.org). The Math Forum is an interactive online educational site made up of teachers, students, mathematicians, and hobbyists from around the world. In the exploration of the successes and failures of the Math Forum, two main questions will be addressed: What has gone into the production of online participation? And how has that participation been sustained and developed? Of course, in order to address these questions, other questions will be raised as well: What defines success for an online educational community? What constitutes participation and what forms of participation are productive for the community? This chapter will explore these questions while taking a more intimate look at the history of the Math Forum and what the Math Forum is.

PRACTICE AND THEORY

The chapter has both a practical and theoretical goal. Practically, it provides an ethnographic look at the development of the Math Forum and how the potential of new media intersected with the early culture of the Internet and the culture of a small elite liberal arts college to produce a unique and innovative organization that is one of the leaders of online education. This is a behind-the-scenes look at the history and development of the Math Forum and is both an educational ethnography and an ethnography of a small creative organization (Bennis & Biederman, 1997).

Theoretically, the chapter looks at the new social spaces opened up by new communication technologies. Unlike much ethnographic research in education and technology that focuses on virtual community (including some of our own), this chapter assumes a social world where people live in hybrid spaces that combine physical interactions with virtual interactions. Encapsulated in the notion of hybrid space is, in fact, a theoretical take on the notion of virtual community. In the early days of discussions of virtual communities, a simple binary was created that was something like "physical community/virtual community." That distinction may be analytically useful in some instances, but many theorists, especially in sociology and communication, have begun to suggest that social cyberspaces are in fact places where people combine their online and offline worlds, places that allow for more complex social groupings and for people to craft more "personalized" social groupings (Kollock & Smith, 1999; Wellman, 2001; Wellman, Quan-Haase, Boase, & Chen, 2002). These new social spaces[1] make possible new ways of defining the boundaries of social groups and hence the imagination of things like the community an individual is part of, relationships with peers and co-workers, and so on. It also makes possible new ways of being and thinking about the self.

As a public space, the Math Forum site affords the possibilities of interaction with others around common, purposeful, desired activity. Its educational impact derives from purposeful activity that helps the participant learn about, get introduced to, and make use of the content in the Forum library, itself built up from the knowledge generated by participants and staff as they worked to solve particular problems. Participant activity on educational Web sites can act at multiple levels and have different forms. It can attract more users and usage of the site as it generates new content for the site through those interactions. Those archived interactions then can be turned into reusable educational content/objects. Archived interactions can be used to help others figure out how to use the content; they also can be used to bring the content within the sphere of the existing educational system and connect it to the formal curriculum. All this should feed back into the content generation end of the loop described above, bringing in more people, new and refined needs and objects, and resulting content to stimulate and be refactored to feed the rest of the cycle.

Participation has been produced on the Math Forum site in a dialectical process. Individuals come with a range of wants and needs that they then shape by imagining the Math Forum site and the Math Forum community in ways that will meet their needs. Of particular interest is the identification of support functions that sustain involvement for a range of site participants. That support may be face-to-face workshops for teacher leaders or novice teachers just learning to incorporate the Internet in their teaching, or online help allowing teachers and students to find the resources they need and help them answer questions that they have. Because the site has interactive services, participation at the Math Forum takes on dimensionality. There are different levels of participation: (1) what the individual brings to the interaction, (2) the dyadic exchange during interaction, (3) and the cultural context(s) and groups within which the person engages the site. Much of our research has been to capture data about interaction at these three levels. Therefore, the texts that have been produced are themselves articulated at different levels for different needs, and the forms of consciousness that have grown out of Math Forum development are also multiple, with the staff's understanding of participant needs growing at the same time that participants are able to think about themselves and their math work differently after working with the Math Forum.

THE EVOLUTION OF THE MATH FORUM

The Math Forum is unique in the newly developing world of online educational communities in that it has grown into both a collection of some of the best math education resources on the Internet, as well as one of the most successful and interactive of educational communities. Currently the Math Forum has over 1.5 million pages of content and 3 million visits a month, which typically might involve a range of activity across the site, including 84,000 page views a month in the T2T (teacher to teacher) teacher pedagogy discussion group, 368,000 page views a month in the Problem of the Week services, and 1.8 million page views a month in Ask Dr. Math. What makes the Math Forum unique is its very personal version of user-centered design. The resources and interactive services have grown out of the "gifts" given by core participants on the site: volunteer mentors, committed staff members, and teachers who have participated in face-to-face (f2f) and online workshops. This amazing demonstration of altruistic behavior, which anthropologists and sociologists call "generalized reciprocity" (Kollock & Smith, 1999; Mauss, 2000; Shumar & Renninger, 2002), has been at the core of creating this robust and multidimensional educational site. Understanding that development and what lessons can be learned from it, is a crucial educational as well as societal issue.

Before the World Wide Web existed, the Math Forum began as the Geometry Forum, a text-based Internet discussion list. At that time the early staff members were thinking about how computers, the Internet, and other related informational technologies could be used to facilitate math learning. These creative early founders of the Math Forum were very aware of the ways that schools, as bureaucratic institutions, stymie mathematical thinking and drive both children and teachers into a mental underground where no one admits their competencies or weaknesses. They further understood that the lack of open conversation made it very difficult for people to improve their ability to think mathematically and hence be good at mathematics. Communication and discourse are key to helping learners develop their mathematical practices and hence their mathematical thinking and learning. Out of that understanding came two main foci of the Math Forum. One focus was to create ways for teachers to use technology so that they could improve their own math skills and meet their personal needs, work more with like-minded people on math, and find online resources. This was the impetus behind many of the workshops. Another focus was the creation of interactive services. The two main services on the Math Forum site are Ask Dr. Math, a question and answer service, and the Problem of the Week (PoW) service, which is a weekly challenge problem service.

A useful way to explore the growth of the Math Forum is to look at the evolving culture of the staff, the workshop process that has been so central to creating a community of Math Forum users, the services that the Math Forum has developed for people to use and contribute to, and then some more recent projects that have grown from the staff's effort to combine workshops and services. Finally, this section will look at the key issues of scaling and sustainability and several of their implications. The successes of meeting some of the communication goals the Math Forum set out created scaling sustainability problems of several types that we will look at near the end of this section.

The Role of the Staff

The early staff of the Math Forum were aware that the Internet created a new social world in that it opened up new spaces, social cyberspaces that allowed for new kinds of human relationships because distance and time could be made flexible. These new social spaces facilitated free conversation that was not limited by institutional norms or subject to institutional hierarchies. This kind of interactional space facilitated the kinds of inquiry-based, problem-based collaborative learning that is advocated by many educational theorists but is difficult to enact in traditional classroom settings. Further, it fit the *habitus* (Bourdieu, 1984, 1990) of these early Math Forum staff members in that it created a new tool for problem solving and getting things accomplished in creative, interesting, and fun ways.

One early Math Forum staff member really enjoyed reaching out and linking to other people. While he may have had some limitations as a staff member in other areas, his real strength was in meeting new people, connecting with their needs, and then helping them to solve problems and use the Internet and the Math Forum to meet those local needs. In one famous story, this staff member, along with some others, was doing a workshop in a school district in Georgia. They were very far from home and when they got to the school they found that it did not have enough Internet access for them to do the workshop. Without missing a beat, this staff member went off to Radio Shack and bought several modems and multiple yards of cable in order to create enough access for the teachers to get on the Internet and do the workshop. He got back to the school and ended up stringing wire outside the building and through windows in order to get the configuration they needed.

In another summer workshop in Philadelphia, teachers were working with the Math Forum in an inner-city school that lacked air conditioning. Again the staff problem solved and brought in old air conditioners and fans that they borrowed from friends and neighbors, and cobbled together a cooling system that made the workshop rooms tolerable so that the workshop could proceed. For these inner-city teachers who were used to resigning in the face of some contradiction that hindered the work they needed to do, it was an eye-opening experience to see the Math Forum staff apply the same attitudes of conversation and problem solving that they used for math, to the solution of practical problems like a building too hot to work in.

This kind of behavior then: (1) fostered a problem-solving environment in Math Forum workshops and activities, (2) set the tone for the Math Forum culture, and, most critically, (3) inspired some of the early teacher participants to become members of the Math Forum community and form the core of a community of practice that helped to develop the Math Forum and make it a flexible learning environment.

To this day, the staff of the Math Forum have retained this innovative, problem-solving culture. They continue to enjoy interacting with those who come to the site to discuss math, and, in fact, engage weekly in math problem solving with one another. The staff meet weekly for the official purpose of creating the content for the Problem of the Week. But in effect, this meeting provides an opportunity for the staff to continue to talk about math and pedagogy with one another, exploring uncharted territory. It is an opportunity for staff to embrace the practices they support. They do so using the Internet and wiki formats, working face to face and also remotely, as groups and as individuals, and then convening synchronously to further the discussion. This is a reflection of the hybrid community that they then encourage with other participants. It is a collaborative, laterally organized, nonhierarchical, idea-rich work activity.

Workshops

One of the ways the Math Forum has influenced teachers and the culture of teaching in a number of schools has been through workshops. Since the Math

Forum began, it has been offering both face-to-face and online workshops as well as workshops that combine both modalities. Initially these workshops were a combination of math and technology workshops where teachers would learn how to use computers and build Web pages, as well as getting ideas about how to teach math with computers and the Internet. Student workshops often were designed to be projects where children learned some math using manipulatives, talk, and also computer applications. These multiple avenues into problem solving provided rich contexts in which students could engage and learn. Later workshops with teachers were oriented more around projects, which was possible especially after most teachers had familiarity with computers and the Internet, and the staff did not have to do as much basic teaching.

The Math Forum workshops were a critical part of developing resources for the site, seeding community, identifying lead teachers, and creating a model for combining online and offline work. The Math Forum staff inspired teachers in workshops not only with their problem-solving orientation, discussed above, but with their support of teacher learning. Teachers in workshops moved from no Web experience to building Web pages and designing online lessons in a matter of 2 to 3 days. This experience was very empowering for many teachers. Teachers also were encouraged to pursue their own interests and to develop projects that were interesting and meaningful to them. This combination of support and freedom had three effects. First, it allowed teachers to pursue their interests, develop interesting and new resources, and make connections with other teachers who were interested in the same things. Second, it helped generate resources like lesson plans for the Math Forum site that could be shared with others. Finally, it helped move some teachers from novices with technology to leaders and mainstays of the Math Forum community.

The workshop process, as well as the way that Math Forum staff tended to work with any person seeking to interact on the site, established the Math Forum's community of practice. There is a lot of talk in the educational literature about communities of practice, but much of this talk is proscriptive: the desire to create communities of practice as instruments to achieve some other purpose. The Math Forum, through its online interactions and workshops, enabled participants to begin as apprentices and then to move on to become experts and leaders in the community. This process of development could occur at the participants' own pace, following their interests, and without many of the institutional impediments that people experience in many educational institutions. Because the Math Forum site established an egalitarian culture and could be likened to a postmodern "band organization" (Renninger & Shumar, 2004), the development of a true community of practice, in which participants apprentice to either Math Forum staff or senior participants at the site, became a very real prospect. In this, it may offer a model for the development of leadership and contributors to the site.

The workshops tended to create very close personal relationships between Math Forum staff members and workshop participants. Staff often would change their original workshop agenda to accommodate the project ideas of the participants. This had the effect of scaffolding participants' development, while producing individualized projects that then became resources on the site. An example of such work is Suzanne Alejandre's tessellation lessons (http://mathforum.org/sum95/suzanne/tess.intro.html). These lessons, which Suzanne began as a participant in a summer workshop, have grown to a much more developed area on her part of the Math Forum Web site. Suzanne went on to develop lots of other online lessons and worked very closely with the Math Forum before she finally became a staff member. While most teachers do not become staff members, several have assumed staff positions at different times.

From the beginning, the Math Forum has maximized the use of a hybrid social space. Creating workshops was a way for the Math Forum to interject its culture into some other local context. The workshops helped to orient both teachers and students to the Math Forum staff's problem-solving orientation. These f2f workshops also allowed staff to demonstrate their commitment to the interests of the participants and to letting the participants define where the workshop would go, given their interests and needs. The online community then became an extension of that f2f work. It is both a temporal and spatial extension. It is temporal in that participants get to continue to work with the Math Forum and can build a long-lasting relationship. The relationship does not end when the f2f workshop ends. It is a spatial extension in that other people and other resources can be made part of the participants' work. The spatial connections can expand in multiple directions, because the Math Forum creates a nonhierarchical, freely branching, horizontal structure. It tends to draw in collaborators and participants in a way that creates more nodes that can articulate with other nodes in a very networked way. Just as online work allows teachers and students to continue the work they began in a face-to-face workshop, so too in reverse does a face-to-face meeting allow some teachers to take on leadership roles in workshops that originally began online.

Services

The early activities of the Math Forum staff also centered around developing several key interactive services, building the collections, and fostering a community of practice with online and f2f workshops as well as with special projects like the Bridging Research and Practice (BRAP) project, to be discussed later. The two central interactive services that began early on at the Math Forum were Ask Dr. Math, http://mathforum.org/dr.math/, and the Problem of the Week, http://mathforum.org/pow/. While we could see some of the discussions as services and some of the projects that developed as providing services too, the two main services are Ask Dr. Math and the PoW. So in this section we will look at these two key interactive services that not only have shaped so much of what the Math Forum is, but are two key ways that the Math Forum encouraged participation in its online site—participation that was used to build a set of online resources that are unique.

Ask Dr. Math

Ask Dr. Math is a question and answer service through which learners can ask a math question and get an answer from a live person trained not only in that area of math but also "tenured" as a math doctor to give answers that are clearly written, polite, and pedagogically sound. The unique features of Ask Dr. Math in the early days were the "tenuring" of volunteers and the building of the archive. The Ask Dr. Math service actively sought volunteer mentors to answer people's math questions; the volunteer staff were and are composed of a unique collection of people, including K–12 teachers, professors, other mathematicians, talented students, and hobbyists. No matter what the individual's level of formal expertise, he or she starts out volunteering in the Ask Dr. Math service as an untenured math doctor. When the volunteer answers a person's math question, the answer is reviewed by one of the tenured math doctors. The volunteer then receives some mentoring. If the answer needs to be changed before it is sent to the original questioner, the volunteer is given the opportunity to make those changes. A tenured doctor then reviews the revised reply again before it is sent as a reply to the original questioner. This internal mentoring process is not observable to the original questioner, who simply gets a thoughtful reply to her or his question. Once a math doctor has successfully sent out replies to people for a while, he or she is tenured and can send out replies without being mentored first. The individual then is able also to mentor untenured math doctors. While the metaphor is tenuring, in fact this is a very positive mentoring process where the model of mentoring gets shared all the way down to the original questioner.

The second activity that the Math Forum staff undertook with the Ask Dr. Math service was to create a library of math information using the best questions and the best answers to those questions. In fact, in the early days of Ask Dr. Math, it was not possible, even with a volunteer staff, to answer all the questions that were submitted. And so the staff strategically chose certain questions to answer, knowing that good answers to good questions would accumulate to build a very specific archive, in which the materials grew out of actual mathematical conversations and so had the look and feel of the consciousness of actors who were addressing math questions in a way that came from a certain knowledge base.

Today, when visitors come to Ask Dr. Math, they are encouraged to search the archive first for an answer to their question before asking a question of a live doctor. This process of building a library out of past interactions not only represents how students might think about math questions and how one might mentor a student asking about some math issue, but it also allows questions and answers to live again as they get reintegrated into new conversations. Furthermore, this reuse process is one of the ways Ask Dr. Math sought to sustain and scale its activities. There is a cost, which is hard to calculate: How much do students benefit from a live mentor and how much are they able on their own to integrate prior conversations into their own learning? This is a critical question all the Math Forum services face.

PoW

The two principles used in Ask Dr. Math, the mentoring of volunteers and the archiving of good interactions to build a library of math resources, are also at the core of the Problem of the Week service, as well as some of the newer services on the Math Forum site. The Problem of the Week began as the Geometry Problem of the Week, but the service has expanded to a math fundamentals PoW called Fun PoW, both a pre-algebra and an algebra PoW, and of course the geometry PoW. The problems are nonroutine challenge problems. They often involve diagrams but are primarily word problems. Students have about a week to submit a solution to the problem. Originally, all students' answers were mentored by a live person who replied to the student, encouraging further thought on the problem even if the answer was correct. Today, only a selection of students, either those who are seeking mentoring or whose teachers want them to be mentored, get mentored replies to their submissions. While the PoW service does not use the metaphor of tenuring, the service has many volunteer mentors, and mentors must be mentored themselves until a staff member feels they have had enough experience to directly send their replies to students without first having them looked at by a more experienced member of the community.

The Problem of the Week began with a single staff member and, like Ask Dr. Math, was very successful in its early days. There were many students around the country who answered the PoW and waited expectantly for a mentored reply to their posting. Some of the children were very good at math, and the Math Forum was one of the few places they could go to do challenging math and talk with others about math. A lot of the children did the PoW as part of their classwork or for extra credit given by teachers who were excited about what the Math Forum was doing. Some of the teachers would type their students' responses in and upload them to the Math Forum in a labor of love.

Like the workshops discussed above, the Problem of the Week gave rise to a hybrid social world of virtual interaction and f2f interaction. On one level, this was done by the users of the online Math Forum problems; it also was fostered by the way Math Forum staff and volunteers talked about problems in their classrooms. For a long time, teachers have been using the Math Forum as a way to bring a different kind of discourse about mathematics into their classes. At a second level, Math Forum staff established personal relationships with particular children and classes, and actually visited schools to meet the teachers and the students whom they had grown close to. Finally, the PoW service began to be included in both the f2f and virtual workshops as a source of problems and as a source of materials for ideas on how students tended to respond to problems.

Unlike Ask Dr. Math, the PoW relied on a model in which all children who wrote in got mentored replies to their problem solving. This was the ideal in Ask Dr. Math too, but at least Ask Dr. Math had something of a scaling plan that involved automating answers through the building of an archive. That automation could justify the short-term problem of not being able to answer every child's question. But with the PoW, the whole principle was built around the notion that children needed to do more problem solving and to develop both the communicative and analytic skills to talk about their answers and how they got those answers. To this end, every child really needed a mentored reply, but there was no easy way to automate this process.

For the PoW, the solution has been to move the service from a free service to a monetized scheme: Students and teachers can buy memberships in the PoW. School districts also can buy memberships for the whole district. This is the only way to access current problems and the problem library. The Math Forum tries to provide members with mentoring for some of the problems, but it no longer guarantees mentoring for all of the problems. This scheme puts only a minimal cost on users for the service, but it is also a scaling back of some of the mentoring services and it certainly takes away from the feeling of openness that characterized the early days of the Internet.

The Ask Dr. Math service and the PoW service were an important part of the Math Forum's history. These two interactive services were key to the effort the Math Forum made to produce participation and make the site more than a set of resources on a Web site. These services attracted a lot of users and made Math Forum a household name in a number of communities. But they also created the first set of dilemmas around scaling and sustainability, which are still part of the Math Forum reality. Questions of how to respond to all of the participants in the services, and which interactions should be highlighted to develop the libraries of the services, were critical to Math Forum development. The early evaluation research we conducted at the Math Forum asked what the participants wanted and what they found lacking in the services. The staff then had to address these issues and decide what was important to users. These early dilemmas of scaling and sustainability continue to haunt the Math Forum, but they were also part of the early dynamism that made the Web site such an exciting place to be.

Projects

From the beginning, the Math Forum reached out and attempted to establish collaborative projects with a number of colleagues and organizations. The founding members took the existing social networks that had in the worlds of math and online education and then built upon those networks. What resulted from that networking effort was a series of projects, some sponsored by granting agencies or foundations, and others that grew out of partnerships with schools or other university groups. In this section I will talk about some of the key projects that shaped the Math Forum as an organization and were central to its thinking about participation and sustainability.

Educational Software Components of Tomorrow and Bridging Research and Practice Projects

Two projects that were implemented at a critical juncture for the Math Forum were the Educational Software Components of Tomorrow (ESCOT) project, http://www.escot.org/, and the Bridging Research and Practice project, http://mathforum.org/brap/wrap/. Both began in the late 1990s and early 2000s, and both involved a collaboration. ESCOT grew out of an NSF project at SRI and the SimCalc Project. BRAP was an NSF project located at TERC, Inc. In each of these projects, the Math Forum engaged as integral players K–12 teachers with whom staff had worked before.

The ESCOT project brought together teams of software designers, educational technologists, and teachers in order to develop software applets, small software applications that would aid in the learning of certain math concepts, and then place these applets within a pedagogical context. The project was innovative in a number of ways, but probably most obviously in the bringing together of teachers and software developers. These are two groups that rarely work with each other and because of their contexts of work have very different work processes. The result of the project was a set of technology-based Problems of the Week called tPoWs. These tPoWs were an important addition to the Math Forum library, but they also helped the Math Forum staff think about new directions in which they might take their work.

The BRAP project began around the same time as the ESCOT project and its primary goal was to give teachers a large voice in decisions about how to bridge research and practice. In workshops the teachers were given a great deal of latitude in shaping the project, and although reticent at first, they grew to enjoy asserting control. After looking at some of the research on discourse in the math classroom and videotaping their own practices, the teachers in the project decided to make discourse the focus of a video paper they produced for the Math Forum site. The Math Forum not only fostered a sense of leadership and independence among these teachers, but the teachers realized, at the moment they began to embrace the importance of their discourse, that discourse as a concept was important.

The BRAP project (and to some extent the ESCOT project as well) helped the Math Forum staff think more about issues of leadership in an online community and how leaders might contribute to the overall needs of building participation, sustaining community interactions, and scaling to manage all the interactions and materials of the site.

Math Tools

The ESCOT and BRAP projects were critical formative experiences for the Math Forum's next major venture, which was the Math Tools project, http://mathforum.org/mathtools/index.html. The goal of the Math Tools site, an NSF-funded project, was to create a digital library of applets that could be used in solving math problems. It was designed not only as a repository, but also as an interactive space, drawing on some of the experience the Math Forum had had with online interaction. Math Tools was set up so that individuals could review the tools and lessons, develop lessons to be used with the tools, and review the reviewers. There was also a discussion space where issues around tools and technology could be discussed by interested individuals.

Math Tools was a very important development for the Math Forum. Up to that point, the Math Forum simply built on the opportunities that had been presented to the staff over time. Math Tools was a concerted effort to engineer an interactive site based on the lessons that the Math Forum had learned over time. In some ways Math Tools is very successful in that it has a dynamic community that contributes to discussions regularly. But in some other ways Math Tools has not been as successful as the Math Forum had hoped. The original vision of the project included doing workshops in tandem with the development of the library. The workshop component had to be cut because of budgetary considerations; thus, the production of participation at Math Tools was done entirely online, by providing funds to some individuals to take a leadership role on the site. Perhaps as a result of the decision to forgo a f2f component, the social interaction around reviewing and rating tools and lessons never reached the kind of density that the Math Forum staff had hoped for.

Virtual Math Teams Project

The Virtual Math Teams (VMT) project, http://mathforum.org/vmt/, is an ongoing NSF-funded project at the Math Forum to study and develop online collaborative problem-solving environments using a chat format and work around math problems such as the Problem of the Week. VMT has developed a chat/whiteboard environment based on Fraunhaufer/IPSI's Concert Chat. The goal of the VMT project is the design of a self-scaffolding online synchronous chat environment where groups of children can work together collaboratively on math problems and increase their collective understanding of mathematics. The project is rooted in notions of group cognition and the idea that knowledge is produced socially and hence is always intersubjective. Further, small groups have a special place in the production of knowledge because of their capacity to work together in an intensive fashion over long periods (Stahl, 2006). The VMT environment promises to provide the Math Forum with an important new service that will appeal to a generation of students more used to IM than e-mail. Moreover, the chat environment has already proved useful to the Math Forum for other kinds of workshops, further enabling staff to create hybrid workshops where some participants are working f2f and others online.

LESSONS FROM THE EVOLUTION OF THE MATH FORUM

Drawing together the lessons that we have learned from the staff, workshops, services, and projects that the Math Forum has offered, we can define principles of participation at the site. First, the site has layers of mentoring and support, from staff members who meet the needs of some participants, to facilitating participants to effectively support one another. Second, the Math Forum has built first-rate, rich and deep math collections out of these powerful interactions between site participants. Third, the collaborative and community orientation of the Math Forum makes it possible to support people in what they want to do, thus making the learning participant centered. Fourth, while the staff support and scaffold teachers in their needs and interests, teachers have become the core of the community. This leads to a fifth principle: real empowerment for teachers, and a sixth: the sharing of and in the Math Forum culture, which helps to break the constraints of bureaucracy in traditional schools.

Collaboration and Culture

The Math Forum culture is built from a community of staff members who are oriented toward problem solving—whether the problems are math problems or problems with getting computers in schools to work or making sure it is possible to run workshops given all the issues encountered when working in schools. The Math Forum staff are equally committed to high-quality mathematics resources and high-quality discussions, as well as thinking mathematically and encouraging a process of inquiry. The Math Forum staff have always put interactions and conversations first, valuing the thinking of individuals and then working to use tools and create contexts where people can have those conversations and rich interactions with mathematics. These characteristics of the Math Forum and its staff make the site very attractive for a lot of teachers. Because it has a culture very different from the culture of most schools, it is a welcome relief from the day-to-day challenges of working in a bureaucratic institution. There are no forms to fill out or hoops to jump through; people can just begin to talk about math. It is empowering to see a group of problem solvers make things work, and so again the Math Forum becomes very desirable because people can begin to see new possibilities for themselves while watching others solve problems and make progress.

From the inception, there have been reciprocal relations between site staff members and site participants, particularly teachers. This work has been carried out both face to face in summer workshops and school workshop activities, and also online as teachers and other participants continue work with the Math Forum that they started in a workshop. There are also online workshop participants who never have met face to face, and individual projects that are begun by a teacher making an inquiry to a Math Forum staff person. As pointed out above, a unique feature of the Math Forum is that the collections are built through interaction with participants; but it is also the case that participants are changed through that interaction. Work with participants changes and enhances the library/site through reconceptualizing and institutionalizing the role of the participant as more than consumer.

Importantly, there are always multiple paths of access between the Math Forum and the participant. First, there are multiple ways of being in touch with participants, for example, newsletter, interactive services (including discussion groups), Web master, workshops, teacher conferences, and so on. Second, there are multiple ways to participate in the Math Forum through workshops and various activities on the site. For example, Math Tools allows participants to contribute tools that can be used with computers or hand-held devices, but it also allows people to review tools, contribute lessons on working with tools, blog on their favorite tools and lessons, and discuss the lessons and tools.

Therefore, while the Math Forum depends on volunteers and leaders to come forward and contribute resources, as well as time and expertise, to the site, the space for that volunteerism is created by giving individuals a place where their conversation can be made important and their interests have a chance to grow and develop. Here we see that the Math Forum as an organization directly influences the kinds of communities that develop on the site. The problem-solving, egalitarian, conversation-oriented Math Forum staff culture is encouraged through the way the staff imagine what the online community(ies) could be. The Math Forum is a place where people can come at any level of math skill and begin to change. In this way the Math Forum is really a community of practice. It allows for the evolution of skills as people go from periphery to center in their participation on the site. In these ways it produces its volunteers. But at the same time, space and a path are created for leaders. Individuals who have ideas are encouraged to explore those ideas. They can become experts in a small area or a large area, depending on the skills they currently have and how quickly they build new skills. As individuals become site participants and leaders, they re-imagine the Math Forum or their piece of it, creating new groups on the site who work together and think together. They also begin to change their thinking about themselves as the community becomes more complex and identities change.

Scaling and Sustainability

Like so many Internet organizations, the Math Forum began as a small group of highly motivated and talented individuals working in one room with scarce resources. This group was convinced of the power of the new technologies and aware that something big was going on. But its members were not prepared for the repercussions of the power of the Internet in bringing people together and creating communities of individuals with shared interests.

As discussed above, a big sustainability issue for the Math Forum was the amount of traffic in the Ask Dr. Math and Problem of the Week services. And in these services we see that scaling and sustainability are two sides of the same coin. As an early player in the math education online marketplace, the Math Forum never had to work very hard to get projects to scale. Rather its larger problem was how to manage the amount of interaction the site did get, especially as the goal was to foster a more personal form of interaction around mathematics. In these two early services, that meant how to answer so many math questions and how to mentor students' problem solving. But in general the question at the Math Forum has been how to encourage interactions that are mathematically rich and lead to greater understanding on the part of the participants. The Math Forum's new online professional development courses in probability and algebraic reasoning have the same problem that the early services had, which is how to provide leaders who can mentor people in these online courses so that the discourse around mathematics can reach a greater level of sophistication and the collective knowledge of the group grows. (This, for me as an anthropologist, is an issue of consciousness, which I will discuss below.)

Above we mentioned some specific ways that the Ask Dr. Math and PoW services attempted to foster sustainability. These services are so labor intensive that they require revenue; thus, the staff has developed several books, which can be purchased, out of the Ask Dr. Math service, and the PoW service is now a paid subscription service. These revenue-generating strategies in part aid the sustainability effort. But the larger effort at the Math Forum has always been to try to get volunteer community support for sustainability. Just like Wikipedia and the open source movement, the Math Forum participates in the Internet ethos of the collective intelligence of the community. But the Math Forum has a very specific set of problems in this regard that are not shared by Wikipedia and the open source movements. In those movements it is the community of experts who come together to produce knowledge collectively and to share that knowledge with others. While there may be problems in those communities as well, they have large amounts of intellectual capital to draw upon.

By contrast, the Math Forum community is a kind of community of practice, in which there people with diverse levels of expertise. There are many math professors and highly skilled math teachers, and even genius children and hobbyists, who participate in the Math Forum community. There are also many novice or apprentice (to use Lave and Wenger's [1991] term) practitioners who need a good bit of support. So the ratio of expert participants to novice participants is very different at the Math Forum than, say, in the open source movement. This is perhaps one of the reasons participation needs to be produced at the Math Forum. It is relatively easy to get people to come to the site to ask a question or seek a resource like a lesson plan. It is more difficult to get novice participants to engage in a mathematical conversation that may end up improving their knowledge and understanding of a particular math topic. Moreover, when those novice participants do come in large numbers (as they have been coming to the new online algebraic reasoning and probability workshops), it is a challenge to have enough "lead" participants who can support the conversation and encourage interaction. Recently there has been a fair amount of interest in online professional development workshops for teachers, and questions about ways in which they are better or worse for teachers (Schlager & Fusco, 2004). The Math Forum's new online algebraic reasoning and probability workshops have begun to identify, through the online workshop process, particular teachers who stand out. These teachers are then invited to a face-to-face materials development workshop where they are given the chance to develop a stronger identity within the Math Forum community. Individuals who have the interest are encouraged to take on leadership roles (with some financial support) in future online workshops.

We can see in this most recent work the way that the Math Forum uses the Internet tradition of drawing on community resources more specific to its needs. It is also a creative use of that hybrid space. Individuals who are engaged in interesting mathematical dialogue are identified and then encouraged to cross over into the Math Forum culture. This is done literally by inviting a virtual participant to come to the Math Forum's physical home, meet with the staff, and then go back into the virtual community. It is through seeding work in this way that the Math Forum continues to produce participation, take advantage of the spatial opportunities in social cyberspace, and foster communication and interaction.

THEORETICAL CONSIDERATIONS: COMMUNITIES, TEXT, AND CONSCIOUSNESS

I conclude with some theoretical insights about the relationship among communities, texts, and the consciousness, both collective and individual, of participants in the communities. The choice of these three theoretical frames grows out of the discussion above. As I said at the beginning of the chapter, the Math Forum staff is about practice: Their goal is to make it possible for people to do problem solving together and to talk about the mathematics in that process. This focus on the centrality of communication is a key feature of the Math Forum's effort to raise the level of mathematical discourse and thinking. On the Internet, this communication produces texts. Hence, textual production and reuse has become a central feature of Math Forum work. It turns out that the potential of the Internet to create reusable text, coupled with the Math Forum's sensitivity to communication, has made it a good site for thinking about communication and textual theory. As the director of the Math Forum has said to me many times, "We did not set out to create community but rather community was the result of trying to encourage more mathematical communication." If the texts take on a life of their own online, so does a group of people who come together around a common interest. In this way, community is an emergent property of the Math Forum's efforts.

Thus, the Math Forum has created a unique model for online communities of practice in which the relationship between community and text is truly changed from models based in the modern era of print and mass media. If in the modern era, text was produced by some author, in concert with a bureaucracy for the shaping and dissemination of that text, at the Math Forum, text is a product of communities of participants interacting with one another and Math Forum staff. That text becomes a living part of the library, where it continues to interact with other participants and other utterances. Through all this interaction, knowledge is built collectively and the library changes, people are transformed, and the community grows. Out of that dynamic interplay of texts and the community of participants produced by those interactions comes consciousness, a consciousness that is the product of human symbolic interaction. It is constituted in part by the collective knowledge held by the community but also by the attitude toward mathematical work and problem solving in general. In short, it is the aspect of the culture that becomes a way of understanding.

Communities

In the 21st century, many more work environments are becoming collaborative spaces where knowledge is produced by groups of autonomous professionals organized in structures that are becoming more lateral and less hierarchical (Wenger, 1998). It is in the context of these changes in many workplaces and within segments of the larger economy itself that Lave and Wenger's (1991) original work on communities of practice caught on. In one sense, it is somewhat ironic that this work, which focused more on traditional trades, would be so relevant to the 21st-century workplace. But, of course, this is precisely the change that the work force has gone through in the developed world. Many of the hierarchical and bureaucratic factory structures are being replaced by models of work that are more apprentice-like in that worker autonomy, knowledge, and skill are increasingly important. But they are not exactly like traditional trades either, as they are knowledge organizations where advanced levels of mathematical, scientific, and technical knowledge must be mastered, used, and developed. Similarly, in many contemporary organizations, establishing the balance between the forms of collaborative interaction and knowledge building that workers engage in with one another, and the bureaucratic forms where activities are structured and recorded, has become a critical issue for companies to address (Wenger, 1998).[2]

New technologies have helped to form fluid linkages (e.g., between work and school) where there used to be abrupt divides. These technologies form rich sociotechnical networks that have come to constitute life in this digital age, and participation in these networks is becoming commonplace. They exist in various stages, forms, and venues: in nonprofit Internet forums, newsgroups, and successful online professional learning communities such as the Math Forum, Digital Library for Earth System Education (dlese.org), and Hawai'i Networked Learning Communities (hnlc.org). They also are evident in diverse and highly profitable enterprises such as multiplayer video games, online courses, and consumer services (match.com, amazon.com, eBay). In fact, the sociotechnical world cuts across socioeconomic and international lines, and public access is increasing.

It is in this context that we have seen the Math Forum take advantage of the potential of the Internet. The drive of the Math Forum to bring people together to talk and problem solve is at the heart of an intentional community that brings like-minded people together who get to share a common identity and allows them to form attachments to meet new needs. These individuals also are then free to imagine themselves in new ways as they imagine the community they are part of as well. These processes are all ones we have explored in depth at the Math Forum (Renninger & Shumar, 2002, 2004; Shumar, 2003; Shumar & Renninger, 2002; Shumar & Sarmiento, 2008). They are also processes that other social scientists have commented on (Kollack & Smith, 1999; Wellman, 2001; Wellman et al., 2002).

The Math Forum has developed into such a large and successful interactive educational Web community that there are different but overlapping groups on the site. The groups that participate in the Math Tools discussions regularly partly overlap with people who work with the PoW regularly and might occasionally overlap with workshop participants as well. Community groups also have a different life-span on the Math Forum site; some are very long-lasting and durable, and others are short-lived and last only as long as the workshop that they are participating in lasts (Levin & Cervantes, 2002).

This suggests that the Math Forum should be regarded not as one big Internet community, but rather as many smaller communities that have multiple opportunities to connect with one another. This complicated social space and all of these possibilities for social interaction create the potential for collaboration, apprenticeship, shared interests, developing interests, skills knowledge, and so on. This is an idea explored by Gerhard Fischer (2005) through the concept of Communities of Interest, which draws on Campbell's (1969) fish-scale model. Fischer argues that many professional communities in an information society are complicated and have different expertise in different areas. In this view, the social space consists of several communities of interest that each focus on one area of expertise. When all these different areas of expertise overlap, like the scales of a fish, they cover a large area. But each one covers only a small area. The different interest groups on the Math Forum site, for example, high school teachers, middle school teachers,

elementary teachers, people interested in algebra, those interested in geometry, and so on, are somewhat like this. Each is part of a specific community
of interest on the Math Forum site, but they overlap somewhat and together
form the larger community that is the Math Forum.

Schools, as they currently exist, will have increasing difficulty meeting
the needs of students in the 21st century. The challenge for schools in the
21st century is that they will need to provide very current and complex content for people to work in a complex world, and at the same time they will
need to encourage people to be reflexive critical thinkers. People will need
to modify the knowledge and skills they have learned over time, as knowledge these days changes at a very rapid rate. People will need to be both critical
thinkers and deep content holders, and also always to be ready to adapt their
thinking.

The Math Forum is an educational community for this new world. Many
teachers and students experience frustration dealing with the limitations of
their schools, in terms of rigid curriculum, lack of collegial support, bureaucratic rules that must be followed, and so on. The Math Forum provides a
welcome set of opportunities for individuals to meet their needs and build
knowledge in a more organic way, and colleagues with whom to do this. As
a subculture, the Math Forum has developed a set of values and practices
that reflect the potential of the new information economy (Renninger &
Shumar, 2004). For the Math Forum, the new technologies have always been
about improving opportunities for communication and interaction. The Math
Forum has always put people first, and meeting their needs with these new
tools. This attitude can be a very powerful incentive for involvement and
cultivating interest and motivation. It is also quite different than the reified
consciousness that permeates many schools. As discussed above, a critical
part of the Math Forum's success has come from not only offering good resources and answers to questions, but creatively blending face-to-face activities with online activities. These hybrid social spaces are an important part
of building community, creating dynamic texts, and allowing new forms of
consciousness to develop.

Text

If the Internet and online educational communities like the Math Forum have
created new hybrid social spaces and the possibilities for new forms of community and collaborative work, the role of text has been transformed as well.
In the early 20th century the Russian linguist Mikhail Bakhtin transformed
our thinking about language by focusing on utterances in social context, and
the social context as constitutive of the utterance. The utterance could be
speech or a written passage from a book, article, newspaper, and so on. What

was important was that the utterance was made alive and given meaning by its articulation in a particular social interaction. Passages of written text are reinterpreted every time they are part of a conversation and set of interactions, as are the speech acts of participants in the social interaction. As many researchers have pointed out recently, the Internet is a perfect medium for applying Bakhtin's notion of utterances and social contexts creating utterances, as every trace of a conversation online can be re-imagined for some future set of social interactions.

For Bakhtin, utterances were motivated by a twin set of forces. On one hand, there are the intentions of the actors and the desire to communicate something in a social situation. On the other hand, there are dynamic forces at work affecting the meaning of words that actors use in social situations; thus, pieces of the context, the backgrounds of the speakers, the ideological and cultural milieu in which the conversation is taking place, the historical moment—all of these things add to the meaning and affect actors' intentions as well (Bakhtin, 1981, 1986; Holquist, 1981; Wertsch, 2002). For Bakhtin, this rich stew is what makes meaning in its social context complex and perhaps even contradictory.

This question of the twin forces in language also raises an important question about agency and the reflexivity of participants in a conversation. If participants unreflectively allow particular ideologies to speak through them in an uncritical way, then certain meanings could take hold of an interaction. For instance, there are powerful cultural discourses that say math is hard, you either have math ability or you do not—it is more or less innate; thus the best way to sharpen math ability is to answer questions competitively, since math is about answers and not process. These powerful discourses in the culture not only are rearticulated by participants in classrooms and problem-solving situations but also affect the meanings of other utterances as they happen in social situations.

The Math Forum's approach to problem solving is one that encourages a lot of conversation and interaction. The Math Forum's culture encourages everyone to see themselves as people who can do math, and it emphasizes that any question or approach has validity. In this way, the Math Forum encourages productive interactions but it does so in a safe, friendly, non-hierarchical way. Further, the Internet, with its lack of social cues, often makes individuals feel safer and more willing to engage in a conversation about math and to discover the mathematicians in themselves. While the Math Forum cannot single-handedly change teachers' and students' views of themselves as not being good at math, it can foster forms of interaction that might lead eventually to such changes.

Text is thus a social product. It is part of the interactive work of the community as it goes about doing what it does. The Math Forum has always been very conscious of itself as a community (or set of communities) that encourages the production of certain forms of text. In the debate in math education between reformed mathematics and basic skills, the Math Forum has always steered a path that tried both to advocate the importance of good mathematics and correct work and answers, and at the same time to foster a discourse of exploration and discovery around math. In order to create good mathematical thinkers, the Math Forum culture has always advocated talking about math. This emphasis means that individuals have to be open to exploration and willing to talk about what they do not know and face that they might be wrong about ideas.

A nice example of both the Math Forum's straddling of the math education debate and its focus on discourse is the scoring rubric that the staff developed for the Problem of the Week service. Encouraged by many teachers and some students to provide a way to score answers in the PoW, the Math Forum designed a scoring rubric that both could give students a sense of how well they did with the math and also encouraged discussion and exploration of mathematical ideas (see http://mathforum.org/pow/teacher/assessown/scoring.html). The scoring rubric goes from novice to expert, implying that math is a process of developing knowledge and skills, not just a numerical score. It also has two main areas, problem solving and communication. This underscores that communicating and being able to talk about math is as highly valued as the actual ability to solve problems. Each of the areas, problem solving and communication, has subareas; therefore, the rubric looks at a child's ability to problem solve and communicate in some detail.

Another nice example of the focus on discourse and text at the Math Forum is the above-mentioned Bridging Research and Practice project. While the BRAP project drew on the Math Forum's experience doing teacher workshops, which always involved textual productions that became part of the site, the BRAP project was a major innovation for the Math Forum. The project produced a scholarly work that ended up being published on the Math Forum site. Further, the paper took advantage of new technologies in that it incorporated videos that the teachers had made of critical discursive moments in their own classrooms.

In such ways the Math Forum has fostered discourse around math and made it central to the community as a whole. But it also has taken a Bakhtinian approach to text in another way. In the late 1990s the Math Forum rediscovered itself as a digital library. It had always been a digital library, but of a very special type. The Math Forum began to build its collections of math materials from the traces of conversations about mathematics in the community. So the Ask Dr. Math archive was built from questions that people had submitted and that math doctors had answered. Likewise, the PoW archive was built from past problems and past solutions that had been written by students as well as the archive of texts written by members to the students doing those problems. Prior social interaction literally was reified, repackaged for use in future mathematical interactions. Text as a product of social interaction thus became part of the rich resources on the Math Forum site. In this way, the Math Forum community could produce a wealth of mathematical ideas, through the individuals and groups that spent time communicating on the site, as well as through the traces of past interactions that were vetted and stored as text objects for further use. On one level, this is no different than the archive of a discussion list or blog, but the text was crafted and archived carefully so that quality mathematics could be displayed and easily accessed for different needs.

The Math Forum pushed the notion of the interactive digital library to show that social space and social interaction are transformed quite significantly in the virtual world. It is not just a matter of getting to material more easily than in the brick and mortar library. These new developments show that human communicative social interaction can be taken to a new level because of these communication technologies and their potential for bringing together people who share interests and expertise, and making the rich communicative interaction available to novices and everyone in between. In the 1970s poststructuralist writers like Roland Barthes (Barthes, 1974) suggested that texts could be "readerly" or "writerly." For Barthes, this was about the way language was coded so that it led readers either to passively read a narrative and follow the "illusions of realism" created by the flow of certain codes or to actively reconstruct the text in a "writerly" fashion. Again, the Internet has shown the tremendous potential of reframing language and other forms of communication. The Math Forum is a digital library that is "writerly" in a new way. Participants create the texts, images, diagrams, and so forth, that form the holdings of the site and then rewrite those semiotic media in a variety of ways to suit new needs in new contexts. This creates a tremendous potential for the individuals and the groups who are part of this process.

Consciousness

For many anthropologists, the philosophical notion of *consciousness* is a term that can be used to label the everyday experience of the social world that is held at both an individual and a collective level. It is perhaps somewhat synonymous with worldview. Consciousness is the horizon of sense making that a group of people engages in and so is not always subject to conscious reflection, although it can be. It is also what the French sociologist Pierre Bourdieu (1984, 1990) described as "tacit knowledge" or *habitus*. Marx, who has had a great impact on contemporary social theory, was aware that much of consciousness grows out of the practices people engage in as part of their encounter with the material world (Marx, 1847/1963, 1939–1941/1973; Marx & Engels, 1845/1974). Habitual forms of activity and interactions with other people reinforce the social norms and pressures on an individual, giving that individual a sense of how the world is structured and that there is power within it.

Work in all societies is collective and produces knowledge that is held collectively. This is true for gatherers/hunters as well as industrialists. But in the postindustrial knowledge society, the social production of knowledge has become increasingly more important for productivity and the way that the society is organized. Many corporations have realized this, and as a result the hierarchically organized corporation is giving way to the laterally organized corporation that supports "knowledge groups" that work together and depend on one another (Bennis & Biederman, 1997; Wenger, 1998).

Further, this transformation from within the economic system is indicative of a deeper transformation in which, as discussed above, an economy of scarcity is giving way to an economy that is more sustainable and based on plentitude. In this new economy, as Wenger has foreshadowed, a new understanding of reification is important and a balance between the interaction of social actors and the reifications of their practice becomes very important. In this world, the relationship of individuals to the collective, specifically individual forms of consciousness to group forms of consciousness (including identity, belonging, and knowledge), is also very important. Groups like the open source community foreshadow a decommodification of the productive process as well as forms of liberation for consciousness.

These are social forces that people experience in a variety of ways. Consumers experience them in the form of cultural products that can be downloaded easily and enjoyed. Whether the individual downloads a TV show, song, or movie, legally or illegally, this is evidence of an economy of plentitude: Everyone can have a copy of the product, with little concern about productive costs. Workers experience these social forces in the way they work, the way they collaborate with colleagues, the ease of communicating across vast distances, and the potential for individual creativity both in terms of the groups they interact with and the ideas they engage with.

Organizations like the Math Forum are fostering this new consciousness around learning as well. In the knowledge society, it is becoming increasingly more important that individuals be reflexive and articulate participants in overlapping, electronically mediated forms of communication that form the backbone of learning and work. These new skills are in increasing demand as more literature begins to point out that what makes some children distinctive is their ability to be very involved in all the new technologies but also to be critical readers, thinkers, and problem solvers (National Endowment for the Arts, 2007; Ortner, 2003). These are the skills that not only will allow individuals to move ahead, but also are needed by a nation moving toward a new form of organization. And these skills require and reinforce new forms of consciousness.

CONCLUSION

From the general literature, we can extract five major effects of the Internet and other new communication technologies. First is the transformation of time. Time has the potential to become more elastic, allowing people to multitask and either increase the speed of communication or slow the communication process down. Closely related to the transformation of time, is the transformation of space. Virtual social spaces not only have made virtual communities more possible but have transformed the nature of physical spaces as well. The transformation of space and time has allowed new forms of community and social interaction to emerge.

A third effect of the Internet is that an economy of plentitude becomes possible, at least in relation to informational goods and services. This economy overcomes the old laws of scarcity and encourages reciprocal exchange and particularly generalized reciprocity. This third effect is something that has deeply troubled the entertainment industry, which always was able in the past to take advantage of the scarcity produced by inefficient means of reproducing books, movies, music, and so on. Now this industry faces a world where easy copying of products makes the cost of reproduction very small and ushers in an era of plentitude.

A fourth effect of the Internet and new communication technologies is the increased possibility for anonymity and disguising an individual's social identity. People not only can hide, with varying degrees of success, their race, gender, and economic status, but also can escape rigid status cultures that may exist in their schools or workplaces.

Finally, a fifth effect is the ability of individuals to transform their identities and the communities they interact with by leveraging the first four effects. All of these effects, it should be mentioned, are really part of the larger transformations of the social, and are consistent with other technological developments in modernity.

Throughout this chapter I have shown how the Math Forum has worked to leverage these five potentials of the Internet in order to produce the participation that we see at the site. As Dewey, Vygotsky, and others suggest, learning is a social process. And further, I would argue it is human nature to learn. We do not have to encourage people to learn; they do it all the time and in all places. But what is a matter of societal concern is what are people learning. Dewey suggested that teachers might want to focus on creating educative experiences, which are ones that: (1) connect to a person's experience, (2) build on that experience, and (3) have social value. From this point of view, learning is a double social process: It is done with others in a social/cultural context, and societies encourage their members to learn particular kinds of things.

Interaction and communication are central to the learning process. Like all of culture, learning is carried out through symbols and discursive interaction. Conversation and discourse take place in social groups.

In this social learning process, thought and knowledge involve the re-imagination of the individual's identity as well as the re-imagination of the knowledge community he or she is part of (Renninger & Shumar, 2002, 2004). Recently Barry Fishman (2006) has argued that technology in the classroom has a lot of promise but there have not been a lot of results yet. I would suggest that is because many schools have tried to incorporate technology within the existing social space, which I have critiqued above. Organizations like the Math Forum represent a dramatic departure in the transformation of social spaces in schools, as suggested throughout this chapter. This transformation has led to what I have called the "production of participation," a theoretical notion that underscores how a new cultural space can infuse bureaucratic institutions with authentic learning communities that meet people where they live and build upon their knowledge in a way that is collaborative. It builds the knowledge of individuals as well as communities and the resources they use. In the process, the communities, texts, and consciousness of social actors are transformed. Further, thanks to the Internet, this kind of cultural intervention can be scaled and provide at least some of the structural needs of schools, teachers, and students.

NOTES

1. While new social spaces also imply alternative temporalities, and time and space are always linked, there is a tradition in the social theory literature of talking about space and the social production of space (Harvey, 2000; Lefebvre, 1974/1991). One of the reasons for this is that social space needs to be imagined (Anderson, 1991) and articulated in particular ways so that infrastructure can be built and social life can be carried out. Changes in the ways we view time, the self and identity, the group and the other, all flow from these social constructions.

2. Wenger, in his book *Communities of Practice* (1998), suggests that in organizations there needs to be a balance between "participation" and "reification." For Wenger, reification is not the narrower concept that grows out of Marxist theoretical thought, but rather a broad term that refers to the ways people and organizations attempt to turn social processes into things. And so reifications are notes of a meeting, but they are also the templates that companies use for workers to engage in certain processes in certain ways. Wenger points out that organizations need

reifications, but if we adhere too slavishly to the reifications, then our ability to creatively interact and take advantage of the knowledge and skills that everyone brings to the table becomes severely impaired.

REFERENCES

Anderson, B. R. O. G. (1991). *Imagined communities: Reflections on the origin and spread of nationalism* (Rev. and extended ed.). New York: Verso.

Bakhtin, M. M. (1981). *The dialogic imagination: Four essays by M. M. Bakhtin.* (C. Emerson & M. Holquist, Trans.; M. Holquist, Ed.). Austin: University of Texas Press.

Bakhtin, M. M. (1986). *Speech genres and other late essays* (1st ed.) (V. W. McGee, Trans.; C. Emerson and M. Holquist, Eds.). Austin: University of Texas Press.

Barthes, R. (1974). *S/Z* (1st American ed.) (Richard Miller, Trans.). New York: Hill and Wang.

Bennis, W. G., & Biederman, P. W. (1997). *Organizing genius: The secrets of creative collaboration.* Reading, MA: Addison-Wesley.

Bourdieu, P. (1984). *Distinction: A social critique of the judgement of taste.* Cambridge, MA: Harvard University Press.

Bourdieu, P. (1990). *The logic of practice.* Stanford, CA: Stanford University Press.

Campbell, D. T. (1969). Ethnocentrism of disciplines and the fish-scale model of omniscience. In M. Sherif & C. W. Sherif (Eds.), *Interdisciplinary relationships in the social sciences* (pp. 328–348). Chicago: Aldine.

Fischer, G. (2005, July). From reflective practitioners to reflective communities. In *Proceedings of the HCI International Conference*, Las Vegas. Available online at http://l3d.cs.colorado.edu/~gerhard/papers/reflective-communities-hcii-2005 .pdf

Fishman, B. J. (2006, July 6). It's not about the technology. *Teachers College Record.* Date Published: July 06, 2006 http://www.tcrecord.org ID Number: 12584, Date Accessed: 9/23/2008 4:19:13 PM.

Harvey, D. (2000). *Spaces of hope.* Berkeley and Los Angeles: University of California Press.

Holquist, M. (1981). Introduction. In M. M. Bakhtin, *The dialogic imagination: Four essays by M. M. Bakhtin* (C. Emerson & M. Holquist, Trans.; M. Holquist, Eds.) (pp. xv–xxxiii). Austin: University of Texas Press.

Kollock, P., & Smith, M. A. (1999). *Communities in cyberspace.* London: Routledge.

Lave, J., & Wenger, E. (1991). *Situated learning: Legitimate peripheral participation.* New York: Cambridge University Press.

Lefebvre, H. (1991). *The production of space* (D. Nicholson-Smith, Trans.). Oxford: Basil Blackwell. (Original work published 1974)

Levin, J. A., & Cervantes, R. (2002). Understanding the lifecycles of network-based learning communities. In K. A. Renninger & W. Shumar (Eds.), *Building virtual communities: Learning and change in cyberspace* (pp. 269–292). New York: Cambridge University Press.

Marx, K. (1963). *The poverty of philosophy*. New York: International Publishers. (Original work published 1847)

Marx, K. (1973). *Grundrisse: Foundations of the critique of political economy*. New York: Vintage Books. (Original work published 1939–1941)

Marx, K., & Engels, F. (1974). *The German ideology, Part 1*. New York: International Publishers. (Original work published 1845)

Mauss, M., & ebrary Inc. (2000). *The gift: The form and reason for exchange in archaic societies*. New York: W. W. Notton.

National Endowment for the Arts. (2007). *To read or not to read: A question of national consequence*. (Research Rep. No. 47). Washington, DC: NEA, Office of Research and Analysis.

Ortner, S. B. (2003). *New Jersey dreaming: Capital, culture and the class of '58*. Durham, NC: Duke University Press.

Renninger, K. A., & Shumar, W. (2002). Community building with and for teachers at the Math Forum. In K. A. Renninger & W. Shumar (Eds.), *Building virtual communities: Learning and change in cyberspace* (pp. 60–95). New York: Cambridge University Press.

Renninger, K. A., & Shumar, W. (2004). The centrality of culture and community to participant learning at and with the Math Forum. In S. A. Barab, R. Kling, & J. H. Gray (Eds.), *Designing for virtual communities in the service of learning* (pp. 181–209). New York: Cambridge University Press.

Schlager, M. S., & Fusco, J. (2004). Teacher professional development, technology, and communities of practice: Are we putting the cart before the horse? In S. A. Barab, R. Kling, & J. H. Gray (Eds.), *Designing for virtual communities in the service of learning* (pp. 120–153). New York: Cambridge University Press.

Shumar, W. (2003). The role of community and belonging in online learning. In M. Mardis (Ed.), *Developing digital libraries for K–12* (pp. 174–187). Washington, DC: ERIC Monograph Series.

Shumar, W., & Renninger, K. A. (2002). On community building. In K. A. Renninger & W. Shumar (Eds.), *Building virtual communities: Learning and change in cyberspace* (pp. 1–20). New York: Cambridge University Press.

Shumar, W., & Sarmiento, J. (2008). Communities of practice at the Math Forum: Supporting teachers as professionals. In P. Hildreth & C. Kimble (Eds.), *Communities of practice: Creating learning environments for educators* (pp. 223–239). Hershey, PA: Idea Group Publishing.

Stahl, G. (2006). *Group cognition: Computer support for building collaborative knowledge*. Cambridge, MA: MIT Press.

Wellman, B. (2001). Physical place and cyberplace: The rise of personalized networking. *International Journal of Urban and Regional Research*, 25(2), 227–252.

Wellman, B., Quan-Haase, A., Boase, J., & Chen, W. (2002, October). *Examining the Internet in everyday life*. Keynote address given by B. Wellman to the Euricom Conference on e-democracy. Nijmegen, Netherlands.

Wenger, E. (1998). *Communities of practice: Learning, meaning, and identity*. New York: Cambridge University Press.

Wertsch, J. V. (2002). *Voices of collective remembering*. New York: Cambridge University Press.

CHAPTER 4

MERLOT: A Community-Driven Digital Library

Flora McMartin

To date, most literature about online communities has tended to focus on the design requirements for building a successful online community, especially with regard to the online tools and design of the learner's experience (Barab, MaKinster, & Scheckler, 2004; Renninger & Shumar, 2002). More rare is the discussion of what it takes to develop, maintain, and sustain the organization behind such a community. When the background organization is discussed, as in Amy Kim's book, *Community Building on the Web* (2000), the organization is described in terms of the types of activities that staff and volunteers must undertake to engage and encourage users to participate in commercially driven online communities rather than educational communities.

This chapter examines how one such digital library, MERLOT—the Multimedia Educational Resource for Learning Online and Teaching (http://www.merlot.org)[1]—successfully has developed and sustained an organizational structure that since 1997 has grown its community of "patrons"[2] by providing professional development activities and learning materials. MERLOT's experience serves as one model for newly emerging digital libraries to design and implement organizational structures (including policies, procedures, and staffing) that align with and reflect the patrons they seek to serve. In MERLOT's case, it strategically aligned its organizational values, services, programs, and business strategies with those of the American higher education system.

OVERVIEW

Contrary to stories of relatively easy acceptance and use of other digital tools or services in higher education (e.g., e-mail, word processing, and spreadsheets), described by Steve Ehrmann (1997) as "worldware," the integration of digital libraries into the teaching and learning process has been neither rapid nor far-reaching. Instead, it has been a slow process in which digital libraries such as MERLOT have attempted to overcome the challenges associated with integration into the workflow of faculty members, instructors, students, librarians, academic technologists, faculty developers, and the wealth of other campus members who seek to improve education and its practice on their campuses. MERLOT stands out as one digital library that has found a means to connect directly with the faculty and instructors who seek to incorporate digital learning materials into their teaching practice and who require some professional development in order to do so effectively. MERLOT has been able to give these instructors access to materials that are becoming increasingly hard to obtain. Such access has become limited, in part because such materials have become part of the "invisible web" (Barker, 2006), being stored in course management systems and other campus systems that do not expose them to the broader public.

The development of online communities as a strategy to support the adoption of digital libraries emerged as a response to a challenge frequently raised by funding agencies:[3] "If you build a digital library, will they come?" MERLOT's community-building model led to the development of a successful community of practice where a small but dedicated group of faculty members have been able, to date, to sustain and grow its collection of learning resources. As digital libraries transition from the informal research world of small, localized research projects directed by individual faculty and located in university research groups, into formal e-learning organizations that can support the demands made by national and international library patrons (Giersch et al., 2004), they must face questions fundamental to all developing organizations, such as: What does it mean to institutionalize a digital library in a higher education setting? What is the value of educational digital libraries? How can digital libraries encourage educational innovation by faculty's and instructors? What kinds of professional development are necessary to support faculty's and instructors' use of and commitment to digital library e-learning communities? How do these innovative organizations stay true to their values and purpose as they transition from innovation to stable trusted resources?

Life cycle theories of organizational development are a useful framework for examining MERLOT's experience in this transformational process and for exploring more broadly how digital libraries as innovative organizations in higher education can become institutionalized. These theories, emerging in the 1980s and promoted by authors such as Quinn and Cameron (1983), track organizations from "birth" through "maturity," laying out the challenges organizations must surpass in order to survive. Judith Sharken Simon's

(2001) recent application of life cycle theory in the nonprofit organizational realm is particularly relevant in describing organizational growth, starting from the digital library "dream" to making it a viable and sustainable organization. Given the primacy of questions of survival that most digital libraries currently face, this framework provides a useful structure for examining not only their formation but also the challenges they face in today's climate for higher education, the challenges associated with introducing and sustaining innovation in this climate, and the challenges facing them as they look toward the future.

ABOUT MERLOT

The Web Site

MERLOT is a complex e-learning organization that provides faculty and instructors access to digital learning materials as well as related professional development necessary to help them learn more about how to use the materials in their teaching. MERLOT's mission is to "improve the effectiveness of teaching and learning by expanding the quantity and quality of peer-reviewed online learning materials that can be easily incorporated into faculty designed courses" (2006). To accomplish this, MERLOT has developed and supports a digital library of learning resources found at www.merlot.org (see Figure 4.1).

The site is a free, Web-based resource that connects faculty, staff, and students to almost 15,000 online learning materials in over 15 different disciplines representing the arts, humanities, and the social and physical sciences, as well as professional schools such as business and education. Unlike many digital libraries, it is not a repository for these materials, nor is it merely a referatory that simply points a patron to the materials. It is both and neither in that it provides off- and online professional development services for its patrons, who are for the most part faculty and instructors in higher education, to learn how to use these resources in teaching. It also invites its almost 40,000 registered patrons to participate in its growing multidisciplinary community of scholars via its discipline board portals.

Patrons can search MERLOT for learning materials related to their discipline. A search results in a listing of learning materials ranging from simple online animations or simulations of a concept, to complex case studies or modules focusing on simple or complex concepts (see Figure 4.2). But the value to patrons is not in these results alone. MERLOT links these resources to a set of quality indicators (i.e., peer reviews, comments by other patrons, assignments, personal collections, and author comments) to help patrons

FIGURE 4.1. MERLOT home page

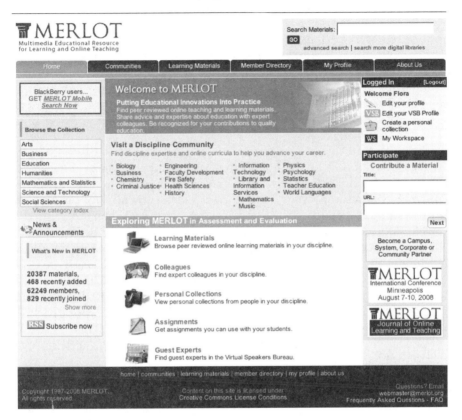

decide whether further exploration of an item is warranted. By examining these indicators, they can determine quickly the value or use of the material in meeting their teaching or learning needs. Taken as a whole, the indicators are a rich set of professional development materials designed to help an instructor or faculty member use the learning material to its fullest as an integral aspect of their online or more traditional in-class courses. These quality indicators include:

> *Peer reviews*, conducted by MERLOT editorial boards, which rate the material based on the quality of its content, potential as a teaching tool, and ease of use.
> *Comments* made by editorial board members or other patrons regarding their use of the material or their impressions of its quality.

Assignments describing how others have used the material in their teaching and the effects of its use on teaching or student learning.

Personal Collections, which are collections of learning materials found
in MERLOT that patrons create and annotate. These collections
can be shared and are searchable, allowing patrons to learn how
others have used them in courses that might be similar to theirs.

Author Comments, which describe from the author's (or developer's)
point of view why the material was developed, how it was used in
teaching, the effects it had on student learning, and tips for how
others might use it.

Patrons not only find materials that may meet their educational needs,
but the quality indicators allow them to learn how others in their field have
used the materials, the results of those uses, and the potential for future uses.
MERLOT's strategy (described in depth later in this chapter) to grow the
collection of learning materials and associated quality indicators has hinged
(quite successfully to date) on encouraging community members to submit
both the materials and the items making up the quality indicators.

In addition to the quality indicators, seen along the right side of the
results page in Figure 4.2, each item in the collection is described in more

FIGURE 4.2. Example of a results (hits) page

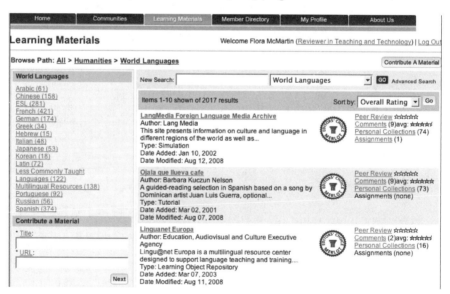

detail with more standard "library card" information, such as location (URL) of the item, author, year created, copyright restrictions, and cost.

In addition to a wide-ranging catalog of learning materials, MERLOT provides patrons with connections to communities of like-minded faculty within their discipline. Each discipline supported by a MERLOT editorial board has a portal page devoted to information about using online resources in that particular discipline (see Figure 4.3). At this page patrons can explore the state of the art of online teaching and learning within their discipline, learn more about how they might contribute to MERLOT, and connect with other MERLOT patrons who share their interests. This scholarly community also may lead them to contribute to the MERLOT Journal for Online Learning

FIGURE 4.3. Example of a discipline portal page

and Teaching (JOLT), or to participate in MERLOT's annual conference, which is designed to bring together this multidisciplinary community of educators.

The MERLOT Community

Begun in 1996 as a project for the California State University System, MERLOT has since become a nationwide e-learning organization centered on meeting faculty members' needs to learn about and use online computer technologies in teaching. Organized as a consortium of state systems of higher education, MERLOT supports a complex organizational and human infrastructure to undergird the services and programs freely available at its Web site. The consortium members[4] provide the human resources that make up MERLOT's core community.

MERLOT's community might best be described as a series of concentric circles (see Figure 4.4). Those who are most involved are found at the core. The core consists of those faculty members, instructors, and staff who receive some kind of support[5] from MERLOT partner institutions for their services. Their role is to seed the development of the site and help build its scholarly community. The next circle is made up of a small but dedicated group of volunteers and contributors who do not receive financial compensation from a partner, but who are motivated to participate because of their sense of belonging to the MERLOT community and their desire to be a mem-

FIGURE 4.4. The MERLOT community

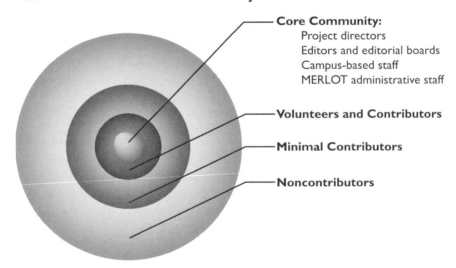

Core Community:
Project directors
Editors and editorial boards
Campus-based staff
MERLOT administrative staff

Volunteers and Contributors

Minimal Contributors

Noncontributors

ber of it. (It is possible that they receive some sort of internal or external reward for their participation, either through recognition within their disciplinary community or from their campus.)

The outer two circles represent those patrons who contribute at successively lower levels, that is, those who contribute minimally; for example, they may submit a comment or assignment, or an article to JOLT, or perhaps present their scholarship at the annual MERLOT conference. In most cases, however, they do not contribute more than one or two items to the collection. The outside ring, the largest of all in terms of participants, consists of visitors who are not registered members and who do not contribute at any level. This group is the most amorphous and least understood. They are the patrons who visit the site, who tend not to become registered users, and who may or may not use the information or materials found there, but who definitely do not contribute back to the site.

Patrons can move closer to the core community by increasing their level of contributions. After completing a short online training program, they also may become peer reviewers (making them de facto members of the editorial boards). Thus, they may participate fairly deeply in the organization even if the institution in which they work is not a paying member of the MERLOT consortium. Formally, however, they cannot become members of the core community, which was designed as a benefit for the paying partners of MERLOT. This design ensures that only members of the consortium provide MERLOT with direction in terms of defining its services, programs, and so forth. The design is also a primary strategy used to achieve sustainability, for it is hoped that in motivating faculty members to move from noncontributors to contributors and eventually membership in the core community, they will demonstrate the value of MERLOT to their institutions, thereby encouraging formal membership in the consortium.

MERLOT's core community, the community behind the community, so to speak, is restricted to the relatively small set of leaders (about 150 people drawn from the approximately 20 partners) in the use of technology in teaching and learning. The core community is made up mainly of project directors, editors, and editorial board members, whose main responsibilities are to build the collection of learning materials and at the same time build the online community by promoting MERLOT on their campuses and through their professional associations (see Table 4.1).

Project directors act as liaisons between MERLOT and the partner institution or system, recruiting and managing the selection of faculty and staff to participate in the community as editors and editorial board members. They plan and implement local strategies (e.g., professional development workshops, trainings, etc.) for creating a community of practice around MERLOT within their states or on their campuses. Project directors tend to be academic

TABLE 4.1. Roles and responsibilities of core community members

Project Director	*Editor*	*Editorial Board Member*
• Act as liaison between partner and MERLOT	• Coordinate and manage the activities of the editorial board	• Find and select learning materials to add to the collection
• Recruit and select editors and editorial board members and members of the library and faculty development communities	• Recruit and train peer reviewers	• Contribute valued-added information connected to learning materials (peer reviews, assignments, comments, personal collections, snapshots)
	• Evaluate peer reviewers and editorial board members	
• Create and coordinate professional development opportunities for faculty and instructors regarding MERLOT	• Manage the development and maintenance of the discipline portal	• Promote MERLOT within the discipline; develop cooperative relationship between professional societies and MERLOT
	• Manage the annual classics award process for the discipline	
• Collaborate to devise and support technology initiatives to promote good use of technology in teaching	• Promote MERLOT within the discipline; develop cooperative relationship between professional societies and MERLOT	• Promote MERLOT at local, regional, and national levels
		• Participate in selecting the annual classics award
• Manage the relationship between MERLOT and partners		
• Participate on the Project Directors' Council	• Promote MERLOT at local, regional, and national levels	• Other duties related to specific roles (e.g., associate editor) including contributing materials to the discipline portal, recruiting, and training peer reviewers, etc.
	• Participate on the Editors' Council	

technology officers at either the campus or state level, so as a group they have extensive expertise regarding issues associated with technology, teaching, and campus acquisition of the services in support of those activities. Because of this expertise, they provide the organization with advice in setting the future direction of MERLOT activities, programs, and services.

Editors (faculty members from partner colleges and institutions) are responsible for leading one of the 15 editorial boards and working with the editorial board members to develop the quality of the collection as well as to promote MERLOT in their campus and professional circles. Together with their editorial board members, they work to build and conserve the discipline's collection, maintain its quality through the peer review process, and build the community of scholars associated with their discipline. While the project directors are essential to introducing MERLOT to potential patrons, and stimulating their faculty to become MERLOT patrons at the core and contributing levels, the editorial board's role is to work with the patrons who use and contribute to MERLOT, to create a community of practice around a particular discipline.

The size of the editorial boards reflects the nature and complexity of the discipline and its discipline's state of the art in terms of using and creating online teaching and learning materials. For example, the business editorial board's collection focuses on accounting, economics, finance, general business, information systems, management, and marketing. This editorial board, comprising the partner-supported positions of editor, four associate editors, and four peer reviewers, also supports a large pool of around 60 reviewers. In contrast, the music editorial board makes no distinctions by type of department, consists of five supported editorial board members, and has only a few volunteer reviewers.

As MERLOT has grown, it has added campus staff to its core community, including librarians, faculty development staff, and academic technology staff. These campus staff members are key players in promoting the use of digital resources with the faculty and instructors on their college campuses.

The last constituency in the core community is that of the MERLOT administrative staff. The staff support the boards through the development and support of online tools, such as the workflow tool that undergirds the peer review process, from submission of an item for review through posting of the review. They also provide both face-to-face and online training for peer reviewers.

Mapping MERLOT to Academic Cultures and Communities

Just as creating the core community was essential in the early life of MERLOT, so too was creating a set of services that would be valued by members of higher education. Innovative organizations in higher education tend to fail because often they are structured differently than others providing similar services, hold strikingly divergent values from those who might make up their client base, or offer services that potential clients do not know or recognize they need (Levine, 1979). In an attempt to avoid these pitfalls, MERLOT's developers designed the core community, Web site and attendant services, professional development programs, and governance to align with closely held academic values. In the first version of MERLOT, the following statements were posted on its home page to reinforce to its patrons that this was a resource designed with college and university faculty and instructors in mind:

- Faculty are, and should remain, in control of the learning process.
- Faculty need better mechanisms to document their contributions to teaching and learning.
- Faculty-led peer review processes are key to expanding the use and effectiveness of digital learning materials.
- States, systems, consortia, and individual institutions can collectively learn and share with each other, thus maximizing their investments in instructional information technology. (MERLOT, 2006)

In posting these values on the home page (see Figure 4.5), MERLOT attempted to show its potential patrons that it could be a trusted partner in the effort to integrate technology into teaching. Through promotion of faculty control of the curriculum and teaching, MERLOT hoped to set aside any fears that faculty-led instruction might be replaced by computers. Instead, it reinforced the need to place faculty and instructors at the center of the higher education enterprise.

FIGURE 4.5. MERLOT home page 2000–2005

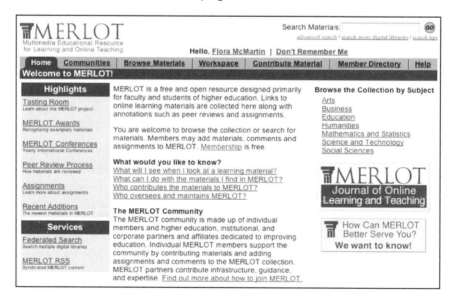

Focusing first on faculty members and instructors, their needs and their values, MERLOT's strategy was to build its community of users by consciously designing services and products strongly linked to an academic culture defined by research, teaching, and service responsibilities that make up a faculty member's career. To make this an appealing resource to these potential participants, MERLOT developers assumed that support of the activities required in the promotion and tenure process would be a strong enough motivational force to encourage faculty members to use and contribute to MERLOT's collection and the site's communication mechanisms.

Since peer review of scholarly work is a highly regarded aspect of faculty work, MERLOT designed a peer review process similar to that used in scholarly journals, but that had the added professional development feature of providing potential users with the actual review. This model allowed MERLOT to introduce an innovation (making peer reviews public) within the well-known, recognizable framework of journal-style peer reviews. This new peer review framework was similar enough to the old one that members of academe could recognize it easily and evaluate it. MERLOT theorized that it increased the likelihood of adoption and use of online learning materials by making these innovations seem similar or familiar. Also, by holding true to the values of academe, that is, the value of excellence in scholarship, teaching, and research, its products and services would be more trusted than those of competing digital libraries that did not have such processes in place. These types of strategies exemplified MERLOT's efforts to build deep connections with individual campuses and schools by tapping into and becoming part of their academic communities.

Academic culture also places high value on the unique identities the disciplines. College departments organize themselves around the disciplines, and universities organize the disciplines into schools or colleges, for example, college of arts and sciences, college of physical sciences, and professional schools. Designers for the initial MERLOT Web site and programs used these organizing principles as a metaphor for the Web site's home page (see Figure 4.1). Knowing that faculty identify most strongly with their discipline, it was extremely important that the disciplines be highly visible on MERLOT's Web site and that, just like campuses, they define the communities of practice within MERLOT. The idea was that when new patrons visited the site for the first time, they should see that it was organized much like their campus, enabling them to find their academic "home" and to search or browse it intuitively.

Mapping MERLOT's services and programs to academic culture provided its patrons with a metaphor for engaging with this new educational resource that was as easy to understand as their own campus. So, for example, chemists easily can find other chemists in MERLOT, just as they might find their colleagues on another campus. Finding and using metaphors such as this are important to the sustainability of an innovation, for if patrons (or perhaps more important, potential funders) cannot understand how to work within the organization, or cannot find their place in the organization, they are less likely to participate.

MERLOT IN CONTEXT: A TECHNOLOGY INNOVATION IN HIGHER EDUCATION

MERLOT's organizational development occurred concurrent with the increasing focus on teaching with technology in higher education in the 1990s. At that time, there was little or no trusted place (library) to go to on the Web where a faculty member or instructor could find online learning materials and learn about their use. (There also was, in fact, very little professional development at the campus level.) MERLOT was at the forefront of the early efforts to collect these items, review them for quality, and make them freely available to faculty members and instructors. It was especially innovative in that it did not rely on grants to fund its services. Unlike models that focused on a specific discipline (e.g., the Math Forum or NEEDS—the National Engineering Education Digital Library), it was interdisciplinary and connected directly with individual campuses to reach its patrons.

MERLOT as an educational technology innovation centered its organizational survival strategies on achieving recognition, acceptability, and adoption by faculty and instructors, campus and systemwide administrators, students, and higher education in general. In addition to attempting to align itself with academic cultures and communities, MERLOT sought to ensure that it was perceived as a high-quality and stable resource by working in partnership with high-status organizations such as the Carnegie Foundation. For example, it developed collaborations around projects such as the Scholarship of Teaching and Learning (http://www.carnegiefoundation.org) that are dedicated to changing the campus culture to shift the balance toward valuing building communities of learners rather than focusing on traditional modes of teaching such as transmission of knowledge. MERLOT also aligned itself with the National Science Digital Library sponsored by the National Science Foundation, successfully receiving funding within that program and participating in the leadership of that effort. This participation showed its ability to be a leader in a field dominated by large research institutions.

At the same time that MERLOT was gaining recognition as a leader in the digital library realm and expanding the partners within its consortium and number of registered members at the site, it was experiencing the challenge of transitioning from an innovator to a trusted academic resource used by faculty, administrators, and students. Like other technology innovations, MERLOT has had to deal with tension between the glacially slow rate of adoption of innovation in higher education and the fact that changes in technology can happen seemingly in nano-seconds. In this environment, innovations in higher education such as MERLOT seemingly face an insurmountable challenge in attempting to encourage wide adoption by faculty members in a culture that has proven to be extremely resistant to change.

A commonly cited measure of success of a website is the number of users. In 2004 MERLOT had fewer than 20,000 registered users, and in 2008 this number has exceeded 60,000. But, how do we assess that growth? Certainly compared to YouTube and MySpace[6] it is meager, yet MERLOT serves a targeted population who will engage with the site for the specific purposes related to enriching their teaching or professional development with online resources.

Critics may claim, as Robert Zemsky and W. F. Massey did in 2004, that e-learning is a failed innovation in higher education because only a very small percentage of faculty are active users; in the case of MERLOT, less than 1% of all faculty members in the United States[7] were registered users. Taking seriously the need to increase its reach to all faculty members, MERLOT realizes that at a minimum it must involve the innovators (between 2% to 3% of the potential population of users) as described in Rogers's seminal work on innovation (2003) and the early adopters (about 14% of the population) to develop the critical mass within higher education necessary to encourage broader adoption (Millar, 1995; Moore, 1991; Rogers, 2003). Zemsky's claim, though perhaps correctly based on his perception that the number of registered users is low, calls attention to the broader questions associated with the use of numbers to judge success.

While the number of registered users is a useful marker, it only tells part of a complex story. They do not, for example, account for the large numbers of visitors who browse the site for material without logging in. A far greater proportion of faculty may be gaining benefit from MERLOT, without joining, or for that matter, without being consciously aware that they are accessing it's resources. While MERLOT can show growth in numbers of patrons and users, this type of measure does not adequately assess the impact of technology innovations such as MERLOT.

Recent research (Harley et al., 2006; McMartin, Iverson, Manduca, Wolf, & Morgan, 2006) indicates that faculty members and instructors avidly searching the Web for digital learning materials search on Google first. To these users, the source of a material or site is often invisible to them because Google has mediated their access to the site. Faculty might indeed be frequent users of a digital library, but only access it through Google, because using its search engine is easy, quick, and fits their existing search behaviors.

This research shows that few of the faculty members who participated in the studies could name specific digital libraries, even though they may have benefited from their use.

Thus, the difference between registered users and guests may be that registered users may have different search behaviors, or may have found value in becoming a patron so that they can contribute to the site as well as browse. Yet both registered users and guests may be deriving benefit in terms of incorporating online resources from MERLOT within their teaching practices.

Another common marker of use is to look at the number of times a resource is accessed. This measure is also imperfect since MERLOT, like other digital libraries that are "referatories" (as opposed to repositories), does not hold the resources at its site. It is impossible to know how many visitors eventually accessed these resources, finding the original source, after leaving the MERLOT site.

Perhaps adoption of innovations such as these in higher education might be bettered measured in terms of "stickiness" as used in commercial Web sites (Gladwell, 2000). Stickiness refers to the frequency of return and length of time spent on a site by a user. Those organizations that can engender loyal users—that is, users who return to the site frequently, stay at it for a period of time, and who contribute to it—may be able to claim that their users derive more value from their site. The measures taken into account to judge "stickiness" relate directly to important aspects of online communities.

Even more difficult to measure, is the metric of success that most education digital libraries would like to show: that use of their resource results in changes in teaching or learning. But digital libraries are so young that they can only guess at how faculty members and instructors use their resources, let alone know how that use changed their teaching or their students' learning. If use is the ultimate indicator of success for a digital library, then new questions must be asked in relation to numbers of patrons, their use of the library, and what that means in relation to educational impact. One might ask, for example, Is it better that a patron spend a long time at a site or is it better that a patron come to a site, get what he or she wants, and leave quickly? Or what about the faculty member or instructor as learner? All too often it is assumed that the contents of digital libraries all find their way eventually into the classroom. But what if patrons use these materials for their own professional development? How might that be measured? The question facing MERLOT and others then becomes: What makes someone invest in visiting a site, return to it, and decide to integrate an innovative teaching practice into his or her teaching repertoire? And once this is known, how can this information help digital libraries market their services in such a way as to create the critical mass necessary to ensure larger adoption?

MERLOT (and other digital libraries) still had to face the problem that, even as technology barriers began to drop (e.g., faculty use of high-speed

Internet connections is more common than not [Ehrmann, 1997; Jones & Johnson-Yale, 2005], allowing for increasingly rapid searches and download ability), to change the way faculty and instructors teach to incorporate use of digital libraries, there first needs to be a market or need for using digital learning materials and obtaining professional development from the site. Digital libraries are in the midst of a conundrum, for they are innovative organizations that depend on the adoption of another innovation, that of the ubiquitous integration of digital learning materials into teaching and learning by a broad segment of their potential patrons.

THE MERLOT ORGANIZATIONAL LIFE CYCLE

The most difficult challenge faced by MERLOT and other e-learning professional development communities is the need for organizational structures and strategies that will allow them to establish themselves and transition into long-lasting organizations while depending on the culture of teaching in higher education to change so as to embrace their services. The rest of this chapter will focus on describing how MERLOT has moved through its organizational life cycle and developed strategies to deal with these challenges.

Organizational theorists (Daft, 1992; Quinn & Cameron, 1983; Sharken Simon, 2001) describe the life of organizations as being akin to that of humans: They are born, live youthful lives, transition into midlife, and finally experience maturity. Younger organizations are typified as being small or medium-sized, and having few rules, few staff, and few budget or control systems, with many overlapping tasks and a highly centralized leadership. The major focus of an organization in these early stages is to demonstrate that its mission can be accomplished and that it is viable. Older, more established and mature organizations are larger; have more bureaucratic structures and many departments with numerous formal leaders; are highly formalized; and use task forces and other integrators to try to break down the effects of bureaucracy. The major focus of mature organizations is to sustain their momentum and (re)designing ways to keep themselves viable in rapidly changing environments without harming or changing themselves in any significant way.

The Role of Community in Establishing MERLOT

In the early stages of an online organization, building community is a critical function to create the market for the organization's product and the people who will volunteer or work for the organization. From its inception, MERLOT's builders envisioned it as a vibrant community of scholars who contributed to a collection of online resources as well as communicated with the "collection" of participants contributing those resources. MERLOT's framers were highly influenced by the notion of *communities of practice*, as advanced by Lave and Wenger (1991; Wenger, 1998; Wenger, McDermott, & Snyder, 2002), in that they established an organizational framework of offline communities designed to support the creation of mirror communities online. MERLOT developed a behind-the-scenes core community to instantiate Barab and colleagues (2004) definition of a community of practice as a "persistent, sustained social network of individuals who share and develop an overlapping knowledge base, set of beliefs, values, history, and experiences focused on a common practice and/or mutual enterprise" (p. 55).

The challenge to this young organization was to build and sustain a community of practice where none had existed previously. Not only was there no community of practice (or professional development) around the use of online digital learning materials, there was no organization (digital library) that collected, organized, or made them available to faculty. MERLOT was an innovation that truly filled this need. MERLOT addressed this challenge by moving from its "cottage industry" model (Otto, Hanley, & Swift, 2004) of serving only members of the California State University System to a national consortium model that it believed to be more scalable and sustainable.

The Core Community

As a small, newly established organization, MERLOT alone could not support the high cost of employees necessary to staff its projects and programs. The core community, then, evolved from the need to leverage resources collectively and was a central "selling point" for potential partners who were eager to be leaders in the development of digital libraries. These partners also felt that it was important to involve their faculties, and they assigned faculty leaders in educational innovation to MERLOT to make up the core community. (They also paid an annual fee[8] and provided MERLOT with onsite professional development and training venues as a means to market its services among faculty and instructors.) MERLOT's success as a digital library has hinged on the core community's building and maintaining the collection of digital learning materials, vetting that collection, laying the groundwork necessary for collaborations with professional societies to help elevate MERLOT's status among the professoriate, and marketing MERLOT to faculty, staff, students, and administrators at the campus and state levels.

This model has led to a successful community of practice within the consortium. Results from a study conducted by the MERLOT Teacher Education Board (Pelaez et al., 2004) regarding the impact of MERLOT community-building efforts among the 15 editorial boards indicated that several of the boards had created such strong communities of practice that the benefits from participating in the community were the primary motivation for continued participation in MERLOT. Findings included, for example, that the financial support and other motivators required for participation by editorial board members were less important than the social networks that had been formed.

The strong core community has served MERLOT well, for as a new project, it was able to build its initial set of collections and services quickly by depending on the energy, enthusiasm, and commitment of its highly motivated core community. This community, infused with the entrepreneurial spirit, helped grow the consortium to the point that in 2003, 23 partners supported MERLOT with the required fees and eight peer reviewers on each editorial board and two editors. The cost of the reviewers and editors was estimated by some at nearly $75,000 (Morgan, personal communication, September 19, 2008). As we will see later, this support waned as partners were forced to address budget reductions for higher education in their home states, forcing them to reduce support for core community members. Such intervening environmental factors, combined with the growing stability of the site and its services, created new challenge for the organization: how to keep the commitment and energy of its entrepreneurial core community engaged in working on the day-to-day work required for MERLOT to succeed when the novelty and excitement of innovation had worn off.

MERLOT's organizational model and values require this type of community involvement, and to date the consortium has successfully accomplished many of the organization's goals. But it is a model that is tenuous, for it requires that the consortium members be highly dedicated and it requires continuous growth in that membership in order to meet the needs of the growing patron community. To meet the growing demands of patrons, the core community also must grow, and that growth depends on the ability of the partners to provide financial support[9] for the core community members. New partners in the consortium allow for the development of new editorial boards or expansion of existing boards. The converse is also true, for if the consortium membership dropped significantly, the number of editorial boards might need to be reduced accordingly.

The Impact of Environmental Factors on MERLOT's Youth

The life cycle framework for understanding the growth and development of organizations is fundamentally a systems approach to understanding organizations. Like living organisms, organizations affected by environmental crises, or by forces applied to one part of the organization, may respond with delayed development or radical shifts in how resources are deployed. In 2002 and 2003, colleges and state systems of higher education in the United States experienced gradual to sharply significant budget cuts. For some MERLOT partners, the financial obligations associated with membership became a significant burden, resulting in withdrawal from the Consortium. By 2005, the number of paying system and institutional partners had dropped almost 20%. Others struggled to continue to work within the consortium but felt that that the financial burden on the partners needed to be reduced. To ease the burden and maintain sufficient financial support, MERLOT froze partner fees at 2003 levels, added campus partnerships as an option, reduced the requirement to support eight editorial board members (peer reviewers and editors) to four, and introduced a plan to recruit and train volunteer peer reviewers.

This dip in resources did not seem to affect MERLOT significantly, for the involvement of the almost fiercely committed core community was within the bounds of the available resources at that time. The shift in the funding environment did bring to the forefront an especially troublesome weakness in MERLOT's organizational design: that because the financial support for the core community was provided by the partners, MERLOT's viability was vulnerable in times of financial austerity. Given the importance of the core community (now understood to be a critical resource for building the patron community), strategies needed to be devised to ensure its continuation and protect it from further decline.

So, at a time when MERLOT had been poised to enter into the transition to midlife (i.e., regularizing its services and programs, hiring more staff, creating budget and organizational procedures), it was forced to rethink its central organizational strategies and assumptions. The primary challenge it faced was that of maintaining its growing reputation in higher education and its expected level of services, while at the same time instilling cost-cutting measures.

The editorial boards were the elements of the MERLOT core community that were most affected by the rethinking of these strategies. The reduction in funding reduced the size of the boards by about half at the same time that MERLOT was gaining exposure and experiencing an increase in the demand for peer reviewed materials.[10] In short, the boards were asked to do more with fewer resources. The solution was to more strongly align the peer review process with that of traditional scholarly journals, whose editorial board members recruit, train, and manage those who conduct the peer reviews. Other members of the core community (e.g., the project directors) were less affected because their roles tended to be more advisory in nature.

The change in the role of the editorial board members brought into focus the need to redefine their skills and expertise to include management skills, presentation skills, and the ability to inspire and recruit colleagues. This skill set was quite different from the previous set, which had centered on skills needed to conduct peer reviews. As a result of the redefined roles and the reduced funding, some boards experienced attrition.[11] However, the strong social networks described in the study by Pelaez and colleagues (2004) slowed and, in some cases, softened the impact of attrition, as members who previously had been paid to participate, now volunteered their time (mainly as peer reviewers). This volunteerism made it possible for the boards to continue their work in finding and reviewing materials.

Entering Midlife: Formalizing MERLOT's Organizational Structure

The revised model for editorial boards moved MERLOT further along its life cycle path toward organizational midlife by formalizing what had been informal organizational structures into bureaucratic structures, and defining the relationship and responsibilities of the editorial board members, peer reviewers, editors, project directors, MERLOT staff, and volunteers. One result of this bureaucratization was that as the roles formalized, there was an increased need for accountability.[12] This need was met by implementing a formal evaluation process for the editors and editorial board members, in addition to the new selection standards described above.

The development of a strong core community, as exemplified by the editorial boards, was perhaps the most significant success of MERLOT's youthful phase. It showed that online communities could emerge through collaborative building of the contents of the site. It also showed that the core community benefited extensively from regular face-to-face meetings and training. The patron community, much weaker and slower to develop, benefited too from professional development activities held at partner institutions and through the annual MERLOT conference, but it has yet to be shown that these activities are sufficient to grow this community either at the desired rate or the desired level.[13] Successful communities seem to rely on regular face-to-face professional development activities, thereby challenging the early design assumption that human mediation would not be necessary for MERLOT's growth (Hanley, Schneebeck, & Zweier, 1998; Schneebeck & Hanley, 2001).

Recognizing this tension, MERLOT implemented a new online service for faculty and instructors as a means for both increasing the number of patrons visiting the site and deepening their involvement in the community. This service delivered professional development, via the discipline portals, to the novice patron community. A portal page (see Figure 4.3) was developed for each editorial board. The portal's content, developed and controlled by the editorial board members, focuses on information on and about teaching with technology within that particular discipline. The aim is for the portals to become the primary source for patrons (faculty and instructors) for material about teaching and technology in their field. The portal design reflects the academic metaphors used in designing the original MERLOT site, reinforcing for patrons the academic nature of the site. It also represents yet another shift in the role of the editorial boards, for while the portals are tools with which to reach out to the community, they also require continual updating and development of new materials.

The portals are a virtual representation of the growing distance between the core community and the patron community. While still a reflection of the patron community, the core community, because of its training and involvement in MERLOT, now consists of experts in the use of the site and online teaching and learning materials. Patrons for the most part are novices in the use of MERLOT and its contents. Further separating the two is a bureaucratic structure that limits deep involvement at the core level to only those who are supported by a partner. So while there is a desire to help patrons gain expertise, there is no parallel mechanism for rewarding that participation. Confounding the MERLOT structural problem is the academic culture, which, to date, does not give credit to faculty and instructors for participation in technology and teaching ventures, and does not know how to give rewards (e.g., points toward tenure or promotion) for participation in online educational communities.

The reduction in funding resulted in a set of decisions that may have accelerated MERLOT's transition into midlife and institutionalization by regularizing the functions of the core community, articulating and enforcing standards where previously there had been few, and forcing the organization to re-examine its fundamental purpose and business plan. One might claim that the events resulted in positive outcomes, for example, renewed focus on building the patron community. At the same time, this reduction had costs for the organization, because as these renewed community development efforts were made, the number of core community members began to dwindle.

Yet throughout this period, the rate of patrons joining MERLOT as registered members increased at a steady rate (in 2005 about 800 new patrons became registered users on a monthly basis as compared with 400 in 2004). As the number of patrons grew, they participated mainly as users of MERLOT's services, not contributors. Peer reviewers continued to submit the bulk of the materials, comments, and assignments. (Notably, patrons have grown the personal collections service, which is designed as a way to store personal materials. However, it is questionable whether the patrons contributing these collections see this act in the same way as contributing, for example, a comment or an assignment.) The needed increase in participation by patrons, which is necessary to make MERLOT the "non-human-mediated service" envisioned by its designers, has not yet occurred. By this measure alone, the community of practice has remained within the core community and has not yet extended into the larger patron community.

Throughout this period of uncertainty and change, positive results have emerged and indicate that MERLOT has been able to create demand in the higher education community for its services and programs. It is able to attract new patrons to grow the community, albeit slowly, and it has been able to maintain its integrity around its core values. That said, MERLOT seems to have been in a state of stasis, making no significant progress in institutionalizing itself as it has been re-examining questions such as: What is the role the core community as it becomes a more stable organization? Is the consortium an effective model for sustaining the organization? What tangible benefits do partners experience and expect to experience by participating in the consortium? What is the core community evolving into? How can the patron community be motivated to participate at deeper levels? What is the impact of its professional development activities? And, as MERLOT evolves, what kind of support will it require to reach its goals?

Transitioning to a Mature Organization

Just as external environmental conditions can affect an organization's ability to transition from one life cycle phase to another, they also can accelerate growth in one area at the expense of another, as MERLOT experienced. Indicators that MERLOT may have emerged from the reduction in stable funding as a stronger, more mature organization are that it has become "large" in the sense of having many patrons, that it has a division of labor requiring a fairly large staff, that decision making is highly centralized in the administration, and that it has taken a more serious approach to planning. Indicators that suggest otherwise are that its core community has remained relatively the same size, becoming somewhat smaller as partners have left the consortium and only a few new partners have joined, and that it has not yet achieved financial stability. Since the major portion of its budget relies on funding from state systems of higher education, its financial support might be considered precarious.

Not only is its current funding model subject to the whims of certain state budgeting processes, but MERLOT continuously must "sell" its partners on the value of its services, which becomes increasingly difficult as faculty and instructors become more Web savvy in general and rely more on Google to find their teaching materials (Harley et al., 2006; McMartin et al., 2006). And while MERLOT has patterned its services to reflect those of academia, its agonizingly slow pace in making changes and its rigid structures may be too resistant to its efforts to militate for change. So, if one of the major motivations for faculty and instructors to participate deeply in MERLOT is to suggest that they will get credit toward their promotion and tenure efforts, but the individual systems, campuses, and other faculty remain resistant to this as a valued service, faculty members and instructors will be less inclined to participate in MERLOT.

Transition from one part of the life cycle to another is, as in life, full of forward-moving steps and equally full of challenges that slow or stop progress. To become a fully mature organization, MERLOT faces numerous challenges to its organizational structure and to the programs and services that have served it well in its developmental phases. Its core community is made up of educational innovators. As it becomes more institutional, the allure of the entrepreneurial spirit that initially attracted this loyal group may dim. The energy that drove this group is ebbing, and new innovations beckon to members, shifting their attention away from what may now be becoming "old" for them. At the same time, the size and participation of the patron group are growing—but is it large and committed enough to take on the essential functions of the core community (e.g., contributing learning materials, comments, etc.)? What kinds of professional development activities are necessary to extend the values of the core community to the user community? What does a community of patrons look like today? Is it different than that envisioned in 1999, and are those differences important? What kinds of services are necessary to support development of an ever-more sophisticated user community? Are there structural mechanisms to encourage patrons to move into more involved roles? What impact would such movement have on the benefits that the partner institutions receive, since it is possible that the majority of patrons are not members of MERLOT partner institutions?

These questions are the challenges of MERLOT's future. If successful in achieving both maturity as an organization and institutionalization as an online service for faculty and instructors in higher education, MERLOT's organizational structures will change and so too will its communities. The structures, as they exist, have been essential to MERLOT's products and services, and ultimately its reputation. Its intensive support for the core community has led to a model for digital libraries that has integrated professional development resources with online educational resources for teaching. Today's MERLOT has not yet achieved its goal of being a community that is self-perpetuating through its Web site, but it has achieved a kind of organizational structure that supports a small, but extremely dedicated core community (Pelaez et al., 2004), which has led MERLOT out of its initial birth stages and into its young adulthood.

Perhaps as MERLOT looks forward to leaving its midlife stage, its mature life cycle end goal of a self-perpetuating community should be re-examined as the desired end point for the organization. Innovative organizations such as MERLOT gain exponentially from the energy of their core community members. But, as the energy of this group wanes, or what once was new becomes more commonplace, the very activities, services, or products that made the organization innovative change to take on the "look and feel" of activities that are familiar (Levine, 1979). This familiarity is in some situations necessary to attract funding for sustainability. Unfortunately, what is the innovative part of the equation must then change, for it becomes the thing that keeps people from adopting or funding it, except in the short term. Organizations are faced with decisions of whether to shift their goals to gain sustainability or risk stability for continued innovation (Kelly, 2001). This is the choice MERLOT faces. The structures, organizations, and organizations that have been essential to MERLOT's ability to be the resource it is today may not be those that support its future.

NOTES

1. Perhaps MERLOT does not fit a strict definition of digital library, as will be evident later in this chapter. It can be viewed as a hybrid between a digital library and a knowledge-generating community, such as Wikipedia. In this chapter, I use *digital libraries* loosely as a term of convenience that describes an online site that is a repository of community-generated information (e.g., comments, peer reviews, etc.) about materials that themselves are held by the author. This aspect aligns MERLOT more with repositories, that is, sites that refer users to other sites. MERLOT aligns itself as a part of the digital library world because of its close associations with several members of the digital library community, for example, the National Science Digital Library and ARIADNE, as well as with the Open Educational Resource community, for example, Connexions.

There are multiple definitions of digital libraries, ranging from loose, informal collections of material that people have made available through the Web, to formal definitions emerging from the research associated with the technology and applications best exemplified by works promoted by the Joint Conference of Digital Libraries. Throughout this chapter, then, digital libraries will be viewed as a repositories, online journals, and communities of users who add to and build new knowledge around the items held in the libraries. This definition looks at libraries as social constructions, not merely as collections of bytes, bits, and software solutions to searching.

2. Borrowing from the library world, I use the word *patron* to describe users who visit these online resources and use them for their professional development.

3. The NSF alone has given well over $100 million since 2000 in support of development of digital libraries for science education. The Carnegie Mellon and Hewlett Foundations also have lent a great deal of support for the development of online tools that support these kinds of services, as well as the supporting projects such as the Open Courseware Consortium (http://www.ocwconsortium.org/index .html).

4. In 2005, MERLOT's partners included the California Community College System, California State University System, Cooperative Learning Object Exchange,

University of Waterloo in Ontario, Canada, Cornell University, Louisiana Board of Regents, Minnesota State Colleges and Universities, Ohio University, Oklahoma State Regents for Higher Education, South Dakota Board of Regents, State University of New York, St. Petersburg College (Florida), Tennessee Board of Regents, Troy State University, University of Michigan, University of North Carolina, University of Wisconsin System, Wesleyan University, and Virginia Community College System.

5. Most support tends to be in the form of release time, summer salary, or travel funds. Support is not standardized—partners provide support in the manner that meets their campus culture.

6. The explosive growth of YouTube and Myspace, and the subsequent rapid rise in their business worth, exemplifies how numbers of users can leap in exceptionally short time frames, given a critical mass of users combined with effective viral marketing.

7. In 2005 there were approximately 1 million faculty members in the United States.

8. Fees for system partners are $25,000/year; institutional partners pay $50,000/ year and provide other in-kind services. In 2004, the campus partnership level was added at $6,500/year.

9. Each member of the core community (editor, editorial board member, or project director) receives some financial support, paid by the MERLOT partner, for his or her work with MERLOT through a combination of release time, summer salary, travel support, etc.

10. All items contributed to MERLOT are first "triaged" to determine whether they merit a full peer review. Full peer reviews can be time-consuming, often taking several months to complete depending on the number of peer reviewers available who have the requisite experience and the number of items in the queue.

11. Because few editorial members had left boards, there was no good transition mechanism in place. In part this is because project directors, not editors, select the faculty and instructors who make up a board. Lack of power to decide who is on a board, along with inability to recruit new members on their own, makes managing boards extremely difficult for most editors.

12. As available funds decreased, there was a greater need for the MERLOT partners to be able to demonstrate the value and benefits to membership in MERLOT. As part of this, project directors and editors also felt the need to make sure that supported editorial board members were meeting expectations.

13. MERLOT runs the trainer-type workshops for faculty development professionals from partner institutions. These professionals return to their campuses and run workshops for faculty about how to use MERLOT. The MERLOT annual conference is also a large professional development opportunity, bringing the core community and the community of volunteers and interested parties together.

REFERENCES

Barab, S. A., MaKinster, J. G., & Scheckler, R. (2004). Designing system dualities: Characterizing an online professional development community. In S. A. Barab,

R. Klink, & J. H. Gray (Eds.), *Designing for virtual communities in the service of learning* (pp. 53–90). Cambridge: Cambridge University Press.

Barker, J. (2006). Invisible or deep web: What it is, why it exists, how to find it, and its inherent ambiguity. In UC Berkeley—Teaching Library Internet Workshops. Regents of the University of California. Retrieved October 8, 2008, from http://www.lib.berkeley.edu/TeachingLib/Guides/Internet/InivisibleWeb.html

Daft, R. L. (1992). *Organizational theory and design.* St. Paul, MN: West Publishing.

Ehrmann, S. (1997). *Asking the right question: What does research tell us about technology and higher learning?* Annenberg CPB Projects. Retrieved October 8, 2006, from http://www.tltgroup.org/resources/Flashlight/AskingRightQuestion.htm

Giersch, S., Klots, E. A., McMartin, F., Muramatsu, B., Renninger, K. A., Shumar, W., & Weimar, S. A. (2004, July/August). If you build it, will they come? Participant involvement in digital libraries. *D-Lib Magazine.* Retrieved October 8, 2006, from http://www.dlib.org/dlib/july04/giersch/07giersch.html

Gladwell, M. (2000). *The tipping point: How little things can make a big difference.* New York: Little, Brown.

Hanley, G. L., Schneebeck, C., & Zweier, L. (1998). Implementing a scalable and sustainable model for instructional software development. *Syllabus, 11*(9), 30–34.

Harley, D., Henke, J., Lawrence, S., Miller, I., Perciali, I., & Nasatir, D. (2006, April). *Use and users of digital resources: A focus on undergraduate education in the humanities and social sciences.* Berkeley, CA: Center for Studies in Higher Education. Retrieved October 8, 2006, from http://cshe.berkeley.edu/research/digitalresourcestudy/report/

Jones, S., & Johnson-Yale, C. (2005, September). Professors online: The internet's impact on college faculty. *First Monday, 10*(9). Retrieved October 8, 2008, from http://firstmonday.org/issues/issue10_9/jones/index.htm

Kelly, T. (2001). *The art of innovation.* New York: Doubleday.

Kim, A. J. (2000). *Community building on the web: Secret strategies for successful online communities.* Berkeley, CA: Peachpit Press.

Lave, J., & Wenger, E. (1991). *Situated learning: Legitimate peripheral practice.* Cambridge: Cambridge University Press.

Levine, A. (1979). *The life and death of innovation in higher education* (Occasional Paper No. 2). State University of New York at Buffalo.

McMartin, F., Iverson, E., Manduca, C., Wolf, A., & Morgan, G. (2006, June). *Factors motivating use of digital libraries.* Paper presented at the annual Joint Conference on Digital Libraries, Chapel Hill, NC.

MERLOT. (2006). About us. Retrieved September 26, 2008, from http://www.taste.merlot.org

Millar, S. B. (1995). *Full scale implementation: The interactive "whole story."* In *Project impact: Disseminating innovation in undergraduate education.* Arlington, VA: National Science Foundation.

Moore, G. (1991). *Crossing the chasm.* New York: HarperCollins.

Otto, J., Hanley, G., & Swift, C. (2004). Distance learning success for the business school: MERLOT's faciliation strategy. In D. Christopher (Ed.), *E-world: Virtual learning, collaborative environments, and future technologies* (pp. 180–194). Reston, VA: National Business Education Association.

Pelaez, N. J., Ashton, T. M., Pollard, C., Moore, J., Guenter, C., Wicks, D., Judd, D., Pearson, D., Staley, R., & Wetzel, M. J. (2004). Keeping faculty online: The case of MERLOT. *Academic Exchange Quarterly, 8*(4), 25–32.

Quinn, R. E., & Cameron, K. (1983). Organizational life cycles and some shifting criteria of effectiveness. *Management Science, 29,* 31–51.

Renninger, K. A., & Shumar, W. (Eds.). (2002). *Building virtual communities: Learning and change in cyberspace.* Cambridge: Cambridge University Press.

Rogers, E. M. (2003). *Diffusion of innovations* (5th ed.). New York: Free Press.

Schneebeck, C., & Hanley, G. L. (2001). The California State University Center for Distributed Learning. In R. M. Epper & A. W. Bates (Eds.), *Teaching faculty how to use technology: Best practices from leading institutions* (pp. 115–140). Westport, CT: Greenwood/Oryx Press.

Sharken Simon, J. (2001). *5 life stages of nonprofit organizations.* St. Paul, MN: Wilder Foundation.

Wenger, E. (1998). *Communities of practice: Learning, meaning, and identity.* Cambridge: Cambridge University Press.

Wenger, E., McDermott, R., & Snyder, W. M. (2002). *Cultivating communities of practice.* Boston: Harvard Business School Press.

Zemsky, R., & Massey, W. F. (2004). *Beyond innovation: What happened to e-learning and why* (Final Report for the Weatherstation Project of the Learning Alliance). University of Pennsylvania.

PART II

Communities Interacting in Targeted Professional Learning Environments

The chapters in Part II discuss projects that have a more targeted professional learning focus than those in Part I. In each case, the participants were chosen because they had specific characteristics in common, and these common characteristics were an important part of the context and design of the community. For example, the virtual conference drew from participants in an NSF systemic change program, which required that projects have a set of common goals and methods. Building on this common language, the conference itself focused on the issue, idea, or goal of sustainability of systemic reform. In the Inquiry Learning Forum, by contrast, the population is science teachers, and there is a unifying goal, issue, and problem: inquiry in the science classroom. The Investigating Physics course has multiple constraints or structuring principles: It is part of a master's degree program for elementary science teachers, so it includes (among other things) a carefully designed pedagogical model, course requirements, and the motivation to succeed that comes from enrollment in a degree program.

Note that all these "constraints" are also supports for the development and functioning of a community. They provide a common vocabulary and a common "grammar" of motives or purpose, with the related criteria for relevance and quality of contributions, and combine with tools and resources (including schedules and other requirements of participation) to support members' contributions. This shared constellation of ideas, tools, purposes, and values is supported in addition by identified offline experiences, which both feed into and are also the explicit ultimate goal of participation in the online activity.

Thus, while the three chapters differ in their theoretical language, they share a sociocultural approach, in which the learning in these three cases is explicitly understood to be situated in the participants' offline practice in a significant and instrumental way, while being mediated by the online tools/structures, as well as by the human facilitators and co-participants. In all three cases, leadership emerges from the participants as they contribute to the discourse. The artifacts created by participants (e.g., narratives, videos, graphical objects) serve as "boundary objects," which document knowledge and facilitate exchange between differing communities.

CHAPTER 5

Designing for Inquiry
as a Social Practice

Rebecca K. Scheckler and Sasha A. Barab

> Inquiry is a mode of activity that is socially conditioned and that has cultural
> consequences. . . . Every inquiry grows out of a background of culture and takes
> effect in greater or less modification of the conditions out of which it arises.
> (Dewey, 1938/1986, pp. 26–27)

The Inquiry Learning Forum (ILF) (http://ilf.crlt.indiana.edu[1]) designed and
researched an electronic knowledge network, the electronic ILF, which supported a virtual community of inservice and preservice mathematics and
science teachers sharing, improving, and creating inquiry-based pedagogical practices (see Barab, MaKinster, Moore, Cunningham, & the ILF Design Team, 2001; Barab, MaKinster, & Scheckler, 2004). Inquiry in a social
setting is the central focus of the ILF, a Web site with over 3,500 registered
members that is meant to support the professional development (PD) of math
and science teachers who are interested in inquiry pedagogies. Founded in
our previous research and consistent with our pedagogical commitments, we
designed the ILF around a "visiting the classroom" metaphor, with the belief that teachers need to be full participants in and owners of their virtual
space. Using the ILF, teachers with a broad range of experience and expertise come together in a virtual space to observe, discuss, and reflect upon
pedagogical theory and practice anchored to real teaching vignettes. In the
context of this Web site, teacher practitioners are encouraged to inquire into
their practice as well as to adopt inquiry pedagogies in their practice. As
teachers inquire into their practice, not only do they have opportunities to
grow and change, but they also develop empathy for their students' use of
inquiry pedagogy. In this chapter, we focus on the social aspects of John
Dewey's theory of inquiry as a source of understanding what we are observing

in the ILF and to help guide us and other instructional designers in future design projects.

The chapter is organized in four sections. First we briefly discuss the role of philosophy in design. Then we describe some aspects of Dewey's theory of inquiry, with emphasis on the social, so that we will have the vocabulary to understand inquiry as a social process. Next we look at data from the ILF and interpret them through a Deweyan lens as a social process. Lastly, we make design recommendations that will encourage inquiry among teachers in an online social setting such as a Web-supported community.

THE ROLE OF PHILOSOPHY IN DESIGN

Philosophy is often the last thing that designers think about when they set to work on an instructional design project. This is unfortunate because philosophy can be a valuable tool in the design and implementation of instructional technology projects. Furthermore, all designers have a philosophy that guides their actions. Making this philosophy visible allows it to be examined, fine-tuned, and tested for consistency. In particular, Dewey's pragmatic ethos gives valuable insights into issues of situativity, social context, and learning that other sources do not entertain as convincingly. Here we use Deweyan and other theoretical perspectives to enhance our ability to design for inquiry as a social practice—especially with respect to supporting teacher professional development. We start with a discussion of Dewey's theory of inquiry and from this build an understanding of how difference within communities can motivate inquiry. Paradoxically, we also consider the strain that difference presents for online spaces attempting to develop into communities of practice. We note the role of emotion as an essential concern within communities that are engaged in inquiry, noting particularly the tension between fear of inquiry in a social setting and the need for trust in the setting of inquiry. Lastly, we suggest ways that attention to the social in Dewey's philosophy of inquiry can enhance instructional design.

The ILF supports inquiry in at least two ways: Its most obvious involvement with inquiry is to motivate the use of inquiry pedagogy in K–12 math and science classes. A subtler but equally important use of inquiry in the ILF is to motivate teachers to reflect upon and thus inquire into their practice as teachers. We concentrate on this second type of inquiry in this chapter. In relation to teachers' inquiry into their practice, we discuss the cycle of equilibrium/disequilibrium—how a situation arises, is resolved, and leads to changed habits (or learning)[2]—within the context of a community of practice, or social setting. Beyond concerns of usability in terms of human–computer interaction, instructional designers interested in community also must focus on sociability.

Sociability, as described by Jenny Preece (2000a), is the support for social interactions that the software provides. Sociability includes policies for membership, codes of conduct, security, privacy, copyright, free speech, and moderators. Using Dewey's theory of inquiry, we expand on the notion of sociability in design to include concern for emotions and support for social difference as well as sameness. But first, to situate the reader in terms of the ways we worked with teachers to introduce the project, we want to relate an incident in a classroom where we were trying to introduce both the Inquiry Learning Forum and inquiry pedagogies to teachers in an elementary school in rural Indiana.

AN INCIDENT TO SHARPEN OUR INTUITIONS

Ten elementary school teachers entered a classroom set up by us to introduce them to the use of axolotls in their classrooms and to using the Inquiry Learning Forum. Several adult axolotls, 5–6-inch-long Mexican aquatic salamanders, were placed prominently in round plastic half-gallon ice cream containers on one side of the room. Other buckets held juvenile axolotls, about one-half inch long, and a petri dish held axolotl eggs floating in water and large enough to see with the unaided eye. Two microscopes, a balance scale, axolotl food in small plastic bags, various dropper bottles of water treatment chemicals, turkey basters, and a stack of clear plastic shoe boxes lined a long table. On the far wall were six computers already on and set to the ILF Web site.

We introduced ourselves, had the teachers introduce themselves, and began a professional development activity that we had used before to introduce inquiry. The lesson was motivated by this statement: "We want to leave these axolotls with you. What do you need to know to allow these organisms to grow and prosper in your classroom?" As teachers asked questions, we jotted them on the blackboard. What do they eat? Can we keep them in these containers? Will they bite? Is that plain water in the containers? What do we do with them on weekends? Before we left that day, we had the teachers register as members of the Inquiry Learning Forum and showed them a special area of the forum where teachers discussed how they used axolotls in the classroom.

On a second meeting with the teachers, we asked them to categorize their questions and give some thought to how they could be answered. The ILF staff answered the questions that we could and then suggested sources of information for others. We gave them time to explore the questions and look through locally available and Web-based resources on axolotls. We then worked with the teachers to set up ways of observing and recording growth rates and development of the juveniles and eggs.

During this second session, we discussed what inquiry involved in elementary grades. One teacher got very excited and blurted out, "Wellll . . . I have been doing inquiry with axolotls [in our sessions] and I could do this with my class (of second graders)." Another teacher (of third graders) joined in, "We could make charts of the growth rates." We encouraged these teachers to share these thoughts and others with the online forum. We stood beside them and guided their re-entry onto the ILF Web site and their use of the discussion forum. Before we left, we suggested they check back on the forum to see what other teachers had to say about these insights. We also left axolotls with them to use in their classrooms.

SOME ASPECTS OF A DEWEYAN THEORY OF INQUIRY

For Dewey (1938/1986), inquiry is cyclical. "Inquiry is the controlled or directed transformation of an indeterminate situation into one that is so determinate in its constituent distinctions and relations as to convert the elements of the original situation into a unified whole" (p. 108). Thus, there are clear steps or a pattern of inquiry that start with doubt motivating reflection which may then proceed through problem statement, hypothesis formation, and action to resolve the original discomfort or disequilibrium while restoring functioning. The end state of the inquirer is not the same as the beginning state, since the actions that lead to restoration of functioning also change the habits of the inquirer as he or she transacts with the environment of the inquiry. Dewey (1916/1980) describes learning as the same cycle of disequilibrium and restoration of equilibrium, and indeed, Dewey frequently discussed an equivalence among learning and inquiry and growth. The "trigger" for disequilibrium that can lead to inquiry and growth may take many different forms, as in the following three instances.

In the professional development sessions reported above, we presented a problem: "How to care for axolotls in the classroom." This was interesting to these teachers, who wish to provide motivating classroom experiences. Thus, in this case the professional development situation (including the complexity introduced by working with live organisms) created a mild state of disequilibrium.

In another instance, some teachers in the workshop were motivated to learn about inquiry because the introduction of science testing to their school system raised for them a need to examine and introduce more inquiry into their pedagogy. Our workshop gave them a situation in which to investigate inquiry, and moreover, helped them by the way we modeled inquiry. Thus, disequilibrium was introduced by the change in testing requirements.

Finally, consider the case of a teacher who had used a set of lesson plans for years and had gotten good evaluations, adoring notes from her young students, and respect from their parents. This teacher noticed a shift in the interests of her students as a result of demographic shifts, changes in popular culture, and finally tumultuous political events (e.g., the terrorism of Sept. 11, 2001). She was also challenged by seeing how another teacher's new lesson seemed to motivate students to engage with a subject that they found difficult. In this case, disequilibrium originated from changes in school culture and society, which led the teacher to question her practice.

A teacher's possible responses to a new sense of "dis-ease" will vary according to her environment and resources. We not only created a sense of disequilibrium in our workshop but also provided ways for the teachers to regain their sense of equilibrium. In the process, we hoped the teachers' repertoire of teaching methods might have expanded; they might have learned how to teach differently and the result is possibly their changed habits of teaching. They also developed some intuition about science inquiry. We encouraged them to use these same inquiry skills to motivate the learning of math, reading skills, Spanish language vocabulary, social studies, and health and hygiene.

While we have focused on individuals doing inquiry, their transactions with their environment are what motivated the sense of disequilibrium and helped resolve the discomfort experienced. We now provide a more formal explanation of features of Dewey's pattern of inquiry, which we will continue to relate to observations of the ILF and to the design of Web sites in support of inquiry. In addition to the pattern of inquiry, we review the concepts of situation, habit, and pluralism, since a situation is the context of inquiry, changed habits are the result of inquiry, and pluralism is the matrix of difference that plays an essential role in inquiry.

In the most general terms, inquiry is a process of doubt, followed by a searching for solutions that resolve the doubt, all occurring in a cultural-historical context (a situation) and resulting in changed habits. This pattern is not a linear prescription for inquiry, but an analysis of what frequently is undergone in the process of inquiry. In many instances, not all parts of the pattern will be identifiable in the existential event, and some parts may be repeated before equilibrium is restored. However, through the process of inquiry, a situation always goes from open and indeterminate to closed and determinant (Dewey, 1938/1986). We as reasoning creatures cannot avoid the process of inquiry in order to live, learn, and prosper.

The key aspects of inquiry, as postulated by Dewey, that we wish to highlight in this chapter are listed in Table 5.1. Of core interest to us are his notions of situation, reasonable doubt, dialogical pluralism, and habit.

TABLE 5.1. Dewey's aspects of inquiry

Aspect of Inquiry	*Description*
Situations	The sociomaterial spaces that constitute the unit of action
Reasonable doubt	A break in the equilibrium of human functioning
Dialogical pluralism	Discussion across difference giving rise to new solution possibilities that might restore equilibrium
Habits	Modification of the self by actions and experiences undergone

Understanding these four aspects is central to understanding Dewey's notion of inquiry and, we believe, provides useful insights into the challenges of facilitating Web-supported communities designed intentionally to support learning.

Situation

Briefly, for Dewey, a situation is not simply a physical place but a conceptual space that becomes bound, that is, conditionally isolated, in terms of the particular issue of inquiry. A situation is a state of disequilibrium of an organism in its environment, and it is a single concept encompassing both organism and environment. In this way of thinking, akin to Gibson's (1986) ecological view, a situation consists of an environment that gives rise to certain possibilities for action (affordances) and whose actualization requires an individual with the requisite abilities (effectivities) to act on these affordances. Dewey's goal is to transform a disrupted situation of emotional distress, cognitive confusion, and embodied need into a dynamic unified whole.

The degree of connectedness necessary to restore equilibrium determines the connectivity that requires attention. For example, let us look at how one prepares dinner. Perhaps hunger or the obligation to provide food for children causes disequilibrium. The boundary for the situation is initially the extent of the kitchen. On entering the kitchen with your hungry kids in tow, you may discover that some essential ingredient, perhaps milk or bread, is missing or inedible. Now the boundary expands to include the local convenience store, and other factors come into consideration. Will the car start? Who will watch the children? Is it snowing out? The weather in the next county is likely to be outside the boundary of concern, although it potentially is included.

When you get to the store, it has no milk because an avalanche closed the bridge to the highway on which milk deliveries come. Your boundary or scope of context may change several times as you solve your problem of no milk for supper and hungry children. In this way, depending on need and attention, situations (for rational beings) always extend beyond the atomic unit but do not expand without limits—the goals create a set of boundary conditions that transact with individual–environment couplings to create boundary conditions (Barab, Cherkes-Julkowski, Swenson, Shaw, Garret, & Young, 1999).

Our teachers' boundaries are dictated by many and conflicting goals. They must motivate students to want to learn. They must ensure that their students do well on standardized tests. They must provide a classroom that is satisfactory to their supervisors, even if inquiry requires more talking than often is considered acceptable. They must teach language arts and numeracy skill that prepare their students for future grades. Their context exceeds the walls of the classroom and makes problem solving in inquiry accountable to a dizzying array of requirements.

Reasonable Doubt

Dewey had a very simple explanation for the motivation for inquiry: the presence of a reasonable doubt. He attributed motivation for inquiry to breaks in the equilibrium of human functioning. Discomfort, curiosity, fear, or any kind of feeling of things being amiss marks the state of disequilibrium. Intuition, affect, hunches, or general unease can all play a part in this initial stage of inquiry. This motivation for inquiry is the indeterminate situation where there is some level of doubt and uncertainty; most important, it relates to some existential situation. This explanation of the initiator of inquiry makes inquiry very commonplace. In fact, one could say easily that inquiry is impossible to avoid since individuals continually must act to meet their needs. Not only is inquiry accessible to all teachers and students, but it also is necessary for maintaining life and health and some type of satisfaction with an individual's state of teaching and learning. Most important, exposure to new ideas and situations (mediated by signs, symbols, and language) is a potent motivator for inquiry.

The next step in inquiry is to make the implicit question of the sense of disequilibrium an explicit question. This question formulation directly follows recognition that a situation is problematic and involves the shift from a precognitive hunch or sense to a fully developed statement of doubt. Dewey was emphatic that the problem must grow out of an actual situation. Any other development of a problem he labeled as "busy work" (Dewey, 1938/ 1986, p. 112). The teachers discussed above were asked to pose specific questions about axolotls. Hearing one another's questions and later seeing them on the ILF Web site motivated more questions. We think that Dewey would have thought these questions were more than "busy work." The answers were necessary to keeping the axolotls alive—a task the teachers were getting ready to undertake in their classrooms with their students.

Dialogical Pluralism

Once a question in need of solution has been stated, then hypotheses or suggested solutions are acknowledged. There is now a shift from the actual discomfort of disequilibrium to the realm of possible solutions. "Ideas [for solutions] are anticipated consequences (forecasts) of what will happen when certain operations are executed under and with respect to observed conditions" (Dewey, 1938/1986, p. 113). They are possibilities or predictions and require examining to decide how they will function as a solution. This examination of possible solutions is an example of reasoning. The perceptual part of reasoning locates a problem, and the conceptual part of reasoning deals with a solution. The solution to a problem always involves action that is based on the existential matter at an individual's disposal in a sufficient way to restore equilibrium. Here action is not merely a physical manipulation but may be mental or affective as well. It is here that reasoning, and gaining other perspectives, becomes central.

We asked the PD teachers to categorize their questions. The categorization had to do with the complexity of the questions and how they might be answered. As a group, they quickly differentiated the simple how–to questions, such as What, when, and how much to feed? These, we seminar leaders could quickly answer. Another category of questions—such as, Where do they come from? How can we tell their sex?—required more information than we could give easily but was available from other sources. A third group of questions—such as, How fast do they grow? When will the eggs hatch? Can we get them to breed?—could be answered best by observation.

Dewey differentiates between existential and the nonexistential components of reasoning as facts and ideas. Whereas the former, most of the time, are based on socially agreed-upon beliefs that have been deemed useful, the latter are negotiated continually. In this way, useful inquiry usually involves interaction with others. However, not all interactions with others are useful. In fact, one of the greatest challenges for Web-supported communities is how to support meaningful interactions with others. Highlighting this challenge, Bernstein (1992, pp. 335–337) differentiates "engaged fallibilistic pluralism" from "defensive pluralism," which pays lip service to others doing their own thing; and from "polemical pluralism," which uses the ruse of pluralism to advance an individual's own agenda; and from "flabby pluralism," which is a voyeuristic borrowing of other orientations; and from "fragmenting pluralism," which promotes communication only with those who already agree with us. For Bernstein (1992), "engaged fallibilistic pluralism" requires responsible listening to others without denying or suppressing their otherness while admitting our own fallibility (p. 336). It means allowing for the possibility of change to occur through listening as well as talking. It means a constant openness and invitation to otherness, a state that may be uncomfortable, threatening, or dangerous.[3] Thus, the task of engaging in fallibilistic pluralism is neither easy nor ensured.

Along with the plurality that funds new ideas, come conflicts. Issues of identity, ego, and competence are part of the inquiry process as deep beliefs and assumptions are exposed to group scrutiny. It is in this way that inquiry, when treated as a social process, is not simply intellectual but also emotional and very personal. There is an inherent tension in inquiry between the need for difference and the risks of exposing difference (Barab, MaKinster, & Scheckler, 2004). Fear shuts down inquiry, and trust motivates it. A balance must be found between the need for diversity and the need for safety. A group sense of trust growing from the familiarity of sustained interactions is a possible solution to the fear and danger of social inquiry, but this also might erode the degree of plurality. Another tactic is to nurture a critical community of inquirers.

Our initial group of teachers was fairly comfortable together and trusting of one another, although they needed to learn to trust us workshop leaders and they certainly felt nervous about posting online. However, pushing the dialogue, so that the PD environment was a place to engage critical questions, happened over time.

Habit

For Dewey, habits are the fusion of belief, body, and emotion (Garrison, 1997). Habits are characterized by inclinations to act, by the shared actions of groups, as well as by interaction with the physical, social, and natural environments (Dewey, 1922/1983). "Habits are the basis of organic learning" (Dewey, 1938/1986, p. 38). As such, they provide continuity in action. "The basic characteristic of habit is that every experience enacted and undergone modifies the one who acts and undergoes, while this modification affects, whether we wish it or not, the quality of subsequent experiences" (Dewey, 1938, p. 35). When habits are disrupted (blocked), they lead to the cycle of inquiry described above. Similarly, the end of an inquiry results in the adjustment of habits.

Habit is a richer term than knowledge, capturing Dewey's conviction that knowing is not simply a cognitive act but involves whole people and is distributed across those situations in which habits are realized. As a term describing meaningful participation with the world, habit is consistent with Pea's (1993) notion of distributed cognition, or Lave and Wenger's (1991) notion of being knowledgeably skillful, or Barab and Roth's (2006) notion of effectivity sets, or Barab and Duffy's notion of "knowing about." Barab and Duffy (2000) suggest that "knowing about refers to an activity—not a thing; knowing about is always contextualized—not abstract; knowing about is reciprocally constructed within the individual–environment interaction—not objectively defined or subjectively created; and knowing about is a functional stance on the interaction—not a "truth" (p. 28). The important point is not whose term one uses, but rather that knowing is treated as a complex phenomenon that includes particular content, ways of acting, a disposition to act, an appreciation for those situations that require action, and even tools and resources that people use when engaged in the act of knowing.

We hoped that our inquiry workshops would help these teachers change their habits of teaching science, but we realized that such a change would take more than a few workshops. We were hopeful that having support from the ILF (discussed next), and from their fellow teachers, would help make a change in habit to using inquiry possible.

THE INQUIRY LEARNING FORUM
AND DEWEY'S THEORY OF INQUIRY

A central research goal of this work has been to understand the design principles that inform the creation, growth, and fostering of a Web-based community of practice in which the value gained from participation—sharing one individual's practice and engaging in dialogue—outweighs the "costs" of participation. The ILF encompasses a large and complex Web site, called the e-ILF, and a group of over 3,500 members who transact with the e-ILF and one another. Videos of teachers engaged in inquiry are a feature of this Web site. The videos show the reflections of a featured teacher on her teaching, her lesson plan, materials, samples of student work, and discussion forums involving the teacher. In addition, the ILF contains more general discussion forums, a library of teaching ideas and resources, smaller work spaces for small-group collaborative editing and discussion, activities for learning inquiry techniques (refer to Table 5.1), and a personal desk for organizing and accessing all the other parts of the Web site. In this section, we use the terminology of Dewey's theory of inquiry to help us to understand and describe inquiry as a social practice in the ILF.

The ILF Situation

The situation is the unit in which inquiry functions. Teachers report difficulty in understanding their unit of action, since there are many influences on their teaching practice, including students worrying about SAT scores for admission to prestigious colleges, state licensing boards, parents' concepts of appropriate teaching, teachers' pedagogical beliefs of what constitutes effective teaching, and, perhaps most persuasive, the results of standardized tests. These all relate to Dewey's concept of the situation as the unit of action, since they define the context where the teacher must function in the performance of complex activities. In terms of public schools, the situation is potentially so large and complex that teachers feel distracted and tend to despair about being able to motivate and engage with students in all the ways that are necessary in order to be effective.

The limits of the situation for teachers' inquiry into their practice are constantly shifting, and sensitive teachers are very cognizant of this, as a science teacher expresses.

> I can't tell you how many students in my advanced chemistry class tell me, "Hey, it's neat that you're letting us solve problems on our own and create them, but you know what? My brother's telling me about Purdue's pharmacy school and if we don't know about . . . we're going to be at a huge disadvantage."

Pressures on teachers come from many sides, including parents, students, churches, boards of education, and politicians. Perhaps this is why teachers often close their doors and try to keep the world at bay. Unfortunately, this is an artificial means of controlling disorder and, rather than maintaining control, leads to a heightened sense of remoteness on the part of the stakeholders excluded from the site of action as well as a sense of frustration and irrelevance on the part of the students in the site of action. In a Deweyan sense, some teachers appear to be having trouble accepting the contingent and changeable nature of the situation of their own inquiry. Sometimes it will be contained by the classroom, but more often it will expand far beyond the classroom (Nespor, 1997). To generalize about the situation of many ILF members is to note the complexity and shifting nature of their contexts. The teacher often closes her door to shut out distractions, yet longs for contact with other teachers. In our front-end analysis for the ILF, the desire to visit other teachers' classrooms was a common request that the ILF was designed to fulfill (Barab, Moore, Cunningham, & the ILF Design Team, 2000), which we tried to provide by means of videos of inquiry classrooms and interactive discussion forums.

The classroom, as the main habitat of the teacher, is notorious for its closed doors, isolation, and lack of connection with the community (Grossman & Wineburg, 2000; Grossman, Wineburg, & Woolworth, 2000). An inservice teacher in our project identified her concerns with not being able to talk with other teachers on a regular basis.

> I think . . . it [communicating with other teachers] is very important. I don't think it happens very much. I think the school systems are not really set up to facilitate that at all. And yet I think it probably is one of the most important ways to get better, to hear somebody else [say], "Well, when this happened in my class this is how we dealt with it," or that kind of thing. So it is important in that I value it.

In response to such needs, the ILF has tried to help teachers escape the isolation of teacher practice by providing online forums to encourage a community of inquirers into that practice. Yet the transition from isolation to community of practice is not easy, even if it is desired. Going from the solitude of the closed classroom to the social and collaborative nature of the ILF is a major shift that arouses anxiety and fear or at least reluctance, as an advisory board member expresses.

> I have not spent a lot of time in anybody's video. Okay? But now that I've met these people, I'll go home and do it. What's missing is I don't want to look at home movies if I don't know the people.

This teacher expresses the relief of making face-to-face connections with the people in the videos and how this motivates his desire to communicate.

Reasonable Doubt

In looking at teachers' responses to the ILF, we found that there is no need to artificially motivate inquiry into practice for classroom teachers. The constantly shifting and conflicting demands of the classroom provide many discrepant events for teachers to ponder.[4] Teachers readily admit that their teaching day creates much disequilibrium and they feel the need to reflect on the course of their teaching day on a regular basis. Almost every teacher we talked to (in semistructured interviews with 15 teachers concerning their professional development) confirmed the desire to reflect on the day's activities and to try to act on their reflection both formally and informally. In a typical response, when asked when she reflects on her teaching, a 7th-grade science teacher said with much conviction, "Everyday, every car ride home from school and every car ride to school." Teachers tell us that reflecting on their day often focuses on ways to make their activities more effective the next time around.

Some teachers make notes for future years, but the number of teachers taking physical action is small when compared with the number of teachers who engage in the thought processes that precede action. In a Deweyan sense, we see the demands of the teaching day as a continual motivation in teachers for the desire to act in ways that will improve student progress. Yet strangely to us at first, we could not easily motivate the discussions that we thought teachers thirsted for. We thought we were giving our teachers opportunities to escape their isolation, to publicly reflect on their disequilibrium, and, as we discuss in the next section, to search for solutions. Yet, we struggled to get communications going, with the Inquiry Learning Forum having a very slow growth curve for many months after the site was launched (see Figure 5.1).

As we found out, while it was our intention to support teacher reform, this was also the goal for many of the teachers. However, the need for innovating practice does not necessarily meet the more immediate needs of teachers; teachers have a need to identify readily available curricular resources in order to meet the day-to-day demands of their teaching (Gomez, Fishman, & Pea, 1998). The ILF, on the other hand, was designed to support a community of inservice and preservice mathematics and science teachers creating, sharing, and improving inquiry-based pedagogical practices through virtually visiting the classrooms of other teachers. This sharing and critiquing were seen as a means of building relations among teachers who shared similar beliefs and classroom practices. The problem is that visiting the classroom of another teacher to "improve inquiry-based practices" is not necessarily relevant to the more immediate discomfort of teachers. Teachers are most concerned about what they will use as a lesson or unit tomorrow or how they will deal with a particular student problem. In contrast, what we

FIGURE 5.1. Inquiry Learning Forum discussion posts per month, from its release on February 2000 through December 2001

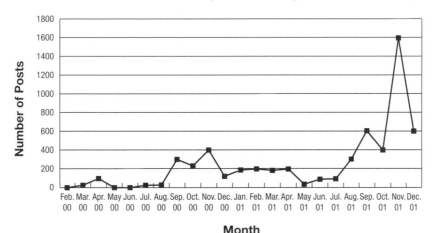

have conceived of as meaningful participation in the ILF is something that may take an extended period of time and require multiple visits and interactions before a teacher even begins to reap any tangible benefits. It is in this way, even for those teachers experiencing a sense of disequilibrium about their current pedagogical practice, that supporting reform through community participation is a challenging process.

While the teaching day is mercilessly social as teachers interact continually with their students, there is a simultaneous isolation from other teachers that tends to continue after school. We see this feeling of teacher isolation in pleas for more community and in a profound sense of frustration at the lack of support for teachers. In an example of the sense of isolation expressed by ILF teachers, an 8th-grade science teacher relates that his most valuable professional development activities occur when his school corporation brings together all the science teachers to talk and try new activities. He said, in relation to this type of activity, "I think it's very important to find out what other people are doing and how they approached a topic or subject or activity and how they work on it. Whether it works, what works and what doesn't work, and then we can try [it] with our kids to see."

This teacher teaches most of the 8th-grade science classes in his school, so to engage in a community of teachers with concerns that he considers relevant, he needs to go outside his building to meetings sponsored by the corporation, which are rare in his yearly schedule.

Pluralism in the ILF

Even when teachers explicitly seek out discussion with other teachers, there are tensions in employing an online community model. In an interview, one teacher's appeal for advice from other teachers was as follows:

> If I wanted to learn something new in the teaching area, I would probably do a couple of things. I would probably ask experienced teachers that I know how they handle things, or if there were things that they knew about that I should look at.

A telling part of this statement is "teachers that I know." Not any teacher will do, but one that is a known entity. This qualification of a suitable source for advice could indicate the desire for a trusted source that will not tell others of the request, or a teacher that is trusted in the sense that he or she understands the context of the asking teacher, or both. As we researchers reflected on this statement, we began to pay more attention to the affective nature of inquiry. We might observe that this request for "teachers that I know" argues against plurality as a requirement for solutions to the problems of teaching practice. Indeed, we did observe a continual tension between desiring both sameness for comfort and difference for the challenge of plurality in sources for inquiry solutions.

The e-ILF includes videos of teachers attempting inquiry lessons in their classrooms. Along with the video of teaching practice, each teacher provides reflections on her teaching. The following is an example of a question that a teacher asked about his teaching in an online video that relates to these reflections:

> I am all for innovative instruction in the classroom but I feel some traditional strategies, like lecture/discussion, still have their place when used in the right proportions. Considering the fact that this introductory lecture provided the background for about a week's worth of activities, do you think it was too long?

Very few of this teacher's reflective questions garnered responses. Of those that were received, most were like the following example:

> I would have liked to see your lecture extended and given as a separate lesson. You were covering so much relevant and necessary information. I felt like you were trying to hurry through information and especially at first you were simply feeding the information, instead of trying to [sic] it from the students. I know that you have limited time, but I think it would solidify student learning and make them feel more actively involved if you could give them time for responses, instead of rushing through the information to get to the lab.

The comment above was made by an ILF staff member, a teacher liaison, as intentional modeling of critical reflection in the hope that this would spur more responses of this nature. This and other attempts[5] to spur more reflective responses in the e-ILF were largely unsuccessful. Teachers talked about lack of time in preventing them from accessing the e-ILF. They also talked about fear, lack of trust, and embarrassment involved in online inquiry; in fact, it was not until the third year, when we developed technical structures for more bounded groups of participation, that we began to see larger numbers of posts.

In general, interviews and observational data show an unfulfilled longing for contact with other teachers and a valuing of self-reflection, but in general our observations also suggest limited willingness to engage in critical feedback through the ILF. Furthermore, our observations and interviews suggest that critical inquiry into one's practice does not happen through any other contexts, either face to face or online. Therefore, we looked for other ways in which the design of the e-ILF could potentially affect participation in a community of practice.

Dewey stressed the necessity of pluralism as a source of diversity that fuels inquiry. We do not dispute this observation. However, we could not avoid the tension that plurality induced in the ILF. As an example of this tension between trust and plurality in the ILF, a math teacher, Karen,[6] who produced two videos of her classrooms for the ILF and was a very active and supportive participant, learned that one of her classroom videos was being reviewed by a preservice class. This math methods class was focused on studying and using Japanese Lesson Study (JLS).[7] As part of the class assignments, the class posted evaluative messages to the discussion forum associated with the video of Karen's classroom. One of the preservice students, Joan, commented that Karen seemed to be following a Japanese script. This was a complimentary comment in the context of JLS, but Karen, not knowing about this technique of lesson development where a teaching script is written and practiced in a group context, interpreted it as criticism and was greatly embarrassed when a state department of education official read the comment in her presence. We note that the differing contexts of Joan and Karen created misunderstanding and a negative emotional response—fear of being ridiculed or sanctioned in the presence of a superior.

Karen was genuinely upset by this incident, enough to complain to ILF staff. She also refused to respond to Joan (although the teacher subject of the video commonly monitored and responded to postings in the forum), a lost opportunity for increased understanding, learning, and dialogue for both Karen and Joan. For Karen, a lack of trust prevented inquiry. She had no knowledge of Joan except that she was a preservice math teacher, and she lacked a sufficient sense of trust in Joan's positive intentions. Status differences between the two women likely increased Karen's distrust of Joan's intentions. Joan missed the opportunity for interchange with an experienced teacher whom she admired and also missed the opportunity to explain the significance of JLS to Karen.

In addition to negative affective reactions, there are other problems limiting social inquiry. Teachers tend to view their own reflective activities separately from groupwork, as shown by this teacher's explanation of the meaning of reflective practice: "I think it is critical. I think in the absence of . . . either collaboration [or] people observing your class, it's like the two main sources of information you have about what is going right and wrong are feedback from students and your own reflections, so I think it is absolutely critical." This teacher and others found it hard to see the ILF as a place for communal reflection and a location to request critical feedback. Among the inservice

teachers who use our site, there is very little participation in this openly reflective activity.

In the case of Internet-based discussion forums, there is certainly the
danger of too much sameness. Some of this sameness of online resources arises
from the capability of search engines to find exact matches for our interests,
as well as our stereotypes and biases. In those settings, we can reinforce our
sameness mercilessly and avoid interactions that otherwise might lead us to
question our assumptions. Yet, too much difference can result in tension and
even flame wars and trolling (Brail, 1996; Herring, Job-Sluder, Scheckler,
& Barab, 2002), as members with different agendas promote conflict and
hostility.

At an ILF-organized Participant Advisory Board[8] meeting, we had some
of our participant teachers engage in a focus group around inquiry, where
they struggled with these tensions of sameness and difference. Here one
teacher expresses delight in the unexpected teaming with teachers who had
different strengths.

> In the 23 years of teaming, I have teamed with six different individu-
> als. I did not get to select but a few of them, and I have benefited
> from knowing every single one of them because everybody has some
> strength that you don't have. . . . [E]very person you meet is going to
> have something they do better than what you do, and you're a better
> person for having spent time with them.

This teacher's view affirms inquiry as a social practice where difference leads
to new ideas and variability in the search for solutions to teaching problems.

Another teacher in that same focus group struggled for a way to describe
the degree of sameness that enables the initiation of dialogue.

> It's very hard to categorize. I could say, I don't know if I can catego-
> rize or put a finger on the kind of person that I want to interact with.
> I know most meaningful relationships with me in my teaching career
> have been those that just spontaneous[ly] emerge out of something
> because not only do we have a shared vision, and we're interested in
> the same things, but we have meaningful conversations with each
> other. I'm not sure what that person's biography is that would make
> it that way, and I don't know if I could, I couldn't read 504 user
> profiles and say, That one. That one. That one.

This teacher sees "a shared vision" as the bond that encourages communication and collaboration, but does not know how to predict that this

sharing will take place. We struggled with issues of sameness and difference in the ILF and made two large changes in design and encouragement of sociability of members. One was to focus on face to face workshops and meetings to foster relationships before members went online. The other was to redesign the Web site to include small workspaces and private discussion forums meant to meet the needs of already congealed communities of practice.

Changed Habits, Restoration of Equilibrium

The ILF is primarily an attempt to conduct professional development online, and at its heart it is a reform project that promotes inquiry pedagogies. Can we see the outcome of inquiry in changed habits? We have examples of preservice teachers' reactions to doing reflection online, we have case studies of teachers who are engaged with the ILF, we have discourse from some teachers over an extended period of time, and we have multiple videos of some of our participating[9] teachers. It is very hard to see change in habits in an online space such as the ILF. Teachers tend to read the online forums more than they contribute to them. We know this from comparing the number of posts to the number of log-ins.

We do see changed practice in the multiple videos of participating teachers. For example, when teachers submitted multiple videos as exemplars of inquiry-based practices, the later ones were invariably more "inquiry-based," according to a rubric we as a community developed, than the first. There were more examples of letting students inquire deeply into the problems and a better use of questioning to engage learners in the problem as opposed to providing solutions. We also see teachers on our advisory board who are trying new practices after resolving the disequilibria that confound them. It is also evident in the perspective of our preservice teachers. Invariably, these preservice teachers initially see the videos as not very useful, highlighting one or two moments of interaction as interesting. However, after being coached by knowledgeable instructors, they notice that the videos are pregnant with interesting interactions and they engage in rich discussions—usually being overly critical. Also of interest is that this overly critical undertone tends to soften after they go out and do their student teaching.

One study in particular highlights the importance of reconceptualizing around Dewey's concept of knowledge as changing habits, as opposed to knowledge acquisition. For example, MaKinster, Barab, Harwood, and Anderson (2006) compared the reflections of and carried out interviews with preservice teachers who were assigned conditions in which they reflected on their student teaching placements either in a private journal, in a collaborative discussion forum involving other preservice teachers, or in a public discussion forum in the lounge area. The private journal group wrote more complete initial reflections, but described the experience as another assignment and attached little meaning or value to the exercise. Students in the private discussion forum posted lower quality reflections, but several students expressed more perceived value in the experience. However, the students in the lounge discussion forum posted even lower quality reflections, but all of these students found significant value in the assignment, the interactions they had with their peers and with the larger community of inservice teachers, and the idea of reflecting on their teaching as a means for personal and collaborative professional development. While a follow-up study would be necessary to determine the long-term impact, we speculate that the students in the more public lounge discussion forum are more likely to have changed habits in the way Dewey conceptualized the term.

Design Implications

Teachers, although cut off from other teachers, still have plenty of contact with both students and parents, and plenty of discrepant events to raise many questions about practice on a daily if not hourly basis. There might even be so many discrepant events in the school day that teachers feel fragmented into reflecting on too many disconnected and vexing problems. Teachers might be suffering from disequilibrium overload. What teachers tend to lack is the space to reflect on these discrepant events and restore equilibrium in their lives and profession. To generalize from Dewey's theory of inquiry, we see teachers having lots of opportunities for disequilibrium, but the part of the inquiry process that often evades teachers is the restoration of equilibrium, with accompanying change in habits. We designed the ILF as a place to allow the entire cycle of inquiry to occur.

In this section, we reflect on both Dewey's theory of inquiry and our experience with the ILF to suggest design guidelines that promote inquiry in a social setting. We focus on two major design issues that became salient in applying a Deweyan lens to our work: the tension between the need for sameness and the need for difference, and the need to pay attention to affect as a part of sociability. It is in working across these issues that we believe professional development can be truly transformative.

Fostering a Community of Critical Inquiry

There is an inherent tension in Dewey's theory of inquiry between sameness and difference. Communication, in a social setting, requires a common vocabulary and array of meanings, and thus a large degree of sameness. However, difference is also necessary to stimulate inquiry and to provide an array of possibilities for solutions. Although this tension is always present in situations of inquiry, it is even more evident in digital spaces such as the ILF, where reification of environment, physical separation of participants, reduced social cues and asynchronous communication channels, and the permanence of the textual medium acerbate this tension (Barab, MaKinster, & Scheckler, 2004). We are brought to consider how to design for sameness and difference, and how both needs must be met in such a way as to not simply allow but encourage inquiry.

With our Deweyan view of inquiry, we want to promote difference within the ILF as a source of variability, ideas, and motivation to change practice. We want to promote sameness for the ability to communicate with and trust social companions. When we look at the opinions of the teachers using the ILF, we see a desire for new ideas but also the need for the comfort of the familiar. We see a strong conflict in these desires for critical engagement and for comfort and familiarity. How do we reconcile these desires? How do we design for both sameness and difference? We make two initial observations. First, we are clearly in the realm of affect where feelings are important to the success of inquiry. Second, we need to find ways to design for *both* comfort and critical dialogue.

Looking back at our successes and failures in fostering inquiry, we note that our small interest groups, called inquiry circles, gave our members both sameness and difference. Sameness arose from common interests that attracted participants to groups or from workshops and other face-to-face meetings that often preceded the formation of an inquiry circle. Difference arose when group members brought experiences and attitudes from other situations into the current group, where they motivated new inquiries as well as provided potential solutions to inquiries. Ensuring an adequate amount of difference in inquiry circles was more difficult than providing enough sameness for trust and cohesion. Sameness and comfort in inquiry circles were rewarded, and we saw more risk taking and critical engagement, particularly when communication in the e-ILF followed face-to-face meetings. Inquiry circles limit difference, but they provide a new stumbling block for inquiry. Along with the comfort of familiarity, there is the risk of too much homogeneity.

Looking back at Dewey's interest in variability as a source of difference and the foundation of inquiries, we struggle with the tension of sameness and difference. Designing Web tools for inquiry entails recognizing the value of difference and not allowing difference to overwhelm the need to foster sociability, form consensus, and foster dialogue. Design is seldom considered in these terms. Yet these issues often overwhelm instructional technology projects—especially those targeted toward supporting the professional development of teachers. They were certainly a largely unrecognized issue in the initial stage of the design of the ILF. In general, as researchers struggle with concern for cultural differences, issues of sameness and difference must be confronted constantly. We struggle with how much sameness is necessary for the democratic processes that are essential to our functioning, and how much we as educators should engage in processes that lead to common grounds for dialogue even when these eliminate cultural differences.

Sameness in Web sites often is identified by users as a source of trust and an absence of fear. Although writers on sociability address affect to a small degree (Kim, 2000; Preece, 2000a, 2000b), this feature of community curiously is ignored in the discussion of communities of practice (Barab, Kling, & Gray, 2004; Barab, MaKinster, & Scheckler, 2004; Wenger, 1998). Need for trust is an issue that continually confronts us as we try to develop spaces that promote inquiry. Our experiences with the ILF indicate much concern with trust. Inquiry is a social process requiring dialogue as well as reflection. In order to support the inquiry of teachers, we need to be very sure that we support the social and emotional aspects of inquiry. We can see how the social-cultural construction of an online space can both limit and encourage inquiry.

Sociability and Bounded Groups

As part of our design experiments (Barab, Baek, Schatz, Scheckler, & Moore, in press) in the ILF, a year after the launching of the Web site we instituted the smaller inquiry circles (10–20 members), which were allowed to function independently of the larger communal space in which there are over 3,500 registered members. Some but not all of these interest groups arose in face-to-face meetings such as workshops or classrooms or have some access to such meetings. All these groups have identifiable facilitators, a statement of identity, and a known and examinable membership list. We suggest that small groups allow development of trust in a more personal and limited setting, limit difference, and provide common ground for dialogue. Difference is limited in the immediate space but is still accessible as links to the larger e-ILF or to the Internet beyond.

Greater development of trust and intimacy is not the only advantage of the inquiry circles. There is also more room for self-determination of the mission of the group and an ease of navigation as resources are brought into the group space via hyperlinks. Our first and longest functioning (3-year duration) bounded group was started to support the Japanese Lesson Study project previously mentioned. This group was composed of preservice math teachers from methods classes, inservice high school math teachers, math education faculty, math education graduate students, and math graduate students.[10] This group, subdivided into smaller lesson-writing task groups, had many face-to-face meetings and also used ILF group editing tools and forums for development of lesson plans when participants were apart. Because this group included classwork, the participants enrolled in the classes could be motivated to post as a class requirement. When postings were not deemed appropriately evaluative and critical, the instructor stripped them of identification and demonstrated how to add content to otherwise ineffective comments. This teaching technique was very effective, and almost all class members followed the instructor's formula for critique: give an opinion, support it with evidence, and end the post with a continuing question or comment (see Scheckler, Herring, & Martinson, 2002).

Some of the liveliest discussions of this JLS group centered on books all the members were reading. Even when these discussions were placed in the larger ILF space, rather than in the bounded group, they continued to get impassioned postings, but only from inservice teachers; this indicates that the poster's status relates to comfort in posting (Herring, Martinson, & Scheckler, 2002) in a more public space.

Even in the intimate space of this group that meets in face-to-face settings, there is discomfort with critical comments, as indicated by this post from Harry, an inservice teacher.

> I am uncomfortable with some of the comments posted in the student work section. I think this is much too public a forum to make what I consider to be negative comments about a student's general performance. I think we should reconsider the way some of the comments about the students are phrased and make some revisions.

Harry seems uncomfortable with status (power) differences of teacher and student as well as with the public nature of comments even in the relatively intimate space of the bounded group. We surmise that although dyadic relationships of critical feedback are commonplace for students, teachers, and researchers, critical dialogue in larger groups is less usual, requiring more practice and structure such as in a critical friends group (CFG).

As an alternative to the intimacy of small groups, adding sociability in design (Kim, 2000; Preece, 2000a) attempts to create a coherent and connected club-like feeling to Web sites, with rituals, identities, participant roles, and earned privilege from participation. These necessary innovations lead to a sense of belonging, but do not meet all the affective needs for trust and freedom from fear and embarrassment, although sociability does serve to provide commonality of experience, which is an aid for communication. In short, sociability does not equate with trust. We trust our advisors and mentors without also socializing with them. We socialize with our peers without always trusting them. In inquiry circles, we see more risk taking and critical engagement, particularly when communication in the e-ILF follows face-to-face meetings. Bounded groups limit difference, but they provide a new stumbling block for inquiry. Along with the comfort of familiarity, there is the risk of too much homogeneity.

CONCLUSION

In this chapter we have shown how Dewey's theory of inquiry can be used to understand the design and implementation challenges of the ILF and online teacher professional development more generally. Specifically, we highlighted those aspects that are central to Dewey's patterns of inquiry (situations, reasonable doubt, dialogical pluralism, habit), noting in particular the social issues of sameness, difference, and affect. Beginning with a brief description of a series of face-to-face workshops with teachers, we then described our theoretical perspective and used this as a lens for examining participation and design decisions in terms of the ILF. Reflecting on our data in terms of Dewey's pragmatic social theory, we derived a number of implications. In our current thinking, online spaces in support of inquiry should evolve out of and enhance face-to-face groups where some level of trust has already been established. An example is the Japanese Lesson Study group that we supported online for 3 years. This is not to say that trust never develops online without previous face-to-face meetings, just that this is a much more difficult route. On a related note, smaller online groups nurture trust more effectively than the larger ILF, but there is a trade-off in less difference in smaller groups. Designers need to be aware of this trade-off of trust and intimacy for difference and find ways to allow the flow of difference in online design.

As we follow Dewey's philosophy of the social construction of knowledge and recognize the role of inquiry in the process of formulating warranted assertions, we come to an interesting insight: *We control the knowledge that we can reasonably engage in by limiting the nature of our social contexts and thereby the type of knowing that emerges.* This insight has implications for those who are not in agreement with the dominant ideology of a society. Because inquiry is social, the social environment can both encourage and discourage inquiry. Online or face-to-face spaces can be constructed so as to encourage inquiry, diversity, and warranted assertions that serve a diverse population. Conversely, they can be constructed narrowly and self-referentially by limiting social contacts to those who agree with us. Either way, we may not be able to fully justify our assertions. The problems of the limited viewpoint may not become fully apparent until adversity threatens our well-being, and then it might be too late to search for a more diverse solution set.

We have come to the point of considering not only the desirability but also the necessity of cultivating a critical community of inquirers so that we, as a community, may order claims in our contingent and fallibilistic world. In the attempt to regain equilibrium in times of doubt, we must be part of the social realm where we hear and evaluate many viewpoints. Speaking to the social needs of the public, Dewey (1916/1980) has two criteria for evaluating a society: "How numerous and varied are the interests which are consciously shared? How full and free is the interplay with other forms of association?" (p. 89). Garrison (1996) describes the consequences of not nurturing a critical community of inquirers, noting how oppressive societies allow only the interests of the powerful few, with the dire result that these societies are slow or unable to change in adverse situations.

In the case of teachers' inquiry into their practice, the greater the plurality of ideas available to them, the more likely they are to find a suitable solution. The less plurality available for teachers' inquiry, the smaller the solution set available to them when put into a state of disequilibrium, leading to frustration, inappropriate responses to student needs, dissatisfaction with teaching, and ultimately burnout and leaving the profession. Meaning itself derives from a community context. Cleo Cherryholmes (1999) says, "Meanings are social constructs . . . because they are consequences of thinking"(p. 36). Teachers, commonly limited to the confines of their classroom by the social practices in U.S. schools, have much to gain by opening their doors and becoming part of a critical community of inquiry (Grossman, Wineburg, & Woolworth, 2000). Their renewed abilities to find meaning as teachers, to search for solutions to difficult problems, and to grow along with their peers are important consequences of the social nature of inquiry.

Dewey's theory of inquiry allowed us to consider the transactive and situated nature of inquiry. The transactive nature of inquiry is important because it speaks to both the process and the product of inquiry, both of which are mediated by the medium through which inquiry occurs. Thus, designers have a tremendously important role when building an online space. They are not simply designing a set of technical spaces, but potentially manipulating social transactions and the resultant meanings for participants. In the entertainment world, those individuals who are responsible for orchestrating and manipulating the sociotechnical configurations are referred to as "gods." Although we view this term as overly presumptuous and arrogant, we appreciate the underlying sentiment and would heed designers of sociotechnical spaces to take their responsibilities seriously. For it is in the transactions that these designed spaces support and constrain that many people will construct real-world meanings that may affect multiple aspects of their lives both inside and outside these spaces.

NOTES

1. This is a password-protected site but anyone can take a tour or apply for a password.

2. For Dewey, habits are where mind, body, and affect come together and, very crucially, are social in nature. Dewey (1922/1983) wrote, "Since habits involve the support of environing conditions, a society or some specific group of fellow-men [*sic*] is always accessory before and after the fact" (p. 16). Learning occurs at this intersection of mind, body, affect, and environment.

3. The dangers of engaged fallibilistic pluralism arise when our dietary, religious, ethnic, or cultural beliefs change, events that might make us rejected by our families and other important social groups.

4. Teachers specifically mention the difficulty of doing inquiry while meeting state and federal standards, the difficulty of doing extended inquiry projects in 45-minute class periods, and the lack of support from other teachers who think inquiry is an "easy" way to teach; teachers also wonder about the suitability of inquiry for special needs students and gifted students. Teachers, of course, also reflect on matters peripherally related to inquiry, such as classroom management issues, licensure and accreditation, balancing the conflicting needs of classroom members, and keeping up with required paperwork.

5. We also attempted to structure times to respond to a particular teacher. All our discussion forums are asynchronous (members respond whenever they wish, not at designated times), and we hypothesized that giving specific times for input when the host teacher would be available might give a greater immediacy to the discussion forums. These attempts were not particularly successful. More successful were posting parties (summer events, complete with refreshments), where we invited teachers to come for a couple of hours to do nothing but post on the forums around the classrooms. This success speaks to economy of attention issues, where time- and space-limited events are more likely to garner teachers' attention, but this practice also eliminates the advantage of the independence of time and place of Internet-based tools.

6. All names of ILF participants are pseudonyms.

7. Japanese Lesson Study is a school-wide approach to curriculum development. As a group, the teachers decide on gaps in their curricula and then devote group time to developing lessons that fill this gap. Lessons are devised by the group and then taught by one member, with the other group members observing. The critique by the observers leads to a new iteration of the lesson, which then is taught by another group member. The teaching–observation–revision cycle continues until the group is satisfied that the lesson is effective. Particularly noteworthy to our discussion, is that the group, not a single teacher, owns the lesson; thus, critique is focused on the lesson itself and not the teacher of the lesson, reducing the affective sting of pointed evaluation.

8. The Participant Advisory Board was composed of teachers (6–8) who were interested in inquiry teaching. The ILF funded two co-present meetings of these teachers each year to advise the ILF on issues of design, usability, and marketing of the

ILF. Even though changing interests and job locations led to a somewhat shifting membership of this board over the 3-year period in which they met, this group formed bonds that we would want to emulate in the ILF at large.

9. Participating teachers is the name we have given to those who have made videos of their classrooms where they were attempting to engage in inquiry.

10. Not all these members remained active the entire time, but there was a core of inservice high school math teachers and math education graduate students and faculty who did. Preservice math education students tended to be active only in the semester that they were enrolled in a class that focused on JLS.

REFERENCES

Barab, S. A., Baek, E., Schatz, S., Scheckler, R., & Moore, J. (in press). Illuminating the braids of change in a Web-supported community: A design experiment by another name. To appear in A. Kelly & D. Lesh (Eds.), *Design-based research II*. Mahwah, NJ: Erlbaum.

Barab, S. A., Cherkes-Julkowski, M., Swenson, R., Garrett, S., Shaw, R. E., & Young, M. (1999). Principles of self-organization: Ecologizing the learner-facilitator system. *The Journal of The Learning Sciences, 8*(3 and 4), 349–390.

Barab, S. A., & Duffy, T. M. (2000). From practice fields to communities of practice. In D. Jonassen & S. Land (Eds.), *Theoretical foundation of learning environments* (pp. 25–56). Mahwah, NJ: Lawrence Erlbaum Associates.

Barab, S., Kling, R., & Gray, J. (Eds.). (2004). *Designing virtual communities in the service of learning*. Cambridge: Cambridge University Press.

Barab, S., MaKinster, J. G., Moore, J., Cunningham, D., & the ILF Design Team. (2001). Designing and building an online community: The struggle to support sociability in the Inquiry Learning Forum. *Educational Technology Research and Development, 49*(4), 71–96.

Barab, S., MaKinster, J., & Scheckler, R. (2004). Designing system dualities: Characterizing an online professional development community. In S. Barab, R. Kling & J. Gray (Eds.), *Designing virtual communities in the service of learning* (pp. 53–90). Cambridge: Cambridge University Press.

Barab, S., Moore, J., Cunningham, D., & the ILF Design Team. (2000, April). *The internet learning forum: A new model for online professional development*. Paper presented at the annual meeting of the American Educational Research Association, New Orleans.

Barab, S. A., & Roth, W.-M. (2006). Intentionally-bound systems and curricular-based ecosystems: An ecological perspective on knowing. *Educational Researcher, 35*(5), 3–13.

Bernstein, R. J. (1992). *The new constellation*. Cambridge, MA: MIT Press.

Brail, S. (1996). The price of admission: Harassment and free speech in the wild, wild west. In L. Cherny & E. R. Weise (Eds.), *Wired women: Genders and new realities in cyberspace* (pp. 141–157). Seattle, WA: Seal Press.

Cherryholmes, C. H. (1999). *Reading pragmatism* (Vol. 24). New York: Teachers College Press.

Dewey, J. (1980). *Democracy and education* (Vol. 9). Carbondale: Southern Illinois University Press. (Original work published 1916)

Dewey, J. (1983). *Human nature and conduct* (Vol. 14). Carbondale: Southern Illinois University Press. (Original work published 1922)

Dewey, J. (1963). *Experience and education.* New York: Collier Books. (Original work published 1938)

Dewey, J. (1986). Logic: The theory of inquiry. In J. A. Boydston (Ed.), *John Dewey: The later works 1925–1953* (Vol. 12, pp. 1–506). Carbondale: Southern Illinois University Press. (Original work published 1938)

Garrison, J. (1996). A Deweyan theory of democratic listening. *Educational Theory*, 46(4), 429–451.

Garrison, J. (1997). *Dewey and Eros: Wisdom and desire in the art of teaching.* New York: Teachers College Press.

Gibson, J. J. (1986). *The ecological approach to visual perception.* Hillsdale, NJ: Erlbaum.

Gomez, L. M., Fishman, B. J., & Pea, R. D. (1998). The CoVis Project: Building a large scale science education testbed. *Interactive Learning Environments*, 6(1–2), 59–92.

Grossman, P., & Wineburg, S. (2000). *What makes a teacher community different from a gathering of teachers* (No. O-00-1). Seattle, WA: Center for Study of Teaching and Policy.

Grossman, P., Wineburg, S., & Woolworth, S. (2000, April). *In pursuit of teacher community.* Paper presented at the annual meeting of the American Educational Research Association, New Orleans.

Herring, S., Job-Sluder, K., Scheckler, R., & Barab, S. (2002). Searching for safety online: Managing "trolling" in a feminist forum. *The Information Society*, 18(5), 371–383.

Herring, S., Martinson, A., & Scheckler, R. (2002). Designing for community: The effects of gender representation in videos on a web site. In *Proceedings of the Thirty-Fifth Hawaii International Conference on System Sciences.* Los Alamitos, CA: IEEE Computer Society Press. Los Alamitos: IEEE Computer Society Press.

Kim, A. J. (2000). *Community building on the web: Secret strategies for successful online communities.* Berkeley, CA: Peachpit Press.

Lave, J., & Wenger, E. (1991). *Situated learning: Legitimate peripheral participation.* Cambridge: Cambridge University Press.

MaKinster, J. G., Barab, S. A., Harwood, W. S., & Andersen, H. O. (2006). The effect of social context on the reflective practice of pre-service science teachers: Incorporating a Web-supported community of teachers. *Journal of Technology and Teacher Education*, 14(3), 543–579.

Nespor, J. (1997). *Tangled up in school: Politics, space, bodies, and signs in the educational process.* Mahwah, NJ: Erlbaum.

Pea, R. (1993). Practices of distributed intelligence and designs for education. In G. Salomon (Ed.), *Distributed cognitions: Psychological and educational considerations* (pp. 47–87). Cambridge: Cambridge University Press.

Preece, J. (2000a). *Online communities: Designing usability, supporting sociability.* Chichester, UK: Wiley.

Preece, J. (2000b). *Shaping communities: Empathy, hostility, lurking, and participation.* Paper presented at the DIAC2000, Seattle, WA.

Scheckler, R. K., Herring, S., & Martinson, A. (2002, April). *Whose community? Gender dynamics of questioning and answering in an online professional development tool designed to promote inquiry.* Paper presented at the annual meeting of the American Educational Research Association, New Orleans.

Wenger, E. (1998). *Communities of practice: Learning, meaning, and identity.* Cambridge: Cambridge University Press.

CHAPTER 6

The Role of Representations in Shaping
a Community of Scientific Inquiry Online

Andee Rubin and Susan J. Doubler

Community building in an online environment is influenced by, among other factors, the general social and cultural experience of online interaction and the more specific disciplinary culture of the course content. Recent research has focused primarily on the first of these: the determinants and effects of the interactions among students and instructor from a situated perspective, which sees learning as occurring within an activity and a context (Brown, Collins, & Duguid, 1989; Lave & Wenger, 1991). This chapter focuses on the second influence on online community building: the culture of the discipline (in this case, the culture of physics) as established through collegial discourse in an online science education course. Indeed, discourse among teachers is the critical activity of the community, the locus of visible learning.

Why is the building of a community of science inquirers relevant to the design of a course in a science education master's program? The science that teachers experience in their own schooling commonly has little resemblance to that practiced by scientists. An emphasis on textbooks, vocabulary, memorized formulas, prescriptive labs, and teacher demonstrations are far removed from the inquiry and quest for understanding undertaken by scientists. These intellectual exercises are designed to provide learners with a collection of facts and concepts, but not with the ability to use science to generate new knowledge. In contrast, the design of courses in the Lesley University/TERC master's degree program was guided by a set of values about science and about learning that more closely reflected the practice of science and simultaneously supported teachers' understanding and discussion of key concepts of the domain with one another. In attempting to create a community of practice that reflected the ways in which scientists participate in the practice of science, we focused on the following aspects of scientific inquiry:

- Doing science involves asking questions, hands-on experimentation, observation, data, and a search for patterns.
- A central aspect of doing science is the communicating of findings and conclusions to the wider scientific community, with supporting evidence.
- Representations of the phenomena being investigated are often used to communicate hypotheses and explanations based on evidence.
- In engaging in this kind of scientific discourse, individuals put themselves and their conclusions "on the line," available for scrutiny by other members of the community.
- The goal (often unreachable) of scientific discourse is to move toward a common understanding, taking into account everyone's evidence.

Discourse is critical. The communication structures and audiences available to participating teachers play a key role in how they collaboratively engage in science inquiry—raising questions, carrying out investigations, and making sense of results. In this chapter, we describe how an online master's degree program in science education provided the representational resources to support teachers' practice of inquiry. We first describe the overall structure and content of the degree program, then focus on the specific course, Investigating Physics. In the context of that course, we look in detail at a series of representations and consider what each added to the teachers' scientific discourse.

DESIGN PRINCIPLES THAT FOSTER COMMUNITY DISCOURSE AND A SCIENTIFIC CULTURE

The context of our exploration is Re-Opening the Science Door, a fully online science education master's degree program for elementary and middle school teachers. The program comprises an introductory 3-credit-hour course, Try Science, and five 6-credit-hour modules. Each of the 6-credit-hour modules consists of both a science course and a coordinated pedagogical course. The science course focuses on a particular science domain—physics, biology, earth science, engineering, or ecology—while the pedagogical course focuses on a particular aspect of teaching—inquiry, children's scientific ideas, curriculum, assessment, equity, or classroom strategies.

Even this basic design reflects the values underlying the program. The science portion of the module is first, immediately putting the participants in the role of scientists, that is, learners of science. This step requires some participants to overcome their fear of science so that they can participate in the individual inquiry that is the core of the course. One of our first design challenges was to "re-open the science door" for these participants, to establish an online environment where it was safe for them to take intellectual risks. To do this effectively, we defined the scientific enterprise as one in which everyone's ideas were valued and in which a "wrong" idea with supporting evidence was much preferable to a bald statement without evidence, even if it was correct.

A module runs for 12 to 13 weeks with a new assignment posted every Friday. Each science session purposely begins with a hands-on investigation both to emphasize the central role of inquiry in science and to allow teachers to experiment on their own, "in their kitchen," and record their own observations. At this point, everyone's data are acceptable, as long as they are based on careful observation. Teachers work independently, offline and away from the computer, for a few days. By Tuesday evening, they report their data and findings to their assigned study group of five to seven people; in the group's ensuing discussion between Tuesday and Thursday, each individual's work becomes part of a collection of data and ideas that the group uses to make sense of the observations. This weekly schedule, which offers clear expectations of when to report and when to discuss data, is pivotal in promoting steady participation among participants. It prevents the all too common syndrome of a minority of people posting for the majority of participants, who read.

Study groups are an essential element of our course design and have proven successful in promoting collegial discourse. Each study group stays together for the entire semester. This provides participants with a small community of colleagues with whom they become comfortable putting their ideas forward, taking intellectual risks, and assuming increased responsibility for one another's learning. Together, study group members aim to find answers to the questions they investigate, by taking into account everyone's data and ideas. Within the group, results are compared, clarification requested, questions posed, and explanations proposed and debated with an eye toward some kind of agreement—or at least agreement on what the unanswered questions are. The asynchronous nature of these discussions supports the science culture; it slows the response time, providing time for reflection, for questions to surface, and for arguments to deepen, as they do in the practice of science.

As the course progresses, participants continue to engage in science collaboratively; they create hypotheses based on their observations, make predictions based on the hypotheses, and collect more data to evaluate these explanations. The structure of the course leads each participant to present evidence with every claim, and the other participants to judge claims by evaluating the reliability and relevance of the evidence. The course investigations provide common experiences and opportunities for teachers not only to understand phenomena but also to develop the associated academic language of science needed to discuss them. In their online discussion, teachers interact with colleagues and with the science facilitators, whose language is often more scientifically advanced. They have the opportunity to consider multiple perspectives put forward in the discussion, and to take on, even imitate, another perspective, including its associated language (Tomasello, 2000). Teachers are expected to communicate and discuss their findings, and the online conversations provide them an opportunity to develop increasingly sophisticated explanations. Unlike face-to-face discussion where conversation moves rapidly and may be characterized by quickly formulated or partial explanations, the asynchronous interactions in Re-opening the Science Door provide participants with time to think, to study others' written arguments, and to formulate and explain their own ideas fully in writing.

Each module is co-facilitated by a scientist and science educator. The scientist-facilitator has a complex task: to use her knowledge of the subject matter to coach participants in thinking scientifically without becoming the "expert." The facilitator responds to the whole study group rather than to individuals. She may remind students to base explanations on evidence, propose a theory for consideration, point out factors participants may have overlooked, encourage discipline-specific vocabulary, or focus the discussion on what she sees as potential problems. These facilitators generally take a low profile, contributing on average about 10% of the discussion posts (Sheingold & Doubler, 2003), so that communication will flow from participant to participant, and learners will come to see themselves as able to think through questions rather than turning to an authority figure for answers. With "a light touch of the tiller," facilitators refocus the discussion and encourage deeper consideration of issues.

For example, in the following facilitator post, we see that the scientist had identified a problem—some teachers were not differentiating between force and momentum:

Dear Copernicans,
    This week you're working with collisions. Some of you have already brought up the term "momentum" in your discussions. Sometimes in everyday language we interchange the terms "force" and "momentum." This is the time to sort out the difference between the two, and to understand more about motions involved in collisions.
    I recommend keeping your velocity data in a chart. Remember that data and data analysis are at the heart of scientific discussions. Be sure to post your data and use [them] as evidence in your discussions.
    As always, I'm looking forward to your findings.

Sam

In general, the course facilitator intervenes sparingly, aware that participants could quickly turn to her as the expert. Her intent is to maintain the teacher-to-teacher conversation that is underway, and at the same time set parameters for productive learning. With time, teachers begin to monitor their own discussion, asking their colleagues for clarification, posing questions, and taking intellectual risks; when this happens, the coaching of the scientists focuses on more nuanced strategies and understanding.

For the first part of the module, participants are asked to assume the role of science learners and to temporarily suspend their stance as classroom teachers. They engage completely in sustained investigation to deepen their understanding of the science at hand. They stay close to the phenomena, build a shared vocabulary, and use representations to uncover patterns in data and to evaluate explanations. Only in the second half of the module do participants reassume their stance as teachers, as they reflect on their experiences as science learners and consider how to create similar opportunities for their students. Their attention shifts to topics such as inquiry, children's scientific ideas, curriculum, assessment, equity, and classroom strategies. Teachers interact with students in classrooms or in smaller groups, then describe their findings to their study group in order to build a shared model of science learning and teaching, much as they attempted to build a shared model of the scientific content.

The two courses within each module are intertwined and designed to be mutually supportive, with the science foreshadowing best practices addressed in the teaching course, and the teaching course using examples from the classroom to revisit concepts investigated in the science (Doubler & Paget, 2006).

THE DEVELOPMENT AND FUNCTION OF REPRESENTATIONS: INVESTIGATING PHYSICS

To see these design principles in action and to consider in detail how representations support the scientific discourse, we look closely at Investigating Physics, the second course module in the fully online master's degree program. Investigating Physics is designed to help teachers extend their understanding of Newtonian physics through investigating the fundamental concepts governing force and motion. In the discussion of the course in this chapter, we focus solely on the science content aspect of the course and not the pedagogical aspect, in order to describe our design decisions and the role that representations play in facilitating scientific discourse.

The content of Investigating Physics can be described succinctly: $F = ma$ (force = mass times acceleration). $F = ma$ is simultaneously an extremely simple mathematical expression and a complex physical relationship with manifestations in our every movement and our every observation of motion. One of the goals of the course is that teachers understand the mathematical implications of F = ma (e.g., that they can find an object's mass if they know the force acting on it and its acceleration, since m = F/a). A more important goal for us, however, was that teachers be able to see F = ma in every instance of motion they observe or experience. In the course, teachers explore acceleration, deceleration, constant motion, forward motion, backward motion, crashes (sudden decelerations), circular motion, the motion of a falling object, and the parabolic motion of a thrown ball. They experiment with balls and carts. They build an accelerometer, out of a jar, a cork, vegetable oil, and string, that can detect and indicate the direction and magnitude of acceleration of any object to which it could be "attached." They learn how to create and interpret graphical representations of motion in one and two directions, moving from firsthand observations of motion through nontraditional representations to the more conventional graphical representations. At each juncture they articulate their hypothesis, describe their evidence, and learn from fellow participants as they grapple with interpreting their data. We describe these steps below.

Firsthand Observation: The Root of Science Discourse

While fostering scientific discourse was a core value, we were aware that such dialogue would not happen without careful scaffolding of the participants' experience. To begin with, scientific discourse requires having some data to represent, talk about, and attempt to model or explain. In Investigating Physics, participants have two primary sources of observational data: experiments that they do as part of the course and observations they make of the physics of motion in their everyday lives. These two differ in that in the course experiments, all participants are working with the same phenomenon—although not always with the same observations, since they do the experiments on their own. Working with the same phenomenon provides a shared experience and eases the awkwardness of initiating conversations with colleagues whom they have never met. In analyzing the motions they encountered individually, participants face an additional challenge of describing the phenomenon in enough detail so that other participants can understand their analysis. We consider examples of each of these kinds of observational data below and provide examples of the discourse that ensued.

Course Experiments

From the very beginning of Investigating Physics, teachers are involved in hands-on scientific investigations that they do with real objects, away from the computer. Before the course begins, participants receive a kit of materials consisting of a low-friction cart, several balls, and some spring scales—simple materials that cost little and could be used in a classroom as well. Each session begins with an experiment that demands close observation; teachers record their results in their journals, which then form the basis for their online report and for online conversations with other participants during the week.

The first investigation invites participants to recall their childhood experiences with a red Radio Flyer wagon. This familiar context, explored by physicist Richard Feynman (1999), provides a gentle entry into physics and sends the message that science is about the everyday world and is accessible to all of us. Participants make predictions based on their childhood experience: "Imagine putting a ball in the wagon and pulling the wagon forward. What happens to the ball? Imagine stopping the wagon. What happens to the ball now?" They then test their predictions with materials from the course kit, record their observations, and share them with their study group, where the goal is to reach a shared understanding of the motion they observed. Since their results and ideas often vary, accomplishing this goal becomes a group effort that may require redoing the investigation, clarifying explanations, and comparing, contrasting, and combining data with colleagues. The power of the group's interaction derives in large part from the fact that all members observed the "same" phenomenon, yet have different observations and data to reconcile.

Motions in Everyday Life

In contrast to the course experiments shared by all the participants, the teachers also share their own experiences of $F = ma$. One of our goals for the course was for teachers to look at their world with a physicist's eye and to see and appreciate the physics of motion everywhere they go. To this end, we established two separate threaded discussion spaces, the physics forum, where participants discuss their experiments, as described above, and the motions in your life forum, in which teachers connect their daily lives to the concepts of the course. We hoped that the latter forum would facilitate the sharing of elusive science concepts that "come to life" in chores (driving children to school, pushing a shopping cart), athletic events (playing volleyball or soccer), vacations (swimming or diving), and relaxing (watching a pet cat jump on the sofa, playing the harp).

For example, in the third week of the course, teachers posted in the "motions in your life" forum events that occurred within their daily lives, in which they could identify constant motion, speeding up motion, slowing down motion, and crashes. One teacher posted the following, describing part of her laundry chores:

Speeding up: occurs when the dryer is turned on; the more mass (due to more clothes or more moisture in the clothes) the slower the speeding up process.

Slowing down: occurs when the dryer door is opened; the more mass, the longer it takes to slow down [My opinion here is different from Joyce's.]

Constant: occurs after the dryer reaches its peak speed. I did wonder if the "balance" of the clothes in the dryer may cause changes, albeit slight, in the constant movement.

Crash: occurs if you open the dryer door and use your hand to stop the motion.

Another teacher regarded her morning coffee with "physics eyes":

Each morning on my way to work I make a quick stop at the local Dunkin' Donuts and order a large French vanilla iced coffee with milk. I then place this drink in my cupholder and try to safely navigate my way to the local highway and ultimately to work. Quite by accident I noticed the motion of the iced coffee when I had to make a sudden stop. The light bulb went on over my head and I decided to discuss this. This interested me because there seemed to be three separate and distinct motions.

The cup remained in a stationary position in the cupholder. This represented the main body of the cart that we used in my mind. The iced coffee mixture sloshed forward and back until an equilibrium was reached. I found this interesting because I felt that this motion represented what the ball did in the previous experiment. The twist came in the difference of the substances (the solid of the ball vs. the liquid of the coffee). The ball had a more visible reaction that ended more quickly. The liquid, while not as reactive, seemed to slosh about and ripple much longer than the 5–6 seconds that the ball bounced My approximation would be 20 to 30 seconds. (It was difficult to get an exact time due to my interest in safe driving.)

In most online courses, personal interactions at best contribute to participants' knowledge and trust of one another and at worst distract participants from the scientific interchange. In contrast, we were able to direct participants' attention to events in their everyday lives to extend the kinds of observational data they could bring to the course and to lessen the perceived gap between science and "real" life. The collegial interactions contributed to the science discourse, and vice versa.

Representations as Resources for Science Discourse

Participants began the course using everyday language to communicate their observations and experiences. However, to refine their ideas and to test their explanatory theories, they needed to use other aspects of the language of science. Recent characterizations of the culture of science have emphasized the many aspects of scientific communication that go beyond text, for example, graphs, mathematical representations, diagrams, tables, symbolic notations, and video (Lemke, 2004). In discussing scientific thinking as it applies to students' learning, Lehrer and Schauble (2006) view representations in the context of modeling, a central component of science. They see modeling as "the construction and test of representations that serve as analogues to systems in the real world" (p. 177). These representations help a learner to interpret evidence, take all evidence into account, systematically consider multiple possibilities, and entertain alternative interpretations of data.

In Investigating Physics, representations serve an additional important purpose. Given that many of the participants' experiences are offline and on their own, they need representations from the beginning to share their observations with the other learners; they cannot rely on the communicative options that are possible when people physically share an experience (e.g., saying, "Did you see how that ball fell?").

Developing a shared representational language is a necessary part of the formation of a scientific community, as the kinds of conversations that are truly scientific need to use the multimodal aspects of scientific communication (Lemke, 1990). Investigating Physics supports participants in developing a set of representations that allow them to make statements that "[rely] on evidence rather than mere examples" (Lehrer & Schauble, 2006, p. 70). While the view of science as the use of shared inscriptions is found only rarely in schools, it is even less common in online settings, even though it is arguably more important in that context. We describe three such representations, two of which we designed especially for the course and one that was adapted from a common graphical representation, and discuss how each representation helped teachers to create a shared scientific language with which to communicate about their observations and offer evidence for their claims.

Strobe Pictures: Taking a Small Step from the Motion

Attempting to observe motion closely presents a major problem: It is over almost as soon as it begins. Most of the motions that participants study in Investigating Physics last 1 second or less. To deal with this problem, we provided teachers with online videotapes of the motions that they could view one frame at a time (i.e., every 1/30 of a second). Slowing down the action increases teachers' ability to observe the details of the motion, but to be able to discuss the motion without the video, they still need some representation that they can see all at once, a record of the passage of time on a single image.

Strobe pictures are made by placing an overhead transparency on a computer screen and marking the position of the moving object in each subsequent frame with an overhead pen, as shown in Figure 6.1. A participant creates a strobe picture of, for example, a cart, by marking with a dot the position of a particular point on the cart in one frame of the video, advancing the video one frame, marking the position of the same point on the cart in that frame with another dot, and so on. When they are done, participants have a representation of the motion of the cart in subsequent frames—all on one transparency. Constant speed is represented by equally spaced dots; speeding up is represented by dots getting further and further apart; slowing down is represented by dots getting closer and closer together. Figure 6.2 is a strobe picture that represents an object speeding up, since the dots get progressively further apart. In contrast with the representations discussed later,

FIGURE 6.1. Creating a strobe picture

FIGURE 6.2. Strobe picture of an object speeding up

there is no explicit graphical display of velocity or acceleration; rather, both have to be inferred from the position of the dots.

What has been distilled from the complex video of cart and ball is a mathematical representation that serves as a common language for teachers to describe and discuss the motions they see. Here is a post from a teacher in Session 1, when the group was just beginning to analyze the motion of the ball on and off the cart. Note how he used descriptions of the distance between tracings to describe the motion that he observed (and the motion that he had not been able to observe without the video!).

> When I viewed the videos, I took a transparency and then traced the ball in each frame. There was consistency in distance between ball tracings for the constant rate of speed and inconsistency when the ball changed rate. The tracings were much closer together when the ball was going very slowly. As the cart was decelerating, the rate of speed of the ball (distance between tracings) was the same as when the cart was going a constant speed. The change in speed came when the ball fell off the cart. Then the distance between the tracings was further on the way down to the table and for the first half of a bounce, then the tracings were closer together than they were on the cart, thus the ball was moving slower than on the cart after the bounce, but faster during the fall. I'm guessing that gravity has to account for that. Truthfully, I was unable to see those nuances without the video, and guessed that it was going the same rate of speed and then slowing down.

Cork Graphs: Combining Pictorial and Graphical Representations

To help teachers move from strobe graphs toward an understanding of how conventional graphs can represent motion and acceleration, we introduced a measuring tool that allowed teachers to "see" acceleration as a measure in and of itself, not just as a change in velocity. The tool was an accelerometer made of a jar, some vegetable oil, a cork, and a string. At rest, the string holding the cork is vertical, and the cork floats directly above the place where the string is attached (see Figure 6.3). Any change in velocity (i.e., acceleration) is indicated by the cork moving away from the vertical. At a constant velocity, even a high one, the cork floats straight up. Teachers nicknamed the accelerometer "Corky" and sometimes used that name in their posts.

After learning to read the accelerometer in familiar motion settings (e.g., the ball and cart), the teachers take Corky on the road—in a car (while someone else is driving!), on a bus, or on the subway—and measure the motion they are experiencing simultaneously themselves. This activity often serves to further teachers' connections between the kinesthetic experience of motion and its symbolic and mathematical representations.

Students' experiences with the accelerometer provide a transition to another nontraditional representation that combines a standard graph showing change in velocity over time and a corresponding picture of the accelerometer as it looked at a point in time (see Figure 6.4). The value of this graph as a transitional representation is that it has a "literal" part—a picture of the accelerometer—and a symbolic part—the graph of velocity over time. Here is an example of a *cork graph* and a teacher's description of the motion it represents.

FIGURE 6.3. An accelerometer, a tool for "seeing" acceleration

FIGURE 6.4. Participant-generated graph that combines pictorial and graphic representation

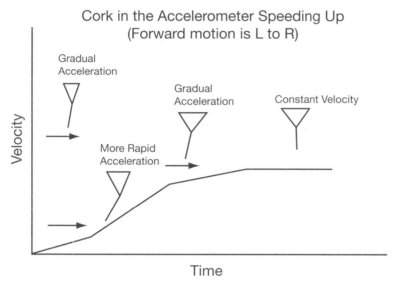

Observing the accelerometer on the cart was quite challenging, as following the cork with your naked eye and trying to make observations while running it through various motions was very daunting. Observing the video frame by frame made the motions much clearer.

Constant motion was the easiest to interpret since the cork stayed in the same position as you looked from frame to frame. . . . [But] I had a very difficult time walking and observing the cork in this middle, rest position. I discussed this in the motions in my life forum. Why is it so difficult to walk at a constant rate? Is it because of the nature of walking, where you are really moving up and down, as well as across?

As far as the speeding up graph, it appeared to me that the cart was traveling at a gradual acceleration initially, followed by a more rapid acceleration. The fact that the cork leaned at a more noticeable angle led to this conclusion. Toward the end of the video the cork was leaning less, indicating gradual acceleration, followed by constant speed, with the cork straight up. In the last frame or two, the string and cork look like they may even be leaning to the left, in the direction opposite the motion, implying some slight deceleration.

A Reflection on Representation

So far we have described two representations that help teachers create their own models of the motions they observe. But we are interested primarily in the way representations are used in a community of science to identify patterns and relationships, and then to argue a point. Without data that are organized to illustrate a point, no scientific knowledge would be generated. The goal of the culture whose formation we supported in the design of the course is to generate public knowledge—knowledge that is widely accepted because it is based on evidence that the community accepts. Representations are a common way in which scientists offer their evidence to be discussed and evaluated. In the scientific community, there are norms about what constitutes a valid representation, how representations are read, and what their relationship is to reality; these are part of the culture we hope students will understand and use.

In order for any representation to be the mediator of scientific inquiry, participants must be able to share it. Many online courses allow participants to post only text, but we realized that without shared representations, teachers would not be able to carry out the conversations that are the basis for scientific inquiry. Finding a tool for creating and sharing graphical representations was not an easy task, since it is imperative that participants be able to create their *own* representations. For example, it might seem that Excel would be a good tool for teachers, since it automatically creates graphs that are universally accepted in the practice of science. In contrast, we were interested in teachers creating their own representations—albeit within the representational language we suggested. Therefore, we provided students with PowerPoint as a drawing tool and with the ability to attach graphs to their posted messages. Our goal was not for teachers to learn about traditional scientific graphs, but to communicate using the language and representational tools of science. We offer this advice to designers of online systems for education: Make it easy for participants to share objects other than text!

Signature Graphs: A Representational
Language to Describe Motion

At this point in Investigating Physics, teachers are well on their way to creating and interpreting traditional change-over-time graphs. But we took one more step to emphasize the importance of understanding the general "shape" of a motion rather than the precise values for velocity over time; we did not want teachers at this point to begin to use graphing software and lose their connection to their experience of a motion. Therefore, we provided teachers with the building blocks of a representational language for talking about motion to support a common understanding of the meaning of the axes of a graph and the general shape of a curve. Our focus was on the shape of graphs and their relationship to one another, not on the exact height of a peak or the exact moment when an object began to slow down. The language we introduced consisted of seven basic motions, each of which has a *signature graph*: constant fast velocity, constant slow velocity, slowing down slowly, slowing down quickly, speeding up slowly, speeding up quickly, and crashing (an extreme version of slowing down quickly). For each motion, we identified a graph shape. The two examples in Figure 6.5 show speeding up and crashing. In each case, the axes are labeled (time on the *x* axis, distance or speed on the *y* axis), but there are no numbers on either axis. For each motion, there is a representation in terms of speed versus time and in terms of position versus time, the latter of which is often difficult for students (of any age) to interpret, especially when the conversation is about changes in velocity.

As the course proceeded, participants mostly created graphs by concatenating signature graphs to represent a complex motion, but many added idiosyncratic aspects to their graphs, as illustrated below. Almost all used a "key," a narrative that described the mapping between the graph shape and the story of the motion. These graphical representations provided the grist for the scientific mill, the source of evidence for scientific claims.

At this point in the online conversation, effective communication required using graphical representations as well as text. In fact, as the next example will illustrate, some posts contained a graph and only minimal text. Using PowerPoint, participants constructed an inquiry practice that required graphs to have clearly delineated and labeled segments to indicate changes in velocity. Graphs automatically generated by standard graphing software were considered less compelling evidence than the graphs participants drew and labeled themselves.

FIGURE 6.5. Examples of signature graphs

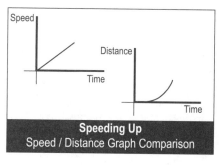
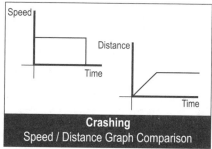

The challenge in creating such careful representations is that it requires participants to attain a deep understanding of the physics, as well as physicists' graphical and vocabulary conventions in describing motion in terms of change of velocity over time. One of the most problematic aspects of representing motion for participants was distinguishing between positive and negative, in terms of both velocity and acceleration, and in how each of those manifested in a graph.[1] Participants had particular difficulty understanding how to think about and represent an object going faster and faster in the negative direction compared with one going faster and faster in the positive direction. An even more difficult puzzle was how to represent an object going slower and slower in the negative direction. How did Irene, Jill, Elaine, and Marie (all names are pseudonyms) use the representational resources available to them to investigate the interaction between velocity and acceleration, especially in the context of changes in direction?

Irene created the graph in Figure 6.7 to describe the complex motion of an accelerometer on a cart. She labeled sections of her graph in several ways. First, she divided the motion into appropriate segments, identified by color and by labels. Red sections (shown by dotted lines in Figure 6.6) are those in which the slope of the segment is negative, green lines (thick lines in the figure) represent horizontal lines, and blue lines (thin lines in the figure) show segments with a positive slope. She also drew the vertical line labeled "stop, zero velocity" in red (shown in Figure 6.6 as a dotted line), presumably because she considered it a continuation of the red motion immediately before it. She was consistent in this color labeling over the course of the motion. However, the text she used to label the graph indicated that she was still

FIGURE 6.6. Irene's complex motion graph

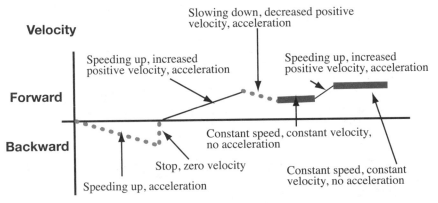

Complex Motion Velocity Over Time Graph

unsure about some of the issues. Her labeling correctly identified whether the cart was slowing down or speeding up in each interval, but she did not know how to decide when acceleration was negative and when it was positive. In addition to the comments she wrote on the graph, Irene included this text below the graph:

> I am not sure what would be negative acceleration and positive acceleration. I think that positive acceleration would denote an object that is speeding up, and negative acceleration would denote an object that is slowing down. I also believe that this holds true no matter what direction the object is traveling, but I am not positive about the conventions physicists use. If I am correct with this, then how is acceleration that takes place with negative velocity differentiated from acceleration during positive velocity? Or is it?

Because of the combination of the capabilities of PowerPoint and the inquiry culture that developed around it, Irene had to explain what she recognized as incomplete labeling on her graph. She knew that her study group's comments on her graph likely would question whether each acceleration was positive or negative, so she laid out her current hypothesis, ending with a specific question.[2]

Irene's graph was posted as part of the discussion, so others in her study group could comment on its details. The presence of the graph made a significant difference in the conversation that followed, because of the commitments Irene had to make in creating it. Her post could not have comprised either a purely textual explanation (which could not possibly contain as much detail as the graph) or an automatically created graph that she might not understand herself. Irene had to make her graph "from scratch," including drawing and labeling the axes. One representational decision she had to make was how to represent the "stop" and change in direction of the cart. Her decision to use a vertical line attracted other teachers' attention.

> *Jill:* The line I found most difficult to interpret and draw was going from motion to a stop or change of direction. I noted your line for this movement is drawn vertical up to the "x" axis. Did you see it as an immediate change in motion? I drew a slanting line because I thought the motion was a change in direction and didn't involve a stop over time. At this point I'm not sure I'm being very clear but any help is appreciated.

> *Irene:* I see the vertical line on my graph as representative of an abrupt change in direction from negative velocity to positive velocity.

Because this switch is so fast, that I feel is best represented as an immediate change, hence the vertical line. This makes sense to me because when I look at the motion of the cart as it changes velocities, I observe that it experiences a 180-degree change in acceleration! This is a substantial directional change, so I would expect it to be a very profound point on the graph. This is simply my understanding at this point, and I could very well be off track here.

The idea of a rapid directional change was problematic for other teachers in addition to Irene and Jill. In a related discussion (about a slightly different motion), Elaine posted the graph shown in Figure 6.8, with a short comment: "I think I did it! Hope it works."

Elaine used different representational conventions than Irene (see Figure 6.7). She labeled her graph segments only in terms of speed, not acceleration. Her labels included an indication of direction of the motion (the arrows) that was to some extent redundant with the location of the line segment it referred to. (The arrows that point directly up or down correctly indicate the direction of the motion, but the arrows at a slant may indicate some confusion about velocity and position.)

In response, Marie posted her graph (see Figure 6.8), accompanied by the following message:

FIGURE 6.7. Elaine's complex motion graph

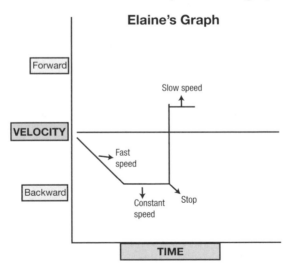

FIGURE 6.8. Marie's complex motion graph

Marie's Cart and Accelerometer Graph

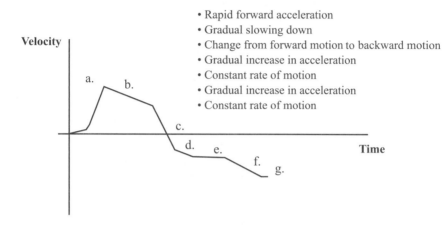

Another area I'm not sure about is the direction change of the motion. I feel somewhere there should be a graph point at 0 on the y axis, because the forward motion stopped, so there is 0 velocity. But instead, the next graph point (taken from my strobe sketch) is below the x axis.

All this being said, I gave it my best and can't wait to compare results.

Marie's graph used different conventions and showed that she had some not completely settled understanding of the representations of velocity and acceleration. She had chosen to label line segments with letters only and describe the motion in a list, so that it was necessary to go back and forth to read the graph. More important, however, was her different representation for the "change from forward motion to backward motion." In contrast to Irene and Elaine, Marie saw this change as a slanted line rather than a vertical one. She also thought there should be a point at 0 on the y axis (this likely means on the x axis, with the value of $y = 0$). Since she was working from the strobe sketch, though, she could see only snapshots of the motion and thus "missed" the turnaround point. When she posted her graph, she was still unsure how to integrate these two perspectives.

PowerPoint provided the representational resources for participants to be explicit about their models in terms of describing, graphing, and labeling the motion. The culture of the study groups included an expectation that participants would use these resources to communicate explicit models of their current hypotheses. We claim that both the representational tools and the inquiry culture were necessary to spawn and support the kinds of scientifically and mathematically rich discussions described here.

Through interactions such as these, graphs in the Investigating Physics course became objects to think with, a common representation (although this continued to be negotiated throughout the course), and the source of a common language. These roles mirror those that graphs play in professional scientific discourse, as both shapers and products of scientific community. Given the importance of graphical representations in scientific discourse, it seems obvious that online courses should make constructing and sharing images simple. Ironically, while online course materials often include fancy graphs, video, and sound, many courses limit students' contributions to text. It is time that online course designers look to the practices and artifacts of science when they attempt to create an environment that affords productive discussions.

CONCLUSION

In conclusion, we return to our design goal: to create a community that reflected the ways in which scientists (in particular, physicists) participate in the practice of science. We note how mathematical representations supported the following three aspects of doing science, in both individual and group contexts.

- Inquiry science involves questions, hands-on experimentation, observation, data, and a search for patterns. In Investigating Physics, representations served as ways to create and record data (using strobe graphs), as well as to suggest patterns. Each of the representations described earlier was used in a different way to reveal and communicate patterns. Strobe pictures required comparing distances between consecutive points, while velocity versus time graphs (primarily combinations of signature graphs) allowed participants to notice similarities between seemingly unrelated motions, such as a ball toss and a ball drop.
- Science requires communicating findings, including supporting evidence, and, therefore, assuming responsibility (at least temporarily) for a scientific claim. We have seen how participants were able to communicate their theories and findings in a variety of ways, culminating in the use of a general velocity versus time graph. The combination of the drawing and text capabilities of PowerPoint made this

kind of communication possible, as the data and theories that participants communicated could not have been presented in either a word processing program such as Word or a graph generator program such as Excel.

- Moving toward some kind of shared view of the physics of a situation would be difficult without also having a common language in which to compare different analyses of motion. Here small differences between representations may be the focus of attention and conversation—and may lead to new understandings and even controversies.

In sum, we believe that scientific communities are only as vibrant as their ability to communicate through a shared language that reflects the values of the discipline—a focus on questions, hypotheses, and explanations grounded in evidence. Such scientific languages must go beyond text to include representations that uncover the mathematical structure of the knowledge. In a face-to-face environment, creating and sharing representations is relatively simple; in an online environment, it can be a challenge, but not an insurmountable one, as we have seen here. Continuing to enhance students' ability to communicate scientifically in online environments will require online educational environment designers, course developers, and researchers to explicitly seek ways of supporting nontextual means of communication, so that students so not attempt to learn science without the tools that support the building of shared knowledge.

NOTES

1. The designation of positive and negative directions is a matter of convention, although it is more natural (and more common) to consider left to right as the positive direction since we read text and graphs left to right.

2. In fact, Irene understood many parts of the complex motion she was graphing. Her main confusion—which she identified herself—was in the interpretation of negative acceleration and positive acceleration. She posited that positive acceleration always indicates speeding up, but her generalization about positive acceleration went too far. Positive acceleration indeed means speeding up if an object is moving in a positive direction. However, if the object is moving in a negative direction, positive acceleration means slowing down. The approach physicists take (which is in fact a mathematical one) is to interpret acceleration not as slowing down or speeding up, but as a change in velocity. For example, positive acceleration is a positive change in velocity, including the case of an object's velocity going from -30 to -10 mph (i.e., going less quickly in the negative direction). Negative acceleration is a negative change in velocity, either slowing down in the positive direction (e.g., 30 mph to 10 mph) or speeding up in the negative direction (e.g., -10 mph to -30 mph).

REFERENCES

Brown, J. S., Collins, A., & Duguid, P. (1989). Situated cognition and the culture of learning. *Educational Research, 18*, 32–42.

Doubler, S., & Paget, K. (2006). Science learning and teaching: A case of online professional learning. In C. Dede (Ed.), *Online professional development for teachers* (pp. 117–135). Cambridge, MA: Harvard Education Press.

Feynman, R. (1999). *The pleasure of finding things out.* Cambridge, MA: Perseus.

Lave, J., & Wenger, E. (1991). *Situated learning: Legitimate peripheral practice.* Cambridge: Cambridge University Press.

Lehrer, R., & Schauble, L. (2006). Scientific thinking and science literacy. In W. Damon, R. Lerner, K. A. Renninger, & I. E. Sigel (Eds.), *Handbook of child psychology* (6th Ed., Vol. 4, pp. 153–196). Hoboken, NJ: Wiley.

Lemke, J. L. (1990). *Talking science: Language, learning and values.* Norwood, NJ: Ablex.

Lemke, J. L. (2004). The literacies of science. In E. Saul (Ed.), *Crossing borders in literacy and science instruction* (pp. 33–47). Newark, DE: International Reading Association.

Sheingold, K., & Doubler, S. (2003, June). What could we mean by "teaching"? In K. Sheingold (Chair), *Teaching your course or someone else's online: Does it matter?* Symposium conducted at the 2003 annual National Educational Computing Conference, Seattle, WA.

Tomasello, M. (2000). *The cultural origins of human cognition.* Cambridge, MA: Harvard University Press.

CHAPTER 7

Structuring a Virtual Conference to Facilitate Collaboration and Reflective Dialogue

Joni K. Falk, Soo-Young Lee, and Brian Drayton

Conferences are a prominent feature of professional life, providing many learning opportunities framed within a shared set of interests and goals (even if broadly defined). As the Internet has become an everyday medium for communication and information exchange, online conferences—organized, thematic group events—have become increasingly common. Within the field of educational professional development, however, little has been written about what design features contribute to effective online conferences, and the human infrastructure that contributes to success.

In this chapter, we offer lessons learned from three virtual conferences that were created for educational leaders who were engaged in the National Science Foundation's Local Systemic Change program. This program funded 90 projects, each dedicated to improving math and science education within school districts across the United States.

While all three conferences are archived on the Web,[1] we describe in detail the last conference, which incorporated the lessons learned from the previous two conferences. We include a description of the conference's design, and the scaffolding and facilitation that took place behind the scenes. We also share ways in which we tried to measure success both in terms of participation and evidence of professional learning. Finally, we draw some general lessons relating to design of such an event, the work that takes place offline to make it a reality, structures and strategies for promoting reflective discourse, and the cultivation of distributed leadership. We hope that these lessons will inform others who are experimenting with virtual conferences.

CONFERENCE CONTEXT AND COMMUNITY

The community for which our conferences were designed was cohesive and yet diverse. It was cohesive in that it consisted of the members of the 90 Local Systemic Change projects (LSCs). As mentioned briefly above, the LSCs were funded by the National Science Foundation (NSF), as 5-year efforts to affect science and mathematics instruction across entire school districts. The program envisioned that the foundation for these transformations lay in teacher professional development, based on the best research and built around inquiry-oriented curriculum materials, thus enhancing teachers' content knowledge and pedagogy in tandem. All projects were mandated to provide at least 130 hours of professional development for each participating teacher, to have systemwide reach, and to engage the school partners in the implementation of systemic reforms that would support the curriculum and teacher learning provided by the project. To a significant extent, therefore, the LSCs shared a common mission.

They were diverse, however, for obvious reasons: Each LSC was built on local partnerships, reflecting local concerns and constraints. Partnerships included researchers and professional developers, education professors and scientists, administrators and classroom teachers. Many of them deployed "teacher leaders" as part of their implementation plan, but there were many different definitions of teacher leaders and their roles. Some projects were deeply rooted in pre-existing partnerships or other joint efforts; others were starting almost from scratch to develop the local alliances and teamwork necessary to realize their vision. Finally, the LSCs were operating in a changing landscape of educational rhetoric and policy: moving from curriculum frameworks to standards, from authentic assessment to the current era of accountability, and with shifting emphases on teachers' pedagogical competence and content knowledge.

In addition, all the LSCs were mandated to develop a plan for sustainability after the time of funding. After all, if these projects were effecting systemic reform in their regions, there should be lasting traces of their work, some of which, at least, should be the result of conscious planning. Yet so absorbing was the work of the LSCs that to a great extent they found themselves moving into later phases of their funding period with no clear idea about what sustainability might mean in their case or how to work toward it.

The LSCs had been talking all along, both offline and online. For the first several years of the program, the NSF convened annual meetings of principal investigators and lead staff from the projects. In parallel, an electronic community, LSC-Net,[2] was developed, under a grant to TERC, to connect all the LSCs and provide a way to exchange news, resources, and discussion about topics of interest to some or all of the LSCs and their staffs.

Thus, this community, which had common points of reference and a diversity of voices, had a lot to talk about, and the issue of sustainability brought particular point to exchanges about many facets of the LSCs' work. Because the annual principal investigators' meetings had been discontinued, LSC-Net remained the one forum that connected all the projects. Therefore, TERC created the sustainability conferences, drawing on its experience and the resources and shared history of LSC-Net, to foster reflective, collegial exchange among the projects around the important questions and promising strategies raised by the challenge of sustainability.

THEORETICAL CONSIDERATIONS: COMMUNITY, PROFESSIONAL DEVELOPMENT, AND COMMUNITY WEB DESIGN

Our design for the conference was shaped by theory about communities as loci of professional development and about Web-based communities.

Sociocultural theorists see learning as embedded in social interactions; associations of professionals (communities of practice) are essential settings within which adult learning happens, with characteristic structures and processes (Lave, 1991, Ruopp, Gal, Drayton, & Pfister, 1993; Wenger, 1998). The scholarship on communities of practice has been seen to have important applications to formal education, with communities of practice a productive way to construe the classroom and also the professional lives of teachers. Diversity of expertise within a community that shares a professional discourse provides the materials for situated learning; this learning is mediated by the social structure of the community, including its typical communication pathways, as it provides for different levels of involvement and leadership. Indeed, some theorists see knowing and participation in community as different aspects of the same process (Wenger, 1998). The community's life and knowledge are present in many forms, including resources, methods, tools, and publications (Salomon, 1998).

Such learning occurs in transactions mediated by the creation and use of artifacts and conceptual structures that are embedded in exchanges within the community of practitioners (Brown & Duguid, 2000). These transactions may convey information, develop research instruments or work plans, accomplish tasks, clarify and elaborate shared principles or practices, or result in the creation of knowledge useful in the field (Riel & Polin, 2004). In a community such as educational researchers and practitioners, characteristics of both formal and informal learning (Lave, 1991; Scribner & Cole, 1973) are present and important, as professionals immersed in the particularities of their work seek to gain from and contribute to a body of analyzed and transferable expertise (conceptual and technical scholarship).

The development of such artifacts often involves collaboration across boundaries (put another way, collaborators from different constituencies or communities); this kind of transaction can strengthen and enrich the quality of the exchanges, but often requires adjustments and negotiations among people with different professional languages and priorities.

Conferences and meetings are events at which any or all of these transactions or negotiations can take place. In fact, an important function of such meetings is to introduce people to one another, to get conversations started, and to change people's perspective about their own work and the field at large. There is an implicit contract, an expectation, that the people you encounter at a meeting will share some points of reference, share some of the same knowledge and values, and understand the conventions of the field. Part of the expectation, however, includes the hope of being surprised by new developments—findings, methods, theories—and encountering leaders in the field who may help to crystallize or extend key ideas relevant to one's own work and the "intellectual capital" on which one can draw.

How can we fit all of this into a virtual conference for professionals engaged in education reform projects? It seems evident from the foregoing that several key elements would be important in such a conference.

1. The attendees should be drawn from one's field, but in a broad sense. That is, there should be many people who share your specific interests and concerns, some who have overlapping interests, but bring other tangential agendas and expertise based on work in parallel fields. The broad construal of the community will affect the potential richness of the exchanges and reflect the complexity of work embedded in overlapping subcommittees.

2. The conference technology should enable attendees to know who is present and to find out something about those people, building relationships as a necessary context for substantive and critical exchange. This is one aspect of "sociability" as articulated by Preece (2000).

3. The conference should be shaped and facilitated to elicit and support intellectual exchange in many modes, reflecting a broad view of professional learning. Substantive presentations will provide the foundation for dialogue, but the format and program should stimulate response and exchange, not only between presenters and attendees, but among attendees as well.

4. The conference technology should provide a variety of formats for the exchange of ideas and conceive of both formal (prepared) and informal (emergent) contributions as valued products of the experience. This means that conference design includes the medium (in this

case, the Web site), program (schedule, format, list of invitees), and leadership and facilitation (by project staff and by participants).

In the rest of this chapter, we describe and analyze how these elements shaped the design of our Virtual Conference on Sustainability 2003, and how this design fostered a successful, 10-day reflective exchange in a diverse community whose members shared both intellectual interests and related, practical, time-sensitive work in education reform.

Conference Design

Length

The virtual conference was a 10-day event. The duration was an important design decision and was dictated by our intent to provide a range of content, produced both by participants and by special invitees, that would stimulate (and indeed demand) reflective reading and consequent dialogue. With most of the content presented in text form (augmented by some audio), attending the conference required time for attentive reading. Since part of the value of the virtual format is that it does not require travel and other dislocations of routine, the extended period of the conference enabled attendees to set aside dedicated periods during the conference to read the postings and reply to threads of interest. It was important for the staff to encourage participants ahead of time to schedule time to visit the site regularly to see new developments; other techniques (described later) alerted attendees to new developments that related to their interests.

Use of a Design Metaphor

The design of the site[3] was constructed using the metaphor of a traditional conference, in order to give the first-time virtual participants a frame of reference about the activities that they could expect to encounter. In a traditional conference, participants typically hear keynote speakers, attend panel sessions, visit poster sessions, have informal discussions with colleagues, and collect resources of interest. The virtual conference built on these expectations, creating visual representations for the keynote, for panels, for a poster hall, for a lounge (to facilitate informal exchange), for the discussants for a resource center, and for an info center. The home page provided daily updates to the conference, directed participants to highlights, and provided a conference schedule. An interactive map appeared on the site (see Figure 7.1). Its purpose was to convey the feeling that the conference was an interactive

FIGURE 7.1. Interactive map of the third Sustainability Virtual Conference

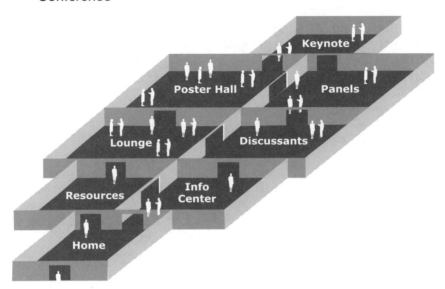

event, through which participants could move easily from one area to another. Photos, audio, and video were integrated to add visual cues, intimacy, and personality to large amounts of textual material. Visual cues and instant messaging helped make individual participants aware that they were a part of a group event.

Asynchronous Communication

The conference relied heavily on asynchronous communication. As described later, the keynote addresses, panels, and poster presentations each had associated threaded discussions that could be sorted by date, presenter, or thread.

Asynchronous communication enabled participants to communicate when it was most convenient for them, and across different time zones. This feature of the site very likely enhanced participation rates and the quality of participation, as people could attend the conference at any time of the day or night. With the discussions preserving the conversations as they unfolded, it was easy to catch up with multiple exchanges on multiple areas of the site, but the asynchronous pace allowed time to think.

Synchronous interactions were possible, but were limited primarily to private messages sent through an instant messaging facility. In addition, however, in the poster hall, an icon informed visitors when a poster presenter was online, and the presenter also could alert visitors to the next time he or she would be present "in person." Thus, although discourse with the presenter was technically asynchronous, the poster hall combined elements of synchronous and asynchronous communication.

Conference Formats

Keynote

Each year, we invited an expert in education reform (Larry Cuban in 2001, Michael Fullan in 2002, Deborah Loewenberg Ball in 2003) to address critical issues in current systemic reform. Keynote speakers presented a short paper along with a short audio introduction. In 2003, we included a video clip as part of the keynote address, and Deborah Loewenberg Ball facilitated a discussion with participants about segments of the video.

Interactive Poster Hall

The interactive poster hall was developed by TERC to simulate the experience that participants have when attending a poster session at a traditional conference. Participants were able to browse through a hall of posters, locate those that were of greatest interest to them, and then engage the presenter in a discussion. In order to actively communicate this metaphor, we created a Flash movie (http://sustainability2003.terc.edu/do.cfm/site/posterhall_movie) introduction that portrayed typical actions that occur at a poster session and introduced the icons used within the virtual environment. Figure 7.2 is one frame of the movie.

Over the 3 years of conferences, 63 posters were presented (from 63 individual LSC projects, thus representing the majority of the projects in the program). The poster hall became more sophisticated with each year's conference, and its development can be seen by looking at the three different conferences in chronological order.

Each poster included:

- Reflections on the project's original vision.
- Reflections from the end of the project, including promoters and inhibitors of sustainability.
- Lessons learned that would inform projects just starting out.
- Questions that the presenter would like to address to visitors.

As mentioned above, in 2003 the poster hall included an icon (silhouette behind poster) that would appear to inform the users when the presenter

FIGURE 7.2. Flash movie, "Introduction of Poster Hall"

of the poster was online. This allowed the users to know when they were likely to receive an immediate reply to a comment or query. This display is indicated in the screen shot in Figure 7.3.

Panel Discussion

Each conference featured three to four panel discussions (e.g., teacher leadership, role of superintendents). Panels had three to five members who each stated their position in a text document and (in 2003) an audio statement. The panelists seeded the discussion by first addressing the issues raised with one another and then opening the discussion up to all conference participants.

Discussants' Reflection

Four experts in the field were invited to discuss and comment on the posters presented and the conference overall. Discussants both stimulated conversation and synthesized and reflected on the conference as a whole. They visited each poster and engaged in a dialogue with poster presenters and visitors.

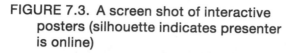

FIGURE 7.3. A screen shot of interactive posters (silhouette indicates presenter is online)

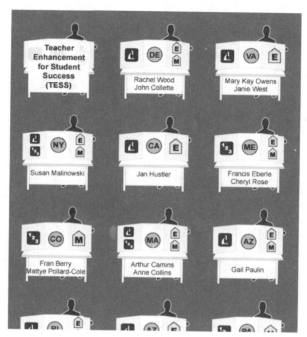

Toward the end of the conference, discussants presented reflections on the conference, and those reflections were associated with a threaded discussion that continued during the last few days of the conference.

Resources

The resource center provided research papers, reports from the fields, and other resources pertaining to science and mathematics systemic reform that were cited in presentations. This area provided links to previous conference contents as well.

Lounge

The lounge, which was created for the 2003 conference, provided a place for participants to have an open discussion on topics not addressed elsewhere within the conference. The lounge also provided a place where participants could find other colleagues who were online at the same time and could send private, instant messages.

Info Center

The info center provided a help desk, where participants could receive general information regarding the conference, technical support, a list of registrants' contact information, and FAQs.

What Worked, and Why?

In this section, we examine the success of the 2003 conference using three points of view: the extent and depth of activity across the site, attendees' comments on the value derived, and qualitative evidence of reflective exchange.

Extent and Depth of Activity Across the Site

The sustainability site software allowed us to track site activity in various ways. In this section, we look at measures: session counts, several page-views, and posting behavior. A *session* is defined as the period from when a participant logs in to when s/he logs out or has been inactive for 20 minutes. If an area is visited multiple times within a given session, it still counts as only one session. A *page-view* is recorded when a person clicks on a page within the site. Thus, it is a rough estimate of the extent (depth within a section, or breadth across the site) to which a user has penetrated an area.

Posting behavior (e.g., frequency of posting) gives yet a different view of activity. As in a live conference, only a portion of the attendees make presentations or converse with presenters of talks and posters. Much of the value of conference attendance comes from hearing and seeing what is presented or displayed. Therefore, it is to be expected that posting will be less frequent than visiting and should not be seen as the key criterion of activity. Yet it does reflect *inter*activity, and in an online setting any post to a discussion or other part of the site adds to the content being created by the community.

The conference invitation was extended to a closed community consisting of 800 affiliated staff working on the LSC projects. Of these, 354 registered for the conference. It was possible to visit the site and have read-only access to the posted content, but logging in enabled registrants to participate interactively, posting to discussions and using site tools to contact other attendees. Of the registrants, 237 (66%) logged in during the conference.

During the 10-day period, the conference received a total (members and guests) of 59,093 page-views and 2,286 sessions. Logged-in members returned to the site an average of 5.7 times during the 10 days and accounted for 36,924 page-views and 1,353 sessions (with an average of 27.29 page-views per session). In addition to logged-in members, 421 guests visited the site; some of them may have been attendees who chose not to log in. Some of these guests returned to the site multiple times; there were 933 guest sessions in total and 22,169 guest page-views (23.76 page-views per session).

It is interesting to note that since the conference ended, the archive of the site (without interactive functionality) continues to receive activity. For example, during the 22-month period between May 2003 and March 2005, the site received 69,705 page-views and 9,644 sessions. Hence, the content created for and during the conference continues to have usefulness even long after the event.

Figure 7.4 displays the number of sessions in which each section of the conference was accessed. As expected, the home page was accessed in the most sessions. The keynote, panels, and discussants' reflection pages followed. The poster hall appears to have been accessed during fewer sessions, and the lounge, info center, and resources were accessed the least.

The page-view count, however, shows a different profile of use (see Figure 7.5). Although the keynote, panels, and discussants' reflections showed a greater number of sessions, the poster hall had the greatest number of page-views. Thus, once people entered the poster hall, they explored longer and

FIGURE 7.4. Session counts by area (N = 7,097)

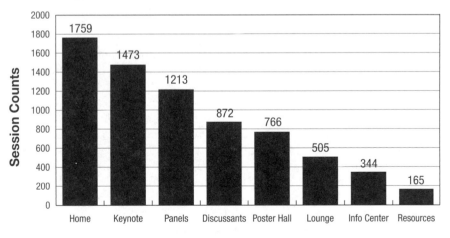

FIGURE 7.5. Page-view count by area (N = 36,924)

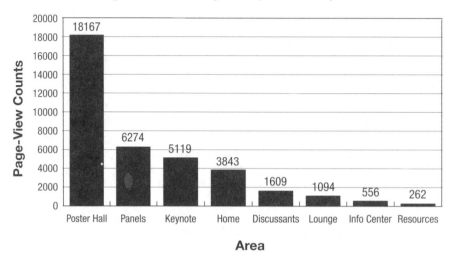

at greater depth. This can be attributed to the fact that the poster hall had a very large amount of material compared with other sections of the site.

Participants were able to contribute during the conference by posting their thoughts in response to the keynote address, the poster presenters, the panel discussions, or the discussants' reflections. Over the course of the conference, 82 of the 237 logged-in participants (34.6%) posted at least one message. Furthermore, most of these 82 participants posted several times and thus made a substantial contribution to the conference content: On average, people who posted contributed an average of 6.8 messages, which yielded 559 posts.

Where did they post? The graph in Figure 7.6 shows that people were most likely to post in the poster hall, even though the keynote was visited more frequently during a given session. This may be due to the diversity of topics addressed within the poster hall. Also, the poster hall conveyed the sense of colleagues conversing with one another, and this may have felt less intimidating than conversing with the keynote speaker.

A follow-up questionnaire explored why participants who had logged in chose not to post; 49 participants responded, and their answers are summarized in Figure 7.7. Time was the most frequently reported answer. The messages that were posted tended to be quite long and well thought out. For example, the messages posted in the keynote discussion ranged in length up to 646 words, with a mean length of 140 words. Composing this kind of message required time to think, reflect, and organize ideas after reading others' messages; it also may have added to the disincentive of time limitation

FIGURE 7.6. Number of messages posted by area (N = 559)

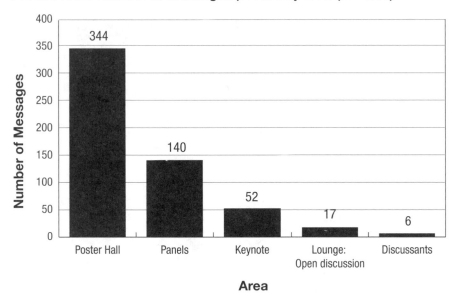

for some people, since long, carefully composed posts may have set a tone or expectation that some may not have felt free to fulfill.

Attendees' Comments on the Value Derived

The postconference questionnaire showed that most participants enjoyed the conference, considering it a useful professional development experience (see Figure 7.8). A high proportion (96%) intended to share the site with colleagues, and to visit the site for reference in the future (89%); this jibes with the postconference usage referred to earlier. In a follow-up question, to which 93 participants responded, 86 (93%) agreed that the conference was a form of professional development for them, because it provided "excellent resources," "new ideas," and "knowledge," and that they were able to learn from others engaged in similar projects. It allowed them to see that other leaders had encountered similar challenges, struggles, and obstacles. Some respondents suggested that it was professional development because it offered them the time to reflect on their work. Still others reported that it made them feel more connected to colleagues and experts in the field.

Comparison with "traditional" conference format. In the postconference survey, participants were asked to describe the advantages and disadvantages

FIGURE 7.7. Reasons offered for not posting

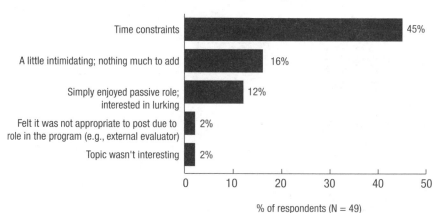

% of respondents (N = 49)

of a virtual conference in comparison with a traditional one. The most frequently cited advantage was that a virtual conference provided flexibility and could be accessed from a distance at different times of day or night. In addition to this added flexibility, the virtual format eliminated the need to choose which sessions to attend: Participant could see it all, at a manageable pace. Furthermore, this relaxation of the constraints of time and space, which shape an individual's navigation of a face-to-face conference, also applies to the

FIGURE 7.8. Reactions to participation

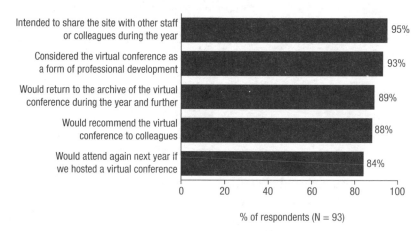

% of respondents (N = 93)

presenters, with the result that more participants can have more access to conversation with leaders in the field. The graph in Figure 7.9 summarizes the advantages reported by participants.

In spite of the above benefits of the virtual conference, participants felt that virtual conferences also had significant drawbacks in comparison with a traditional conference (see Figure 7.10). The major issues mentioned are: (1) the time delay in communication that is primarily by correspondence, which lacks the dynamic of a face-to-face exchange; (2) the much reduced opportunity for serendipitous encounters; and (3) the loss of the focus that results from physically being at a conference, away from quotidian duties and schedules. A comparison between the advantages and disadvantages suggests that the two formats present attendees with trade-offs whose cost/benefit balance may shift depending on many personal factors.

Evidence of Reflective Exchange

Another measure that contributes to our evaluation of the conference's success is whether it engendered reflective discourse. We bring examples here from the poster hall, from the panels, and from the discussants' reflections.

FIGURE 7.9. Advantages of a virtual conference

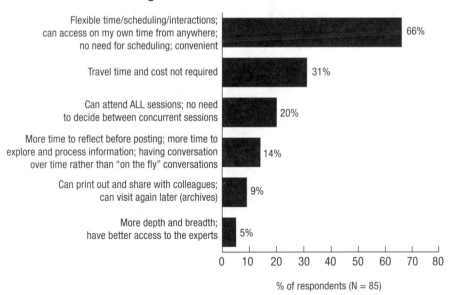

% of respondents (N = 85)

FIGURE 7.10. Disadvantages of a virtual conference

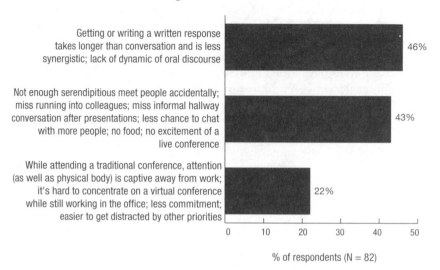

% of respondents (N = 82)

Poster Hall

The poster hall elicited reflective discourse in two important ways: the development of the posters themselves, and the discussion of the posters during the conference. Before elaborating on each of these points, we should point out that members of this community had rarely had an opportunity to tell anything like the full story of their projects or to hear others' stories. The principal investigators' meetings certainly had brought forward interesting cases, but since these meetings happened early in the LSC program, projects had not matured to the point that initial plans could be evaluated for strengths and weaknesses, nor could the likely outcomes be examined for various kinds of impact. By focusing each year on projects coming to the end of funding, the conference presented full accounts, including both retrospect and prospect. These accounts were timely for the community, because there were later cohorts of grantees that could profit from the experience of each year's presenters. Thus, these reflections had direct value to colleagues still shaping their work, while also providing valuable insights about many aspects of systemic reform, useful for future work.

The posters as reflective artifacts. In order to facilitate the presentation of posters, and also the analysis of them for research purposes, TERC designed a simple, standard format for the posters. Each one needed to first state the project's original goals, and then provide reflections on how the project developed over time and the successes and challenges encountered. The third section was "suggestions for other projects," and the final section was to offer questions for discussion with visitors to the posters. This format elicited not just descriptions of project activities, but contextual information essential for others to interpret the projects' findings. The posters also demanded that the presenters critique their own work and invited further dialogue with colleagues.

The first section, in which the project's goals were set forth, also provided rich contextual information about the specific challenges and conditions in which the project operated. For example, one poster noted:

> What distinguishes [this project] from most other LSCs, however, is that we had to make [our program] happen simultaneously in 40 small, rural school districts scattered across about 40,000 square miles in Missouri and Iowa. Much like the strategy devised by small-scale farmers in the Midwest almost a century ago and still used today, we developed a "cooperative" plan in which the small districts could join forces and through which our project staff could effectively and economically provide services.

The section on reflections was notable because in almost all the posters, presenters described both successes and challenges, difficulties, and failures in aspects of their projects. In the poster quoted above, the presenter addressed the challenge that caused the most difficulty in implementation and required a significant alteration in project tactics. Changes in leadership and funding at the district level have multiple effects on a long-term project such as this LSC, as they shape whether teachers feel free and encouraged to take part; this project has had trouble keeping teachers involved as envisioned. The project intends to negotiate more explicit commitments, which fit into existing district structures.

> Our biggest challenge to date has been dealing with changing school district administrations and shrinking district budgets. The generally accepted premise that lasting, systemic curricular reform takes 3–5 years or more does not adequately account for the fact that school districts often change superintendents more frequently. Considering that the initial plans for our project were laid 2 years before our official start, about half of the superintendents who signed on 5 years ago and agreed to support the systemic effort are no longer in the control room. . . .

The problem of superintendent turnover and shrinking budgets are problems enough of their own, but they also make it difficult to involve in the reform efforts the teachers who don't have a primary responsibility to teach science. In a reform targeting the pre-K–6 science curriculum, the involvement of all certified staff in a building is critical because the curricular areas and teaching strategies are so tightly interwoven. . . . The truly effective way to bring everyone on board is to get the full backing of the administration, starting with the superintendent, and to make the science reform a major part of the contract-time professional development—as would be done in an adoption of a new reading or math program. This contract-time strategy is where we plan to focus in our last 2 years of the project.

That there would be surprises, miscalculations, setbacks, or roadblocks in such large, complex projects would be expected a priori, but there is an understandable reluctance to tell such stories, especially when the audience includes funders and colleagues who also may be competitors. The willingness of participants to discuss challenges and failures was an important contribution of the conference, because such openness is rare, yet essential if colleagues are going to learn from each other's experiences and build on the knowledge of the field.

The desire of the presenters to be helpful to their peers, and to examine their experience for lessons learned, was facilitated by the TERC staff behind the scenes in two important ways. The first was the design of the poster itself, which embodied a presumption that both positive and negative stories were a necessary part of the whole account of any project. The second, however, was the staff's discussion with poster presenters during the time the posters were being prepared. The staff read each poster to see whether all the elements deemed important for rich exchange were present, and if some aspects of a presentation seemed underdeveloped (e.g., the "challenges"), they raised questions with the presenters, who then would revise their posters.

These negotiations, and the poster preparation, took place in a context of trust and mutual respect, and it is this quality, embedded in LSC-Net as well as the sustainability conference itself, which enabled the free exchange that resulted. This atmosphere of trust was the product of 3 years of collaboration between TERC/LSC-Net staff and the LSC community. This cultural element, in turn, shaped the access control features of the site, which helped ensure that everyone coming to the conference know "who was in the room," and knew that they were colleagues facing kindred issues. The poster presentation set the stage for the discussion, by which the community carried the reflection forward. Unlike a face-to-face poster hall event, the virtual poster hall offered the opportunity for participants not only to converse with the presenter, but also to engage in asynchronous conversations with other participants who had visited the poster earlier in the 10-day event.

Reflective exchange in the poster discussion. While the exchanges at many of the posters were requests for amplification or clarification, some stimulated extended conversations on topics raised on the posters—or on topics emerging from the interests of the visitors. The poster format required the presenter to pose a question for visitors to discuss. For example, the presenter of the poster quoted above posed the following question:

> Science experts, whether paid or volunteer, who are not accustomed to working with teachers (especially elementary teachers), have a difficult time making their science relevant and comprehensible at workshops or in special presentations despite their best intentions to do so. What strategies have you used to prepare science experts to work with teachers in your enhancement projects?

The question, on how to integrate science experts into the elementary school setting, had not otherwise been addressed in the poster. It formed the center of a long series of messages, 17 posts from nine different people. The visitors' posts touched on ways to help scientists understand how inquiry pedagogy looks in elementary school, the use of memos of understanding to shape the scientist–school partnership, and how classroom exchanges (teachers to the scientists' classrooms as well as the other way around) could help bridge the cultural differences and build a sense of real collaboration. Hence, the poster served as a stimulus for broader discussion and dialogue among community members. The interactions elicited new material from both presenter and visitors, and the material was both conceptual and practical—the mix that nourishes the working professional.

When we examined the discussions that attended each poster, we found that some were more vibrant and reflective than others. Although conversation flowed not only between visitor and presenter but also between visitors who had left comments, it was clear that the poster presenter played a significant role in facilitating the discussions. Figure 7.11 indicates that in most cases the poster presenter was active and responded frequently to comments and queries. The number of posts ranged from 6 to 25 with a mean of 15. Overall, presenters supplied approximately 55% of the posts in the discussions.

Panelists

Panels provided another format that successfully prompted reflective discussions. These panels differed in format from most conference panel discussions,

FIGURE 7.11. Presenter posts in poster hall

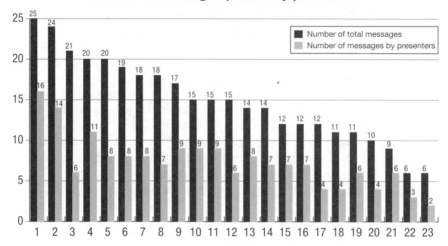

**Number of total messages versus
number of messages posted by presenters**

since the panel members were tasked with raising questions on their specific theme in an opening sentence, and setting them in context to help the participants join an exploration, rather than presenting full accounts of their own ideas on the subject.

The panel topics were chosen by TERC staff, on the basis of conversations with LSC members over the preceding months. During these conversations, we also sought suggestions for panel members from within the LSCs, and this proved to make an important contribution to the success of this part of the conference, as it enabled a range of voices to step forward in leadership roles within the community.

In the 2003 conference, one of the three panels addressed "teacher leadership." The identification, training, and deployment of teacher leaders were a central feature in the strategies of many of the LSCs. There was a robust literature by leaders in the field on various models of teacher leadership, but rather than recruit such leaders to present to the conference, we constituted a panel composed of five teacher leaders from within the LSCs. These thoughtful panelists posed the following challenges to the community:

1. How can the transition from teacher to teacher leader be made smoother and more effective?
2. How have teacher leaders dealt with competing curricular demands and competing reforms such as high-stakes tests, which sometimes divert teachers' attention away from the goals of the reform?

3. How have teacher leaders monitored and assessed teacher growth? What data are most useful to collect?
4. How have teacher leaders dealt with teacher resistance?
5. How have LSCs managed to sustain their teacher leadership model after the grant funding has ended?

These questions, and the brief presentations by the panelists, stimulated a remarkably wide-ranging conversation, 66 posts long, involving 17 different participants. While some of the posts began as simple responses to the prompts, they rarely were straightforward, factual replies. Each person answering had to reflect to some degree on the context out of which she was answering, and her interpretation of the essential elements of the questions. Thus, the variations in ideas and implementation within the LSC community were brought forward, enabling some of the negotiation of meaning that characterizes a vibrant professional community.

Second, the teacher leadership panel was not an abstract exploration of the meaning of teacher leadership. The panelists' opening statements and the participants' responses were grounded in their own experience of teacher leadership. As a result, they naturally related their experiences as teacher-leaders to specific topics of concern to them, such as teacher collaboration, Japanese Lesson Study, the intersection of science and the rest of the curriculum, the use of graphical organizers, contending with high-stakes testing, and systemic reform. In the exchange below, we see that teacher leaders use this discussion to explore pragmatic issues they are facing. One participant wrote:

> It is widely accepted that teachers in changing their pedagogy require time and opportunity for reflection. This is often best facilitated when there are people who facilitate, support, [and] encourage this kind of thinking and discussion. This translates into SPACE in the schedule, PEOPLE like teacher leaders or department chairs or somebody to help keep the process rolling—and SPACE and PEOPLE translate into MONEY. From an administrative point of view, all of these are reflective of a VISION. So how successful have your districts been in negotiating to preserve this vision, even when new "competing initiatives" must be accommodated?

This brought forth a trenchant reply:

> The $64,000 question! All this translates into money, money that is being cut from our budgets at an alarming rate. I know our program is in the current budget proposal, as our value has been proven in our district, BUT it remains to be seen if the school board will pass it.

One of the ways we are negotiating to preserve this vision is by integrating our initiative with the "competing initiatives" that are vying for the same shrinking funds. As our state moves toward standards-based education, we feel we have a foot in the door with our professional development program. By presenting this to our school board curriculum committee, along with our progress in improving student learning, has given us a slight edge in keeping us in the budget for the upcoming year.

Exchanges like these are not often thought of as professional development, yet the issues of school culture and governance that are addressed exemplify real-world conditions and competing values, which professionals must understand and take into consideration.

In another thread, the teacher leadership theme led into a pragmatic exchange of craft knowledge. One project had addressed the competition for time in the curriculum between science and literacy that the state testing regime had created by developing a science strand in the literacy program. One responder affirms this strategy and describes in succinct terms both the challenges they face and tactics they are adopting. The response also reveals a key aspect of this project's understanding of teacher leadership: It is exercised in part by exemplifying innovations in practice.

Sounds like ideas we're trying! We do see progress—slow progress—and yet most teachers agree they need to address more than one content area at a time. . . . We hope to work on those issues this summer with a group of teacher leaders, grades K–5. Our goal is to have about 20–25 teachers work for 3 days investigating writing and math opportunities that are either embedded in the science or linked to the science. Then, those teachers will have the background to support their colleagues at their schools as they dig deeper into integration.

Discussants

Some conferences, such as the American Educational Research Association (AERA), arrange to have scholars serve as discussants for specific sessions, for example on responding to a set of papers. We employed a different model for the sustainability conference, in which the discussants provided stimulus throughout the period and across all conference events. They were asked to bear in mind the goal of fostering discussion and exchange. In this role, they had a subtle influence on the content and tone of the conference.

Towards the end of the conference, they posted a page or two of reflections in response to the conference. Their contributions brought an otherwise rare element into the community's discussion, because they were the comments of experts learning about the LSCs for the first time, from the LSCs themselves, at a time when there was little or no knowledge of them outside the program, since research on the projects and the program was still in process.

One discussant begins his remarks with a reflection on the value and impact of the LSC program as a whole:

> What comes through most clearly is that the LSC program is working; that is, it's doing what it was intended to do: to increase the amount of materials-based, "inquiry" science in classrooms, mainly through the infusion of funds to provide extensive professional development and the use of the newer (mostly) nontextbook curriculum materials. I think it's no small accomplishment to provide professional development for hundreds of teachers in an organized way; to develop systems for acquiring, distributing, and refurbishing science materials; and to get busy teachers, under enormous pressure to improve literacy, to devote precious time to actually have science happen in their classrooms. You've all managed this, and it's a tremendous achievement. Not every NSF-sponsored program can make this claim.

Beyond this, however, the discussants each brought their own viewpoints to bear. One discussant whose research focuses on teacher professional knowledge posted 4 questions that she thought were important for the LSC community to consider:

> I'd like to raise four issues for our collective consideration, based on the reflections you have stimulated in me:
>
> 1. Broadening our conception of "practice"
> 2. Rethinking the role of critique, dissent, and resistance in learning and change
> 3. Using the connections between curriculum and instructional improvement
> 4. Attending to equity and the teaching and learning of mathematics and science

In her comments, she both offers her own ideas on the topics she introduces, and also incorporates her responses to other discussants' reflections. She and the other discussants thus exemplified the scholarly tone and collegial discourse that the conference sought to foster. They set a tone that encouraged the participants to reflect at several levels: first, on feedback that they had received on their own presentations; second, on the ideas and questions emerging during the discussions and presentations; and finally, a sort of metacognitive reflection on the accomplishments and open questions of the LSC program as a whole and of the systemic reform enterprise of which the LSCs were one example.

LESSONS LEARNED

Putting together a virtual conference requires a combination of envisioning content to be shared (e.g., assessing teacher content knowledge), formats (e.g., poster hall) that will facilitate that sharing, and the tools that will enable these formats (e.g., audio, threaded discussion). In addition, it is about working closely with community and scaffolding the experience that the participants will have. Much of this work happens before the conference begins and it affects the layout of the site, the schedule of events, and the content that eventually appears. Another tier of scaffolding happens during the conference. This scaffolding welcomes and orients the participant, ensures the continuation of discussions, highlights interesting events, and provides syntheses of topics discussed. In this discussion, we revisit some of the behind-the-scenes work that contributed to the conference's success.

Contextualization Within a Community

The participants all had some common background (participating in a Local Systemic Change project) and all shared some common goals and challenges. They knew, even before the conference began, that they could learn from one another's experience. Some community members knew one another, whereas many others did not, but the majority had been within shouting distance of one another at NSF-sponsored conferences, and all had been engaged in a year-long electronic community built for this constituency.

Of the 237 participants, 56 were engaged in thinking about, preparing for, or contributing to the conference before it began. These 56 people included keynote speakers, panelists, poster presenters, as well as discussants. In preconference communications with each of these groups, TERC organizers requested their support in providing leadership within the conference through interactive participation beyond their individual poster or presentation. The data support that individuals involved in preconference planning felt increased ownership and responsibility. They were indeed more likely than other participants to post, and they did so in all conference areas, not only in the one in which they were presenting a panel or paper. These leaders represent 24% of logged-in participants, and yet they posted more than 65% of messages during the conference.

While online leadership may emerge spontaneously, our experience suggests that work needs to be done behind the scenes to encourage this leadership to emerge.

Program Design

In the planning of a face-to-face conference for educators, pedagogical values often influence organizers' decisions as to content, logistics, and timing. For example, an organizer might consider the proportion of time given to lecture versus breakout sessions, where discussions are more likely to take place. S/he will take care to plan how to introduce each day's session, decide how long to make breaks, gauge appropriate time for questions following lectures, and decide whether sessions should have moderators or discussants. Each of these decisions will have an impact on the participants' experience.

Many of these decisions, at first glance, do not seem relevant in the virtual environment. For example, people will take breaks when it suits them and will join in the conference when they have time. Discussions, following a keynote address, can continue over a period of days and therefore do not need to be carefully scheduled to the minute. Nonetheless, the virtual environment requires just as much (if not more) planning and scaffolding of the users' experience.

Without the benefit of traditional conference welcome speeches, plenary events, or face-to-face interactions, the virtual conference organizer needs to consider how people will be oriented to the conference, how they will be welcomed and recognized, and how they will understand what is expected of themselves and others. While the asynchronous virtual environment creates a greater degree of freedom for participants, as they do not need to choose between conflicting sessions, they still need a clear understanding of how the conference will unfold. Participants need to know what to expect on each day of the conference, what will change and what will remain, timelines for participation, as well as clear expectations for synthesis and closure. These parameters, when carefully set, allow the user to know when to return to a panel or discussion and when to assume that the event is over.

This scaffolding of the user's experience is at least as important as the formats (text, audio, video, threaded discussion) employed. In the sustainability conference, orienting information was provided to the user through three channels.

- *Daily schedule:* The daily schedule allowed people to see at a glance what was available as well as what would be coming soon. In brief, on day 1 the keynote and poster hall commenced. On day 4, the second keynote and the panels began. On day 7, discussants offered reflections. On day 10, the conference ended.
- *Changing home page:* The home page explained what types of activities were being offered, and directed participants' attention to hot topics and events.
- *Personal introductions:* TERC staff welcomed new participants to the conference through an instant message, acknowledging their presence, and offered technical support if needed.

Orienting and welcoming the user is still only the beginning of scaffolding the conference attendees' experience. As we planned the conference, we thought about which formats (e.g., the poster hall) would require multiple visits, and how to encourage participants to return to areas that they had already visited to read new posts as the discussions progressed. Further, it was important to have many voices from inside the community (panelists) as well as some new expert voices from outside (keynotes). Lastly, it was critical to assign the role of discussant to experts who could reflect on the experience as a whole, point out highlights, and provide closure.

The Interaction Between Technical Formats and Behind-the-Scenes Facilitation

Formats such as the keynotes, panels, or poster hall are each created by combining elements such as text, video, audio, and a threaded discussion. These tools are easily available to a developer. However, successful interaction with each of these formats is largely dependent on facilitation that is mostly invisible to the user. This entails significant preparation with presenters before the conference, as well as a good deal of facilitation during the conference event.

Offering a virtual keynote address creates interesting challenges for the presenter as well as for the user. In this instance, the keynote was not videotaped, but rather was presented in text format, accompanied by the presenter's photo and an audio introduction.

Speakers were unsure what a "written keynote" should look like. Although in text form, it needed to be more interactive and friendly than a journal paper. The length and level of detail needed to be crafted more like a talk than an academic presentation. Achieving this new tone of voice in written format often requires editing in terms of format and length. In 2003, the decision was made by the presenter and organizers to divide a long keynote into two shorter addresses. The first part was introduced on day 1, the second part on day 4 (while leaving part 1 still available to those who logged into the conference midstream).

Poster hall submissions all addressed four major topics: the original project vision, reflections on what promoted or inhibited that vision from being realized, lessons for new projects, and questions that the presenters would like visitors to address. This common format gave very different projects the ability to address some of the same issues, and allowed for comparisons to be drawn in terms of challenges and strategies. Not surprisingly, some of the poster presenters at first submitted posters where successes were mentioned but inhibitors were not. During an edit and review process, organizers contacted the presenters and encouraged them to revise their posters to include the obstacles and challenges that they encountered. A sense of trust in the community and gentle prodding from organizers allowed presenters to share their obstacles. This resulted in posters that were far richer and more captivating to visitors. Participants expressed that they were gratified to see that they were "not alone" and that others were grappling with similar issues.

Panel topics were chosen to address key issues that this community of educational leaders were grappling with. The most active panel ended up being one on teacher leadership. The panelists for this discussion were five teacher leaders who were nominated by their projects. In past virtual conferences teachers were reticent to post, in comparison with superintendents, principals, evaluators, and principal investigators. However, asking these five teacher leaders to become panelists changed this dynamic and empowered many other teachers to actively join the conversation.

Each teacher leader introduced the subject with a short audio presentation. This audio was taped over a phone line, and panelists were carefully coached to make sure they all used a common format. The panelists introduced themselves, spoke of the two key issues they hoped to discuss, and then offered some sort of invitation for people to join in.

Discussants (who were preselected and given a stipend for their efforts) helped to pepper the discussions with interesting insights. Finally, toward the end of the conference (day 7), each of the four discussants offered summary comments. These comments addressed themes that they observed in the panel and keynote discussions as well as in the poster presentations. These expert comments brought some syntheses and reflection to the conference as a whole.

Finally, as we enumerate the conference elements that enabled reflective professional discourse, we must note the participants themselves. We designed the conference, and keynote speakers, panelists, discussants, and presenters helped to facilitate it, but it is the practitioners in the community that serve as each other's most important resource.

Our aim of creating a multivocal, democratic, and interactive experience around key questions of practice drove our thinking about the design of the site, the conference program, and the work of facilitating each type of participation. This study serves as a starting point to expand our understanding of online communities of practice, including similarities and differences in the ways people interact in the online and offline environment, the advantages and limitations of online interaction compared with face-to-face interaction in a knowledge-building community, and the design features that can promote desired interactions and overcome limitations of current reflective discourse within an online environment.

NOTES

1. http//sustainability2003.terc.edu, http//sustainability2002.terc.edu, http//sustainability.terc.edu
2. www.lsc-net.terc.edu
3. The sustainability virtual conference software was developed by TERC in Cold Fusion using a PostgreSQL database that operated on a Linux server. End users accessed the Web site through common Web browsers on either Macs or PCs. Certain multimedia elements incorporated Macromedia Flash. A sophisticated "back-end" administrative area allowed researchers to track individuals' activity on the site.

REFERENCES

Brown, J. S., & Duguid, P. (2000). *The social life of information*. Boston: Harvard Business School Press.

Lave, J. (1991). Situating learning in communities of practice. In L. B. Resnick, J. M. Levine, & S. D. Teasley (Eds.), *Perspectives on socially shared cognition* (pp. 63–82). Washington, DC: American Psychological Association.

Preece, J. (2000). *Online communities: Designing usability, supporting sociability*. Chichester, UK: Wiley.

Riel, M., & Polin, X. (2004). In S. A. Barab, R. Kling, & J. H. Gray (Eds.), *Designing virtual communities in the service of learning* (pp. XX–YY). New York: Cambridge University Press.

Ruopp, R., Gal, S., Drayton, B., & Pfister, M. (Eds.). (1993). *Labnet: Toward a community of practice*. Hillsdale, NJ: Erlbaum.

Salomon, G. (1998). *Distributed cognitions: Psychological and educational considerations*. New York: Cambridge University Press.

Scribner, S., & Cole, M. (1973). Cognitive consequences of formal and informal education: New accommodations are needed between school-based learning and learning experiences of everyday life. *Science, 182,* 553–559.

Wenger, E. (1998). *Communities of practice: Learning, meaning, and identity*. Cambridge & Cambridge: Cambridge University Press.

Epilogue

Brian Drayton, Jon Obuchowski, and Joni K. Falk

The chapters in this book have explored a multitude of approaches to professional learning within online community environments, each of them consistent with a view of learning as a socially conditioned (or even regulated) construction of knowledge, contextualized by the learner's purposes and needs, and available resources. It has been shown that the designers and vision-keepers of these spaces play an indispensable role throughout the life span of these communities—even while the inhabitants/users/learners of the spaces collaborate in the creative work, so that they are in a significant way co-authors of their professional learning environment.

In this concluding chapter, we reflect upon four themes, emerging from these studies, that seem to us of particular interest for scholars and for designers of electronic communities: (1) the human infrastructure; (2) types of success; (3) theory and the theorizing of community; and (4) the future of professional learning communities.

THE HUMAN INFRASTRUCTURE

This book had its genesis in conversations about the human dynamics in the working of electronic communities for professional development. While much has been written about the design of such communities, and about the facilitation of online forums, important parts of the story had not yet been told. These chapters have demonstrated the many ways that the designers of these projects must continue to work purposefully behind the scenes, acting on the basis of their vision of professional learning. Long after the site is launched, and after a common online culture has taken shape, the developers continue to shape the tools, formats for exchange and collaboration, and the nature of online events, to support a vision of professional development. We have come to think of this behind-the-scenes influence as leaving an "invisible imprint," which is often surprisingly easy to overlook and difficult to assess in terms of its impact on the communities' experience. The chapters in this book reveal the many forms this imprint of intent, purpose, and inquiry can take.

Framing by Inquiry, and Vision-Keeping

Each of these communities can be seen as the result of an inquiry about professional learning, in the context of a particular kind of endeavor—inquiry-based classroom teaching, systemic reform of math and science education, the incorporation of new kinds of resources into university practice, the doing and learning of mathematics, and so on. The initial question, and the proposed solution, continue in each of these communities as a motive and reference point. Witness the effect that a consistent reference to a version of Dewey's inquiry cycle has on the way that problems, situations, and insights are framed and exchanged within the Inquiry Group, as described by Bruce.

A crucial behind-the-scenes role is precisely the monitoring of how, and to what extent, tools, events, and processes promote or inhibit fundamental goals and visions of the project. This reflective role goes far beyond techniques of facilitation, which have been well described in many publications over the past 20 years. For example, Rubin and Doubler make the case that the core content of their master's course, the process of science, shapes the way the short-lived community of students is formed during an online course. The rules of evidentiary dialogue, drawing on science data and theory, affect not only what is communicated, but the form in which the exchanges can take place, for example, words (including narratives), data, and graphical representations. While the teachers participating in Scheckler and Barab's Inquiry Learning Forum (Chapter 5) rely heavily on textual as well as face-to-face exchange, their interactions are contextualized in their classrooms, by means of virtual (video) tours of their spaces. The structure for these video presentations, and for the commentaries surrounding them, is itself an intervention, as it provides a template for teacher talk.

In contrast, MSPnet, while providing many modalities for individual voices, also by its very nature provides ways for whole projects, or teams within projects, to represent themselves and broadly disseminate their work to a large audience. Thus, the site supports the very real, but often overlooked, importance of dissemination and publication as professional learning experiences.

The Importance of Resources and Artifacts

Objects such as topics to communicate about, tools to communicate with, and products of community interactions in many forms are essential ingredients in the complex process by which a community becomes visible and alive in the online world. Professionals, always struggling with the problem of too much to read, see, and hear, prize recommendations by their peers and evidence that a colleague has found a particular article or tool (such as an observation protocol) valuable to his or her work. Work behind the scenes, with the community vision in mind, contributes to the search for, the representation of, and the acquaintance with a growing body of resources in this sense. The "library" function, central to MERLOT, and (in different ways) to MSPnet or the Math Forum, offers immediate value to the community, providing a venue for meaningful collections to be assembled, browsed, searched, and archived.

Moreover, in the communities described in this book, the resource collections are the result of community life. The participants contribute indispensably by their posting of reports, sharing of research and references, and engagement in discussion forums. For example, in MSPnet, members post to discussions, add to the library, post comments on items in the library, post reports for the public, create libraries of working documents for internal project use, and contribute video products, among other things. In MERLOT, trained participants review resources being posted and add comments and advice on the use of digital resources. In the Math Forum, participants build the content in various ways, such as posting problems and solutions or exchanging ideas about pedagogy in discussions. Behind-the-scenes work in this connection includes the well-understood techniques for moderating discussions, but also the development of criteria for what should be included, metadata to facilitate organization and searching in a large collection, decisions about how material will be rated or valued, and strategies to coax participation and promote online leadership. In addition, the facilitators may undertake to re-purpose community contributions or to disseminate them for new occasions.

Beyond this straightforward collection and use of resources, however, the exchange of resources has additional sociological value in building the texture of the community. It helps create ties of collaboration and collegial association, and supports the development, or critique, of community values around qualities of the shared work. The development of a rich collection of resources by a diverse community makes visible the varied interests and insights that exist in the community. Just as individuals who move between communities can act as "brokers," bringing together elements from differing professional cultures, so resources can function as "boundary objects," opening conversation and inquiry between communities. Bearing this in mind, those working behind the scenes can solicit and use resources so that diversity can engender dialogue and debate.

The Development of Emergent Structure Within the Communities

In each of these Web sites, the designers have provided structures for the establishment of personal presence—a way to instantiate the ideas of membership and peer relations. This sort of built-in sociology, often facilitated by the metaphors used to orient new users, embodies some assumptions about the nature and structure of the community being served (or brought into being) online.

As members use the site, mastering its functionalities and incorporating it into their work, they test the limits of the model, making visible the limitations or constraints that the facilitative structures impose. Then the behind-the-scenes work needs to accomplish two things: (1) helping members move past the constraints, and (2) incorporating the insights gained by actual use into the revision of the site's characteristics, if possible. Thus, as use flourishes, the users drive a reshaping of the community structure. The nature of their collaboration with the behind-the-scenes team will determine the actual flow of feedbacks and responses.

Community members are not always well served by collaborative structures as originally envisioned by designers. Care must be taken not to over-design sites (Barab, Kling, & Gray, 2004). Yet even in the most flexible sites, facilitators need to guide and support members' productive use of the architecture. In several studies described in these chapters, the behind-the-scenes role of monitoring and facilitation led to an iterative design process that allowed for new collaborative structures (e.g., emergent groups) to take hold. This dynamic feedback/design process is evidence of real community life and sense of shared ownership.

TYPES OF SUCCESS

One of the questions the authors considered as they reflected upon their communities is the nature of success. In the field of education in general, this question increasingly has implied a quantitative answer. It is therefore important at the outset to recognize that several of these communities have had significant impact in quantitative terms. The Math Forum, MSPnet, and MERLOT have involved millions of visitors participating at different levels. In their more circumscribed spheres, the other projects too have shown the basic signs of success, which we might term *presence* and *persistence* of use by their intended constituencies (what McMartin, in Chapter 4, calls "stickiness"). Quantitative measures such as sessions, page counts, membership numbers, and others provide evidence that the targeted communities are making use of the environments and resources present on the site.

Sustainability, continuation after the "venture capital" phase (e.g., the end of grant funding), is another type of success explored in these projects. For example, it is a high priority for MERLOT, which is still seeking a stable transition to this kind of maturity. The Math Forum is making a similar transition: While Drexel University is providing a continuing home for the site, the Math Forum now has in place a business plan that includes both free material, and content and functionalities available only to subscribers. The online master's degree program in which Investigations in Physics is an element has been incorporated into the regular curriculum of its host institutions, such as Lesley University, where its life cycle will unfold in the fashion of such academic entities.

Yet these chapters make clear that such communities, as cultural phenomena, should be considered also from the point of view of their meaning or implications—in relation, therefore, to the goals and purpose of the designers, implementers, and formative participants, and to the value for other current and future communities. Success in these terms is harder to measure.

For many of the projects described in this book, one crucial and lasting measure of success was the value to the community: in some of the projects, the quality of the discourse that emerged; in others, the accumulated resources and record of activity as well. In MERLOT, the "digital library" aspect is particularly central; in MSPnet, collaborations and discussions are important as well, but there was from the beginning the intent to create an archive of the whole NSF Math and Science Partnership experiment in systemic educational change. The Math Forum also exhibits this kind of achievement, an accumulation of resources as a result of community interactions.

Each of these sites is concerned with the learner who is a socially situated agent, whose learning is both stimulated and supported by collaboration, exchange, co-creation, debate, and reflective discourse. The learners could be said to follow Huberman's (1993) "independent artisan" model, seeking information or insight according to their own needs and situated in the specifics of their work. And yet there is evidence that in these communities discourse often moves beyond practical, informational exchanges to conversations on ways of evaluating and critiquing both methods and purposes. Conversations include theoretical reflections (How shall we make sense of this? What is the value of it? What goals have we for these activities, in relation to our more general purposes?). When made an explicit part of the discourse, and the "work" of the community, they can give rise to the questions and ideas that enable innovation within a site, or adoption of the tools by new constituencies, or both, a process that Bruce explores in some depth in Chapter 2, providing an interesting view of how to gauge success.

An important question, whose answer will be approached only by successive approximations, is, "How can we demonstrate, or provide evidence of, this learning?" While we can name the tools that might help answer this question—social networking methods, discourse analysis, and other qualitative methods—an inherent and ineluctable problem remains, because the impact of the learning in all these cases is to be sought in the life and work of the participants, and is not necessarily visible on the Web sites.

THEORY AND THE THEORIZING OF COMMUNITY

What is the role of theory in these chapters? Despite the apparent diversity of theoretical approaches, we have suggested in the Introduction that in fact we can see a productive convergence and theoretical dynamism. Both the convergence and the dynamism represent a constructive achievement of the field and also allow us to descry some areas requiring reflective caution.

Convergence

The theoretical diversity in these chapters reflects an underlying consensus about core approaches to understanding—and working within—such learning communities. All of these authors, despite their differences, share the common language of "situated theory," which draws on sociocultural insights derived from European thinkers such as Vygotsky and Leont'ev, and those influenced by them (e.g., Lave, Wenger, Scribner, and others), as well as on Dewey's ideas about culture, technology, inquiry, and individual and social growth.[1] These seminal ideas, transformed by application and experiment, provide an increasingly coherent grounding for critique and reflection at three crucial stages of development of electronic communities—design, facilitation, and reflection about communities and learning.

The sociocultural paradigm brings key values, which are evident throughout this book. In addition to its view of learning as embedded in social interaction, it assumes a continuum between the person and her milieu—including collaborators, designers, and clients, tools, resources, and the people who shape them and are shaped by them. Dewey and the activity theorists are drawn upon by some of the authors to take in larger aspects of the situation in which action and learning take place, including the important, dynamic role of purposes or tasks, which typically are the references from which importance or relevance is derived.

Dynamism

While theory can underlie a blueprint, or be used as a diagnostic/analytic/forecasting tool, it also can be used as a tool for meaning making and for growth and experimentation. Thus, we see in some of these chapters evidence that the ideas that undergirded the design and implementation phase of the sites need to be supplemented in understanding what happens when people use the sites to actually build and use their learning community.

The general framework just outlined gives a clear sense of the role of the social setting as the place within which learning is fostered. It articulates the role of differential expertise in a community and explains how learning takes place for each individual while also contributing to the group. But note that in each chapter, we see more than a description of a "clockwork community," built on certain lines at first and then released to find its way in the world.

As we have emphasized, the behind-the-scenes work includes observation, reflection, and action by some elements of the community (most often the designers/project leaders) to enhance the effectiveness of the community as a learning space. It is in this phase that we see theoretical dynamism, as developments within the communities push the authors to reach for new theoretical ideas which extend the sociocultural foundations of the community approach. For example, Bruce and Scheckler and Barab draw on Deweyan resources for critique and revision of their communities. McMartin draws upon theories of organizational maturity to understand what problems and opportunities confront MERLOT. Rubin and Doubler refer to the community of practice theory in describing the postulates of their work. Yet changes in their learning environment are necessitated by ideas from the philosophy of science and from theories of science learning which emphasize the crucial role of graphical representations in science discourse. In each case, the employment of new theoretical ideas reflects emergent phenomena. As large and complex community sites such as the Math Forum and MSPnet evolve, they are influenced by the constant developments in Web culture. These developments, both internal and external to the communities, challenge founding assumptions about how to conceptualize community and demand theoretical innovation.

Theorizing Community

A central idea that is employed in each of these chapters is *community*, and its cousin, *community of practice*, that immensely evocative term of Lave and Wenger's. As sketched in the Introduction, Lave and Wenger, and their companions in the field, developed from their studies of workplace cognition a theory about how learning is related to (or even constituted by) participation in a practice, in which interaction and collaboration are structured by common tasks, common tools and techniques, shared history, and shared (negotiated) standards of value. Their understanding of growth (learning) in a practice, from peripheral (and novice) forms of participation to core (and mastery) participation, clearly has stimulated thinking and imagination in the development of electronic communities. In reflecting on the collegial networks described in this book, however, we may ask whether perhaps the community of practice framework has been applied so broadly as to lose its explanatory and analytic value.

In the first place, to what extent can communities of practice be created as an instrument of policy, or an experimental intervention? A key element of the Lave and Wenger theory is the element of shared history. In operational terms, the dimension of time spent in professional association makes possible the development of negotiated standards and values for the practice that forms the basis of the group. It also brings with it the development of structures, processes, and relationships that reflect individuals' connections and purposes, in the overall context of a shared enterprise or practice. Membership in an organization, or on a "community Web site," is not yet the same as relationship or collaboration; it merely sets the stage for creative association.

In the second place, the notion of what a "practice" is, around which a community of practice takes shape, is ill defined at best. In the studies that gave rise to the concept, the communities of practice studied included such groups as butchers or tailors; blacksmiths or fishermen; or by an imaginative extension, members of Alcoholics Anonymous. These groups had several things in common: They worked at the same kind of task (not always "for a common purpose") and the tasks involved characteristic tools, jargon, techniques, typical problems to be solved, and so forth. Learning relationships sometimes were formal apprenticeships, but often were more casual exchanges of tips and advice. One's status as novice or master/expert could be characterized by one's participation in the typical activities of the practice, and in terms of the typical tools, techniques, responsibilities, and so on.

In creating a Web site to foster collegial exchange, this model may offer insight about what processes and resources, and what kinds of interactions, should be allowed for, facilitated, and even built into some of the structures of the site. An essential ingredient for success, however, is the recognition among members that they have things to learn and teach with one another. This means that, in addition to the element of time, people with common practices need to find one another, in ways that are rich and flexible enough that collegial exchange happens. Once again, membership on a Web site does not yet constitute professional relationship, except in the most rudimentary sense.

A collegial network serving a very large and diverse population is therefore hard to construe as a community of practice and is not likely to succeed on those terms. Yet such large sites, such as MSPnet or the Math Forum, can and do enable communities of practice, or other associations, to form and function, for shorter or longer periods of time. They can be designed with this possibility in mind, and the recognition that community is something that grows and that its members constitute by their choices of activity and association.

From the point of view of a participant in these projects seeking to learn to do their work better, the important questions are quite direct: What kinds of interactions are available to me in this space, and what kinds of people may be encountered? Shall I find in this place people who are experts/leaders in the field, from whom I can learn? Shall I find tools for my own work, and news from the field, that is, news about meanings or techniques that lead to innovation in my practice? Will we see examples of practice from which I can learn? Can I expect a long-term experience over time, in which my own practice can change in the direction of expertise, defined over a reasonably recognizable range of issues, techniques, operations, knowledge, and purposes?

The answers to such questions are important in shaping the quality of the professional development that may be possible within the bounds of the community. They also provide some conceptual structure to facilitate the new participant's initiation—which from the participant's point of view is the process of understanding what is available at this place, and how she can take advantage of it and incorporate it into her workflow.

With the evolution of the World Wide Web—and communications technology—over the past decade, a very different approach to the idea of electronic community has emerged that builds on the idea of social networks (on- and offline) and is elaborated, for example, in the work of Barry Wellman and his colleagues (e.g., Garton, Haythornthwaite, & Wellman, 1999; Wellman, 1999; Wellman & Haythornthwaite, 2002; Wellman & Potter, 1999), as well as Harrison White and other scholars (Mandel, 1983; White, Boorman, & Breiger, 1976). This approach is based on an empirical investigation of the ways in which people actually are connecting currently through networks of many kinds, the ways they are construing community, and the ways that their technology use seems to be following that construal.

In a valuable study using this approach, Wellman and Potter (1999) suggest that several important paradigms of "community"[2] can be discerned in sociological thinking over the past century—although it is worth bearing in mind that aspects of all these paradigms co-exist in our thinking, as in our daily experience. We can summarize their analysis of the historical development of conceptions of community as follows: Community was seen first and most primitively in spatial terms, but sociologists came to realize that the most important boundaries experienced by most people are primarily cultural. Further investigation brought the realization that, in fact, each individual participates in multiple cultures, and even within the same culture individuals experience, in a sense, their own version of it. (This is analogous to the distinctions that sociolinguists make among language, dialects of a language, and idiolects, or "personal dialects," within the language community.) More recently, views of community in terms of boundaries and belonging have been succeeded by ego-centered models, in which the individual's community is seen in terms of social networks, which are constituted by ties of varying strengths. These ties take concrete shape as various kinds of interaction or exchange, cohering around a center defined by the individual actor.

As we will discuss in the last section of this chapter, such relational, individual-centered concepts of community have important resonances with developments in the technology available for collegial networking. For online learning communities, this approach bears all the hallmarks of an effective theory: It fosters useful description of the facts, proposes interesting explanations for the facts, generates productive questions, and helps drive interesting, concrete applications and experiments.

Yet social networking theory is not by itself adequate to the needs of the learning communities portrayed in this book. If community of practice is not a complete fit, owing to the fluidity with which individuals form collegial relationships within and across "practices," social networking theory does not take into account the shared purposes, values, resources, and techniques that provide the center of gravity for professional learning. Hence, a broader sociocultural or sociotechnical vocabulary is required for the kind of analysis that is essential to the design, facilitation, and evaluation of collegial networks—the ways that individuals participate, the tools they use, the activities and institutions that contextualize their learning, and the resources they create, deploy, and exchange. This view based on individual action and relationship seems to comport usefully with Fischer's "community of interest" approach discussed by Shumar and Bruce, and the synergy between these two theoretical approaches merits some further exploration.

Both the community of practice/interest and the social networking paradigms, however, can lure theorists of community to a kind of hyper-theorizing, spinning conceptual webs that then have their own imperatives. Theory building often is a powerful and constructive process, which allows people in a field to take stock of achievements and advances. Yet it must be borne in mind that a theory is first and foremost a tool for further inquiry (Dewey, 1929; Hickman, 1992) and must be tested against the data on which it seeks to shed light.

Therefore, while insights from structures such as community of practice theory or social networking theory are immensely useful in thinking about communities designed to support learning, we need to avoid the temptation to make Procrustean distortions that might be necessary to "fit" a complex and innovative entity such as MSPnet or Investigating Physics into a pre-existing frame, to identify it as a *kind-of* something, rather than first seeing what it is, or least how it behaves, on its own terms.[3] Otherwise, the theoretical constructs lose heuristic value, and the phenomena being studied also may not be elucidated, because the effort to fit the construct obscures aspects of the actual case.

Theorists and practitioners behind the scenes of online learning communities must reflect iteratively on the phenomenological details of our community: Who is talking to whom, using what genres and media, about what questions and techniques, for what purposes? This allows us to explore purposes and goals alongside tools—in fact, keeping the relationship between ends and means, but also including at all times the learning and other purposes of the persons actually acting in and through the community space. It is only in doing this, and then confronting the results of this "natural history" with theories we find apposite, that we actually can answer the question, "Are we seeing the development of truly new methods for professional learning?" We believe the answer is "yes," as community Web sites develop the richness and complexity to bring more and more of the diversity of human learning-in-community onto the Web and support the formation and evolution of collegial networking in its many forms.

THE FUTURE OF PROFESSIONAL LEARNING COMMUNITIES

Pioneering electronic communities developed a great deal of user loyalty in the early years of the Internet. Alternative communities were rare, and those that emerged often lacked the critical mass necessary to make them attractive. The subsequent explosive growth in Internet users, and in the number and variety of online communities, chipped away at this loyalty through the sheer volume of options. This resulted in a shift away from users' making use of (and thus identifying with) a single online community to their utilizing and identifying with several communities.

More recently, a new wave of "social network" online communities, including Facebook, MySpace, and others, has begun shifting users' online community identification away from intrinsically defined communities to their own personally centered web of relationships. Each person is central to his or her own self-created community, into which the person may invite friends in social, academic, or hobbyist networks. In this way, no one need feel peripheral to their most important communities; this changes a key dynamic of the classic community of practice theory, legitimate peripheral participation. The ability to create an individual's own groups certainly influenced many of the projects described in this book, as they moved from predefined communities to the creation of models for emergent communities, and from a top-down to a bottom-up approach.

Personally centered networks will push the future of online community experience even further, as interacting individuals will create their own meta-sites that are not limited by community boundaries. Through a variety of synchronization and aggregation technologies, users will become ever-more comfortable with customizing their online experiences around a combination of tools, communities, and resources drawn from multiple sites, networks, and communities. They will rely on RSS feeds, subscription functionalities, and sophisticated notification systems to track their interests, groups, and friends across site boundaries. Further, they will track this information through integrated technologies that include and may combine laptop, PDA, phone, TV, and so on. These decentralizing trends will span all aspects of the online community experience, from end-user devices to the software interfaces through which users experience these communities, to the back-end services that power them.

On the hardware side, perhaps the most important trend is the increasing proliferation of personal mobile hardware (primarily around PDAs, smartphones, and ultra-portable laptops). Online communities will need to tailor their offerings with the mobile-based experience in mind, which is distinguished by a lack of general-purpose inputs (i.e., mouse and keyboard), constrained screen size, and other trade-offs necessary to enable computing "on the go."

Another aspect of the growth in mobile computing will be the need to accommodate styles of communication native to the mobile experience, which increasingly will influence community interactions online. An example of this is Twitter, a popular online community based around "micro-blogging"—each Twitter blog entry consists of no more than 140 characters. This radical brevity is based directly in the text-messaging style of communication, in which conciseness and directness of discussion are not only encouraged, but necessary. While mobile-focused online communities such as Twitter are currently the exception, their popularity is likely to greatly increase as users computing time shifts toward a mobile basis. Whereas until now many applications or environments have been devised on laptops, and then translated to mobile formats, in the future the influence will flow in both directions.

As a result of increased use of mobile computing, it will become very desirable to create seamless synchronization experiences across devices (e.g., sharing address book information across your cell phone, work laptop, and home desktop). It also will be important to integrate data provided by end-users' "personal services" (whether these are addresses hosted by Facebook or MSN Live, photo albums based on Flickr or Snapfish, or personal files hosted at Amazon S3 or Rapidshare) within community spaces. Finally, there will be the need to provide shared data to third-party services. Hence we can expect that attractive online communities in the near future will provide a combination of immediate and integrated access to personal data, a high degree of personalization, and the ability to leverage community-based data within other applications and services.

As user-centric systems become more influential, professional communities will need to reorient the way that they measure use, value, engagement, and success. As community boundaries become more permeable, we will no longer be able to measure participation rates by member page-views, session counts, or similar statistics.

Does this mean that professional learning communities such as those described in this book will lose their purpose or utility within such a user-centric virtual reality? We believe that the answer is "no," and the reason lies in the inquiry-rooted nature of professional learning communities. In the future, such communities will still originate in a question, a recognition of a need, a new possible response, and a proposed pathway to realization of this vision. This inquiry, which is rooted in human perception and social context, provides professional learning communities with an identity and purpose, which, while largely conceived of by the designers behind the scenes, are further shaped and developed by contributors in an interative process.

It is this conceptualization of identity and purpose that not only lets people know whom will they be engaging with, but what they will be engaging about. It is through this intentional interaction around a subject area that shared values are negotiated, information is exchanged, and learning happens. Thus, the creation of a purposeful community, with its attendant structures, resource types, and definition of an initial interest group, stands as an invitation to join the inquiry and to take advantage of the support, continuity, and metacognitive attention that the designers provide.

While individuals can create their own communities, track their own documents, and share with whomever they please, they do not necessarily get to be in contact with those they admire (experts in the field) but do not know. They do not get to "overhear their conversations" as they do in communities such as MSPnet and the Math Forum, where there are discussions in which there are always more people reading than posting. As has been mentioned before, diversity drives learning, both by introducing new voices and by making visible within particular practices in the community a "zone of proximal development"—areas of potential growth and inquiry, supported by the persons and resources of the community at large.

As the chapters in this book show, the growing edge of educational technology, from a social point of view, does not lie in the technology alone, but in the way it is explored and deployed by people gathered together online for the purpose of inquiring, accomplishing, and learning.

NOTES

1. The appearance of Dewey as a resource in exploring learning and community in sociotechnical settings is particularly interesting, as there is evidence that his ideas were in fact contributory to the development of the Russian sociocultural thinkers (see Prawat, 2000).

2. They point out (p. 51) that these typologies are generally developed on the basis of theory. Of course, there is the danger of reification, that is, the treatment of philosophical constructs as if they had some physical reality "out there," when that itself is an empirical question. Yet Wellman and Potter go on to typologize, using their valuable insights about individual-based social networks.

3. This is reminiscent of the intellectual problem posed to biology by the advent of the populational thinking that lies at the heart of evolutionary thinking about the nature of species. Before Darwin, a species was treated as a type, an idealized entity, of which each individual was seen as an imperfect realization. This view cast variation as a problem to be explained away, or an accident of ontogeny—to understand what a species was, it was necessary to abstract from all the variety to find the underlying ideal. Darwin did away with this idealization, and instead said that the population is what there is, and all there is. Variation is part of the essence and also part of the change. This then allowed a great efflorescence of insight about evolution, adaptation, the interaction of nature and nurture, and the nature of many ecological processes.

REFERENCES

Barab, S., Kling, R., & Gray, J. H. (Eds.). (2004). *Designing for virtual communities in the service of learning.* Cambridge: Cambridge University Press.

Dewey, J. (1929). *Experience and nature* (Rev. ed.). New York: Dover.

Hickman, L. A. (1992). *John Dewey's pragmatic technology.* Bloomington: Indiana University Press.

Garton, L., Haythornthwaite, C., & Wellman, B. (1999). Studying on-line social networks. In S. Jones (Ed.), *Doing internet research* (pp. 75–106). Thousand Oaks, CA: Sage.

Huberman, M. (1993). The model of the independent artisan in teachers' professional relations. In J. W. Little & M. W. McLaughlin (Eds.), *Teachers' work: Individuals, colleagues, and contexts* (pp. 11–50). New York: Teachers College Press.

Mandel, M. J. (1983). Local roles and social networks. *American Sociological Review, 48,* 376–386.

Prawat, R. S. (2000). Dewey meets the "Mozart of psychology" in Moscow: The untold story. *American Educational Research Journal, 37*(3), 663–696.

Wellman, B. (Ed.). (1999). *Networks in the global village.* Boulder, CO: Westview Press.

Wellman, B., & Haythornthwaite, C. (Eds.). (2002). *The internet in everyday life.* Malden, MA: Wiley-Blackwell.

Wellman, B., & Potter, S. (1999). The elements of personal communities. In
   B. Wellman (Ed.), *Networks in the global village* (pp. 49–81). Boulder, CO:
   Westview Press.
White, H., Boorman, S., & Breiger, R. (1976). Social structure from multiple net-
   works: I blockmodels of roles and positions. *American Journal of Sociology,*
   81, 730–780.

About the Editors and Contributors

Joni K. Falk co-directs the Center for School Reform at TERC, a nonprofit research and development institution aimed at improving math and science teaching and learning. Her work has focused on creating and researching electronic learning communities. While the communities described in this book (MSPnet and LSC-net) were developed for leaders engaged in educational change, she has also created an electronic community to connect middle and high school girls in a mentorship program with female scientists (Eyes to the Future) and is currently developing a community for higher education faculty and graduate students engaged in interdisciplinary science education (IGERT Resource Center). Her recent research interests include studying schools implementing an inquiry-based approach to science teaching and schools experimenting with ubiquitous computing environments in order to enhance science education.

Brian Drayton, an ecologist and science educator, is co-director of TERC's Center for School Reform. Since 1986, he has developed curriculum for high school general science (*Astrobiology* [2005]) and ecology (*Ecology: A Systems Approach* [1997] and *Biocomplexity and the Habitable Planet* [under development]). In addition to curriculum development, his concern for inquiry in science education has led to classroom research on science teaching and professional development for elementary, middle, and high school teachers. In parallel with these strands of work, he has been involved in the development, facilitation, and research on electronic communities for teachers (LabNet), students (The Global Laboratory, Eyes to the Future), and for systemic reform in science education. He has collaborated with Joni Falk on LSCnet, MSPnet, and the Virtual Conferences on Sustainability, as well as on many of his other projects.

Sasha A. Barab is a professor in learning sciences, Instructional Systems Technology (IST) and, cognitive science at Indiana University. He also holds the Barbara Jacobs Chair of Education and Technology, and is the director of the Center for Research on Learning and Technology. His research has resulted in numerous grants, dozens of academic articles, and multiple chapters in edited books, which investigate knowing and learning in its material, social, and cultural context. His current work involves the research and development of rich learning environments, frequently with the aid of technology, that are designed to assist children in developing their sense of purpose as individuals, as members of their communities, and as knowledgeable citizens of the world. See http://QuestAtlantis.Org for an example of this work.

Bertram (Chip) Bruce is a professor in library & information science, curriculum & instruction, bioengineering, the Center for Writing Studies, and the Center for East Asian & Pacific Studies at the University of Illinois at Urbana-Champaign. During 2007–2008, he held a Fulbright Distinguished Chair at the National College of Ireland. Professor Bruce's research goals include contributing to a conception of democratic education through research on community inquiry through collaborative work, the theory of inquiry-based learning, drawing especially upon scholarship of the American pragmatists and the history of Progressive Education, and research on the affordances and constraints of new media for learning, encapsulated by the term technology-enhanced learning.

Susan J. Doubler is co-leader of the Center for Science Teaching and Learning at TERC (an educational research and development center for K–12 mathematics and science learning) and associate professor of science education at Lesley University in Cambridge, Massachusetts. Her main focus is the interface of science education and technology, with the aim of using the latter to further inquiry-based science learning and teacher professional development.

Soo-Young Lee received her Ph.D. from the University of Michigan in science education and educational technology. From 2001 to 2005, she was a senior researcher at TERC, Inc., where she was engaged in research on several electronic communities, including MSPnet, LSC-net, the Sustainability Virtual Conferences, and Eyes to the Future, a Web-mediated science mentorship program for middle-school girls. Since 2006, Dr. Lee has been a research fellow at the Korea Research Institute for Vocational Education and Training.

Flora McMartin is a founding partner of Broad-based Knowledge (BbK), a consulting firm focused on evaluation of the use and deployment of technology-assisted teaching and learning. Prior to her work with BbK, she was the director of Member Services and Evaluation for MERLOT, where she directed the development, implementation, and evaluation of services for users and MERLOT partners. Her research interests include studying the impact of computer-mediated learning on student learning and faculty roles, the impact of assessment as a means for developing collaborative faculty work groups and organizational change related to institutionalization of innovative academic departments and programs.

Jon Obuchowski is a lead engineer developing Web-based applications at TERC in Cambridge, Massachusetts. His work has included a variety of community-based Web sites, focusing on both online and offline communities, including TEECH-LSC (http://teech-lsc.terc.edu), LSC-Net (http://lsc-net.terc .edu), the Virtual Conferences on Sustainability of Systemic Reform (http://sustainability2003.terc.edu), MSPnet (http://mspnet.org), and Eyes to the Future (http://etf.terc.edu and http://speakout.terc.edu).

Andee Rubin, senior scientist at TERC, has done research and development in the fields of mathematics, educational technology, and online learning for over 25 years. Her recent research has focused on how students and teachers develop statistical reasoning, how video can be used to introduce ideas of movement over time, and how mathematics can be integrated into informal settings, such as zoos and aquariums. She is the author of *Electronic Quills: A Situated Evaluation of Using Computers for Writing in Classrooms* (with Bertram Bruce, 1993) and editor of *Ghosts in the Machine: Women's Voices in Research with Technology* (with Nicola Yelland, 2002).

Rebecca K. Scheckler is an educational technologist in the Waldron College of Health and Human Services at Radford University in Radford, Virginia. Her research focuses on the social effects of digital technologies, particularly in terms of race, class, and gender. Dr. Scheckler is currently investigating the social construction of aging in the era of computers and the co-construction of nursing and caring for nursing faculty and other graduate prepared nurses. She has published on women in computer related careers, feminist pedagogies of distance education, and the effects of design on participation of women in online discussion forums.

Wesley Shumar is a cultural anthropologist at Drexel University whose research focuses on virtual community, higher education, and ethnographic evaluation in education. He is author of *College for Sale: A Critique of the Commodification of Higher Education* (1997). Since 1997 he has worked as an ethnographer at the Math Forum. He is co-editor of *Building Virtual Communities: Learning and Change in Cyberspace* (2002). He is principal investigator on The Math Forum's Virtual Fieldwork sequence, and co-PI on the Virtual Math Teams (VMT) project, a five-year NSF project investigating the dynamics of online and face-to-face collaborative problem solving and problem creation.

Index

2712
gift

2712
gift